WHOLE COOKING
and nutrition

AN EVERYDAY SUPERFOODS APPROACH TO PLANNING, COOKING, AND EATING WITH DIABETES

by Katie Cavuto, MS, RD

with Peggy Paul Casella

American Diabetes Association

Director, Book Publishing, Abe Ogden; *Managing Editor,* Rebekah Renshaw; *Acquisitions Editor,* Victor Van Beuren; *Editor,* Lauren Wilson; *Production Manager and Composition,* Melissa Sprott; *Interior Design,* pixiedesign, llc; *Cover Design,* Jenn French Designs, LLC; *Author Photo:* Sarah Alderman; *Food Photography,* Renée Comet; *Printer,* RR Donnelley.

Printed in the United States of America
1 3 5 7 9 10 8 6 4 2

The suggestions and information contained in this publication are generally consistent with the *Standards of Medical Care in Diabetes* and other policies of the American Diabetes Association, but they do not represent the policy or position of the Association or any of its boards or committees. Reasonable steps have been taken to ensure the accuracy of the information presented. However, the American Diabetes Association cannot ensure the safety or efficacy of any product or service described in this publication. Individuals are advised to consult a physician or other appropriate health care professional before undertaking any diet or exercise program or taking any medication referred to in this publication. Professionals must use and apply their own professional judgment, experience, and training and should not rely solely on the information contained in this publication before prescribing any diet, exercise, or medication. The American Diabetes Association—its officers, directors, employees, volunteers, and members—assumes no responsibility or liability for personal or other injury, loss, or damage that may result from the suggestions or information in this publication.

Madelyn Wheeler conducted the internal review of this book to ensure that it meets American Diabetes Association guidelines.

⊗ The paper in this publication meets the requirements of the ANSI Standard Z39.48-1992 (permanence of paper).

American Diabetes Association titles may be purchased for business or promotional use or for special sales. To purchase more than 50 copies of this book at a discount, or for custom editions of this book with your logo, contact the American Diabetes Association at the address below or at booksales@diabetes.org.

American Diabetes Association
1701 North Beauregard Street
Alexandria, Virginia 22311

DOI: 10.2337/9781580406093

Library of Congress Cataloging-in-Publication Data
Names: Cavuto, Katie, author.
Title: Whole cooking & nutrition : an everyday superfoods approach to
  planning, cooking, and eating with diabetes / Katie Cavuto.
Other titles: Whole cooking and nutrition
Description: Alexandria : The American Diabetes Association, [2016] |
  Includes bibliographical references and index.
Identifiers: LCCN 2015043270 | ISBN 9781580406093 (alk. paper)
Subjects: LCSH: Diabetes--Diet therapy--Recipes. | LCGFT: Cookbooks. l
Classification: LCC RC662 .C387 2016 | DDC 641.5/6314--dc23 LC record available at
http://lccn.loc.gov/2015043270

dedication

This book is for Ashli and Hudson.

With a very full heart, I thank you for loving me, for believing in me, and for inspiring me to relentlessly pursue my passions.

mythja/Shutterstock.com

table of contents

Rutabaga and Turnip Fries with Peach and Mango Chipotle Ketchup p. 149

acknowledgments

I am immensely grateful to have had the opportunity to write this book—my first cookbook. I feel overwhelmed with joy knowing that this dream has become a reality. From the time I was little, food has played an important role in my life. Growing up in a large Italian family, food was an integral part of every family gathering. My grandmother and grandfather (Mom-Mom and Pop-Pop) owned a luncheonette, and I have vivid memories of my time in their kitchen. Cutting potatoes for homemade french fries was one of my favorite jobs. As for my other grandmother, it was impossible to visit her without eating something. She wasn't setting the world on fire with her culinary skills, but she had mastered the staples. She made my grandfather the same chocolate chip cookies with walnuts and raisins, every single week for the 60 years they were together. If you ask my siblings and I about our favorite dish that she made when we were kids, we would unanimously agree on mashed potatoes or "Grandmom's Soup," which was a very basic version of Italian wedding soup that we ate at the holidays! Simple and pure, that is how my grandmom cooked, and I still appreciate her cooking because food doesn't have to be fancy to taste good! Speaking of simple, my grandpop—a butcher by trade—had such a simple spirit. My fondest memories of him have to be the way he savored his food, especially his homegrown tomatoes and the navel oranges he coveted during the winter months. Talk about tasting every bite! He was a man who understood how to be present and experience joy in even the most simple of situations. I try to emulate this ability, and I encourage you to do the same as you read through this book. My parents inherited this simple cooking style from my grandparents, and while I did not grow up eating gourmet meals, I am grateful for the fact that family dinners were a priority in my childhood home.

What sparked my interest in cooking and nutrition? Honestly, when I was a high school gymnast, I did not have the healthiest relationship with food. I began cooking for myself, often so that I could better control the food I was eating. Fortunately, after my gymnastics career ended, I ended up in culinary school and cooking positively transformed my relationship with food. Cooking became an emotional outlet for me and a way to express my love—both for myself and for others. Now, in my nutrition and culinary services practice, I aim to inspire others to find comfort and joy in cooking as a way to redefine their relationship with food. I hope this book inspires you in the same way!

I truly believe that a healthy lifestyle is achievable and that good-for-you food can be approachable, delicious, and satisfying, and now I have the opportunity to share this reality with all of you!

A monumental shout-out to the many people who poured their hearts into this book: your support, time, talents, and efforts are palpable. A very heartfelt thanks to all of you, especially:

- Ashli, Hudson, Mom, Dad, and the rest of my family. Your belief in me gives me the courage to pursue my dreams. Thank you for your unending support and your patience as you taste-tested my new recipes!

- Peggy! Wow! I could not have done this without you. Thank you for ALWAYS believing in me! I am beyond grateful for your writing and editing assistance and all of the hard work you put into this project from the very beginning.

- Sally, my agent. This book would not exist without your guidance and perseverance.

- My friends, interns, and employees! I am forever grateful for the time and effort you put into testing these recipes and providing me with valuable feedback so that my readers can now enjoy them! I also want to thank you for your constant encouragement and positive energy; it always keeps me going.

- My creative team. Thank you to Renée Comet, Lisa Cherkasky, Jen Kane, and Kathy Hedgwood. You captured the look and feel that I envisioned for this book. From photography to food styling and graphic design…I am in awe of your talents.

- The American Diabetes Association, for giving me the opportunity to write this book. Oh, and my amazing editors, Lauren Wilson and Rebekah Renshaw, who tirelessly worked with me to bring this book to life!

part 1

cooking and nutrition

Grilled Peaches with White Balsamic and Mascarpone Cream p. 237

eat this way, every day

Let me set one thing straight right from the beginning: this is not a book about dieting! Why don't we just erase that word from your memory? This is a book about food—nourishing, delicious, approachable, joyful food that I know you are going to love! Yes, you have been told that you need to follow a diabetes-friendly "diet" but that is really no different than the kind of healthy eating pattern everyone should strive to follow. The dietary recommendations for people with diabetes shouldn't feel like restrictions; they are an opportunity to broaden your culinary horizons and embrace a fresh, nourishing way of eating, and I am here to show you how! While there are specific nutritional concerns that come with having this disease—most notably blood glucose regulation and weight control—the kinds of foods that are recommended for people with diabetes are the same foods *everyone* should be eating, regardless of whether or not diabetes is a concern. When people are diagnosed with a disease like diabetes or heart disease and are subsequently encouraged to change their diet to one that is prescriptive for the illness, it can feel like a punishment. But in the moments that we find ourselves feeling deprived or punished, we should instead change our focus to one of self-love. When we love ourselves as we love others, we naturally want to take good care of ourselves. A healthy diet rich in nourishing foods is one of the best care-giving tools we have, and when we care for ourselves in a healthy way something miraculous happens—we feel good!

As I was saying, a diet for people with diabetes is really no more than a healthy eating plan. For instance, the principles of a healthy eating plan likely include limiting processed foods, sugars, saturated fat, and refined carbohydrates, and focusing on eating whole grains and fresh ingredients like fruits, vegetables, and lean proteins—these are the same, foundational principles of an eating plan for people with diabetes. While the fiber from whole grains, fruits, and vegetables may benefit people with diabetes, it also decreases the risk of heart disease, aids the digestive process, and may help prevent certain cancers. Plus, when you increase your intake of fresh fruits and vegetables and kick processed and high-sugar foods to the curb, you provide your body with a host of antioxidants and other vitamins and minerals that may prevent diseases and other serious conditions. And that's just the beginning of what a healthy diet can do for you.

Nutrient-dense foods nourish our bodies, and we thrive. That's why, as a dietitian and wellness advocate, I stay away from the word "diet" altogether and encourage clients to find joy in food; instead of giving into feelings of deprivation, I encourage them to slow down and taste their food, savor each bite, and eat with revelry. While "dieting" suggests blindly

9 principles for healthy eating

1. **Ditch dieting and deprivation.** Say good-bye to calorie counting and the misery of stepping on the scale. Banish the negative associations you have with food, dieting, and yourself. Instead, set an unwavering goal to nourish your body and be compassionate to yourself even if you stray—it happens to the best of us! This simple mantra will help you rebuild your relationship with food, create more nutrient-dense meals, and feel more satisfied in your food choices. Ask yourself why you eat and separate emotional triggers from physical triggers such as hunger and health. As for those emotional triggers, you can tend to them with non-food tools like engaging in an activity you love (taking a bath, reading a book, taking a walk, or simply finding some time for a few relaxing breaths). For now, keep your focus on nourishing your body with foods that make you feel good!

2. **Eat whole foods.** Whole foods are far more nutritious than their processed and packaged counterparts, and they are void of additives, preservatives, and non-food ingredients. Want to weed out the processed foods from your shopping cart? Ignore the front of the package, which is essentially all advertising, and head straight for the ingredient list. Then ask yourself the following questions to weed out the less nutritious options:

   - *Can I purchase all of these ingredients in the grocery store?* If not, you should look for a healthier option that contains more whole-food ingredients.
   - *What ingredients would I use to make this product at home?* Look for a similar product that contains only the foods you would use to make it at home.

   Remember: Ignore the front of the box—it's an advertisement. Read the ingredients and check out the nutrition information to decide for yourself if the product is as nourishing as the label claims!

3. **Limit sugar!** Sugar is lacking in nutrients (the same goes for refined carbohydrates). A great way to decrease your sugar intake is to avoid processed foods as added sugars live abundantly there. Choose to enjoy small amounts of natural sweeteners like raw honey and grade B maple syrup (remember: quality counts!), but retrain your taste buds so you can enjoy even the slightest amount of sweetness. When you do use natural sweeteners, make sure to keep an eye on the portion size and carbohydrate count. Oh, and avoid feeding your emotions with sugar—it won't change them!

4. **Indulge…in good-for-you foods** such as colorful vegetables, nuts, seeds, and fruits as well as smaller amounts of high-quality animal proteins, whole grains, and legumes! I always weigh out the risk-to-benefit ratio of a nutrition recommendation and, thankfully, when it comes to eating more vegetables, it is a total win! Vegetables are at the top of the list when it comes to protective, nutrient-dense foods—so go ahead and eat up! When you fill at least half of your plate with colorful vegetables, they crowd out other, less healthful foods. This is a great meal planning strategy for people with diabetes!

5. **Switch it up.** People often ask me, "What is the best vegetable, nut, seed…to eat?" and my answer is always the same: there is no *one* super food. Each food has its own unique nutrient profile and because a healthy diet should be composed of a variety of

nutrients, it's a good idea to eat a variety of ingredients! (See pages 25–43 for a list of 85 everyday superfoods to stock in your kitchen.)

6. **Feel good.** Enjoy foods that make you feel good both while you're savoring each bite as well as a few hours after eating. Avoid foods that cause you discomfort in any form, be it physical or emotional discomfort. Remember that nutrition is not one size fits all! Find healthy foods that work for *you*.

7. **Heal your gut.** A healthy belly is often the foundation of a healthy you! There are billions of healthy bacteria in your gut that aid in digestion and support your immune system. An unhealthy diet as well as some medications and antibacterial products, such as soaps and wipes, might deplete the army of good "bugs" in your gut. You can help them flourish by eating a healthy diet rich in colorful vegetables and fermented foods such as kimchi, sauerkraut, miso, kefir, and more.

8. **Cook.** The best way to control what you eat is to prepare it yourself, and cooking can be a really rewarding experience. Let go of the notion that you need to spend hours in the kitchen to prepare a meal. Start with something simple that feels approachable and easy, like most of the recipes in this book! They are meant to be easy and are perfect for everyday use!

9. **Savor.** It is no secret that we prefer foods that taste good, but when is the last time you truly tasted your food? You never need to feel deprived if you revamp the way you enjoy food. Be mindful during your meals—chew your food and taste each bite. Try to engage all of your senses and revel in the enjoyment of whatever you are eating.

mythja/Shutterstock.com

following a set of distinct—often limiting—rules that feel like a short-term fix, adopting a "mindful," nourishing lifestyle empowers individuals to think their choices through and use common sense to guide their eating decisions.

So whether you have diabetes or simply want to improve your eating habits and overall health, you're already on the right track with this book! In the pages that follow, I'll walk you through the basics of diabetes nutrition and teach you how to establish better eating habits and feel empowered by your food choices. It's my hope that you will be inspired by the list of 85 everyday superfoods I've included beginning on page 25. In the following pages, I'll give you all the tips and tricks you need to eat mindfully and enjoy a healthier, more joyful, well-nourished life.

living with diabetes

If you have recently been diagnosed with diabetes, you might be feeling scared or overwhelmed. Yes, diabetes is a serious condition. And yes, you will have to make some significant changes to your lifestyle. But here's the good news: by following a few simple guidelines, you can drastically reduce the effects of this disease and remain in control of your own well-being.

Diabetes is a metabolic disease characterized by high blood glucose levels. When we eat, the body converts the carbohydrates in the food into glucose (sugars). The pancreas then produces a hormone called insulin to help transport the glucose to cells throughout the body, where it will be used as energy. However, if you have diabetes, either your pancreas does not produce enough insulin or your body does not respond properly to the insulin it produces, and the glucose builds up in your bloodstream.

Type 1 diabetes occurs when the body's immune system attacks the insulin-producing cells in the pancreas. This form of diabetes requires daily insulin injections and can be managed through diet and exercise. Type 2 diabetes, which is much more common than type 1, occurs when your body's cells resist the effects of insulin. This form of diabetes is often diagnosed in adulthood and can usually be controlled by making healthy food choices, exercising regularly, and taking medication (if prescribed by your doctor).

While type 1 diabetes cannot be prevented, the insulin resistance that causes type 2 diabetes can be prevented and, in some cases, even greatly improved by making changes to your diet and daily routine. *The key is to achieve and maintain a healthy weight, reduce stress, ditch refined carbohydrates, processed foods, and sugar, and focus on eating whole ingredients.* Diabetes-friendly foods include: beans and legumes, fruits and vegetables, fish and seafood, lean meats and poultry, healthy fats, low-fat dairy, nuts and seeds, and lots of whole grains.

Of course, you will need to schedule regular appointments with your doctor if you've been diagnosed with diabetes, and you may be prescribed medications depending on the severity of your condition. But by adapting to a healthier, more nourishing way of living, you can take control of this disease and enjoy a very normal, healthy life.

Cool Weather Cobbler p. 224

rebuilding your relationship with food

Imagine if we all put as much thought into fueling our bodies as we do into, say, buying a house or maintaining our social media accounts. The impact on our personal wellness and the national food system would be staggering. If we stop and think about why we *should* eat (to nourish our bodies) versus why we often *do* eat (because we're bored, tired, sad, excited, etc.), we'll make much better choices, filling our plates with nutrient-dense foods and, eventually, losing the desire for junk foods altogether.

At the most basic level, we need food to survive. Yet for so many people, food can evoke all kinds of deep-seated emotions, from love, joy, and comfort to guilt, shame, and sadness. That's why, when I meet with clients for nutrition consultations, I like to swap out the word "healthy" with the word "nourishing," and teach them how to rebuild their relationships with food from the ground up. My nutrition philosophy is this: nourishment has nothing to do with deprivation and everything to do with mindfulness. When you break down external triggers and take the time to appreciate the foods you eat (for their taste, texture, and nutritional benefits), the kinds of foods you are drawn to will change for the better.

So how do you set the foundation for a nourished lifestyle? Start by asking yourself these two important questions:

- What does food mean to you?
- Why do you eat?

However you express your answers to these questions, it's important to be honest with yourself and to embrace each answer. The better you understand your own triggers when it comes to eating, the easier it will be to break them down and establish a new relationship with food. If you find yourself responding to these question by writing things like, "I eat to feel happy" or "I eat when I'm worried or sad," delve deeper into these feelings. Does eating french fries really make you feel better? What is it about ice cream that makes you feel less stressed? Sadly, eating to feed our emotions usually just exacerbates the negative thoughts in your head. Talk back to those negative thoughts and choose joy and acceptance instead.

I love repeating the mantra *"I deeply love and accept myself"* to help combat negative self-talk.

While emotional triggers may compel you to eat, the most important reason to eat is to provide your body with nourishment so that you can live and thrive. When you learn how to simplify your connection to food and focus on the well-being of your body, you'll be much more motivated to create a nourishing plate at each meal. This is the basis for what I call "mindful eating," the practice of understanding our bodies, living consciously, and making choices that benefit our health.

Here are a few ways to rebuild your relationship with food and adopt a mindful way of eating:

- **Ditch your scale.** I encourage you to stomp on it, burn it (not really), and in the end, throw it away! Let's be honest—how many times have you had a positive experience with your scale? I'm sure you can count them on one hand. For most people, stepping onto the scale, which some people do daily, is like walking up to a firing squad. It is rarely a good feeling, so why do we continue to beat ourselves up? Create a positive environment for yourself and focus on what you eat and how you feel instead of that number on the scale, which usually makes people feel terrible about themselves. Choose self-love instead!

- **Recognize your triggers.** When you find yourself facing the vending machine, pause before you hit the button and think about why you're craving that candy bar. Is it because you're really hungry, or is it because you're bored, upset, or feeling down? Acknowledging your triggers *in the moment* will help you learn to address them in healthier ways. If you're eating because you're sad, go write down your feelings or talk to someone instead. If you're bored, find something else to do—choose something you love that truly fills your soul.

- **Take a deep breath.** Breathing slows you down and creates space and clarity in your decision making. When you are feeling overwhelmed, a deep breath will calm your spirit, and when you experience a sudden craving, it will help ground you and provide a clearer understanding of what is really going on. Take deep breaths before, during, and after your meals to

deter triggers other than hunger and to help you make the best decisions for your body.

- **Create a peaceful environment.** Try eating a meal with no distractions. Turn off the TV. Sit at a table…by yourself. Learning to eat alone, in silence. Paying attention to the process of eating will teach you how to be more mindful when distractions do present themselves.

- **Experience your food.** Every time you eat, take the time to appreciate the texture, aroma, and flavor of your food. Instead of hurriedly shoveling down a mouthful at a time, try to chew each bite at least 20 times. This simple exercise can completely transform the way you experience your meals. Like deep breathing, chewing mindfully will slow you down, allowing you to engage with your body.

- **Eat only until you are satisfied.** After each bite, ask yourself how your stomach feels. Are you satisfied? Did you eat too much? Rate your hunger using a scale of 1 through 10 (1 = famished, 5 = satiated, and 10 = full), and stop eating when you feel satiated, but not full. This will help you learn how much food you really need to nourish your body.

- **Be grateful.** It's pretty amazing when you think about the healing capabilities of food—onions and garlic may guard our bodies from cancer and blueberries may help lower blood pressure. When we're grateful for the nourishing properties of the food we eat, we're more likely to create meals centered on whole, pure, unprocessed ingredients.

- **Indulge.** Avoid feelings of deprivation by focusing on the "haves" instead of the "have nots." Fresh fruits and vegetables and other whole foods are vibrant in flavor and texture, and packed with nutrients to boot! Think about all of the delicious and nourishing foods you can enjoy!

chew your food

When was the last time you were really conscious of chewing your food? It may seem trivial, but chewing with awareness is one of the key components of mindful eating. It helps you slow down and truly savor the flavors, textures, and aromas of the food you eat. Chewing with awareness can keep you from overeating, and it can have a significant positive effect on your health, too.

At your next meal, pay attention to the number of times you chew each bite and your natural reflex to swallow. If you find yourself chewing only a few times between bites, slow down and increase that number to 10 times, then 20 times. The more you chew, the easier it is for your body to digest your food and absorb nutrients, and this can help reduce your risk of bloating and other digestion issues and optimize the health benefits of the foods you eat.

a mindful eating exercise

Sit at your table with your food in front of you. Make sure this space is free of distractions (turn off the TV, put your phone away…you get the point!) Move yourself into to a comfortable seated position with your feet firmly grounded on the floor. Begin by placing your hands in your lap and closing your eyes. Take a few minutes to bring your awareness back to your breathing.

Inhale through your nose and exhale through your mouth to allow the body and mind to settle. As you breathe in, feel the air filling up your lungs, expanding your rib cage, and nourishing your body. As you exhale, soften your belly and feel all of the air exit your body. Allow your body to be still and relaxed.

On your next exhale, slowly open your eyes.

Now, take a moment to simply look at the food in front of you. Does the food evoke any emotional response? If so, recognize what you are feeling—not with judgment but with curiosity instead. Return your focus to the food in front of you. Without touching the food, take a moment to appreciate it. Where has it come from? Consider the hard-working people who produced the food. Try to imagine the different ingredients that make up this food as well as the sunlight, the soil, and/or the animal that nourished or helped create it. Imagine the food's origins—the natural growing environment and the people who took part in bringing the food to your plate. This is a good time to appreciate the fact that you actually *have* food on your plate. Fostering a sense of gratitude is the foundation for a healthy relationship with food and the basis of most mindfulness practices.

Take notice if your mind starts to wander or if you are feeling impatient and eager to take a bite. Perhaps you're thinking of all the other things you need to do. You may even be thinking this is exercise is odd or interesting. Whatever you are feeling, be aware and simply reflect on it without judgment. As many times as you need to, gently bring the focus back to your breathing to ground yourself; repeat this as many times as you need to. Then turn your attention to the food in front of you.

Now, touch your food. Notice the texture, the temperature, and perhaps the color(s) as you pick it up. Gently squeeze the food, even break a piece off and note its characteristics. Is it soft, hard, smooth, or rough? Does touching this food evoke any emotions or thoughts?

Begin to move the food toward your mouth but do not eat it; engage your sense of smell. Does the smell evoke any emotions, memories, or anticipation? Note your thoughts. Is there acceptance of the food as it is, or maybe some resistance to certain aspects of it? Notice whether or not your mind rushes to judge the food or makes any associations. Pause here with your eyes closed and experience the moment.

Now, without chewing, put the food into your mouth. Notice the way it feels, the texture on your tongue, and the temperature. Slowly, take the first bite. Notice any changes in the way the food tastes. Chew this bite of food at least 10

times, noticing changes in texture and flavor. Do you feel an urgency to swallow? Notice if your mind starts to wander, and if it does, gently bring your attention back to the experience.

As you chew the food, notice any sounds that you hear. Listen to how the food sounds as you chew and the sounds of others around you. As you swallow the food, take note of the way it feels as it moves through your throat, down to your stomach.

Repeat this exercise with another bite of food. Notice any sense of urgency you may feel to rush the process. Be aware that your breathing may change depending on your level of comfort with the experience. Notice other physical cues like satiety or fullness. Notice any emotions you feel—such as joy, bliss, awe, or excitement—as you continue to taste and appreciate each bite of food you take.

This mindful eating exercise might seem very foreign to you. That's okay! I remember the first time I did an exercise like this. It was hard not to laugh because there were aspects of it that felt, well, strange! Remember, you are allowed to laugh or feel funny! The point is for you to become more engaged in your eating experience—that doesn't mean you have to be 100% serious the whole time.

get physical

Exercise is an essential part of any mindful, nourishing lifestyle. Exercise can help with weight loss, which is generally an integral component of diabetes management. It can also help you improve your blood glucose control, reduce your risk of heart disease and stroke, and, most importantly, make you feel good! Exercise releases endorphins, which have been shown to boost peoples' moods and even improve self-esteem.

Don't worry—you don't have to run a marathon to reap the benefits of physical activity. The idea is to get moving and stay active, and the best way to do that is by doing activities that you enjoy. Go for a walk around the block during your lunch break at work. Turn on your favorite playlist and dance it out at home. Sign up for a yoga class. Walk the dog. Join a community sports team or a running group. Whatever the activity, aim for at least 30 minutes of exercise each day, either all at once or broken up into 10-minute segments. Be gentle on yourself. It may feel hard at first, but, like most things, it gets easier with practice and persistence. Don't commit yourself to perfection either. Set reasonable and achievable goals and understand that if you miss a day (or even a week) this does not make you a failure. There is no need to throw in the towel. Simply start where you left off. Every day is a new opportunity to make healthy choices.

If you feel overwhelmed, that's okay. You are not alone. Here are a few tips to keep you motivated and having fun while being active:

1. **Schedule it.** The best way to ensure that you take that first step is to schedule it, just like you would a business meeting or an outing with a friend. Look at your calendar and actually commit to a certain time of day and, to start, 1–2 days during that week.

2. **Post reminders.** This is less about reminding yourself to go take a walk and more about reminding yourself *why* you should! Positive reminders act as motivators to get you off the couch and on the move. Try writing things like, "I will sleep so much better tonight if I go to the gym," or "I always feel great after a good workout."

3. **Think of it as you-time.** Let's be honest, life can get hectic. Exercise, if only a 10-minute walk, can offer you the time and space to be alone and decompress. Plus, moving your body helps to free up any negative energy that may feel stuck inside you. Shake it out!

4. **Choose something fun.** Exercise should be fun! If it feels like torture then you are not likely to stick with it. You don't have to run on the treadmill and resent every minute of it to reap the benefits of "moving." Think outside the box. Dance with your kids. Hike in the woods. Try an exercise video in the comfort of your own home. Whatever it is, make sure you are enjoying it. If you like what you're doing, you have a better chance of staying motivated.

5. **Buy new sneakers.** I know this may sound silly, but most people feel like they can run an extra 10 miles in a new pair of running shoes. Buy yourself some workout gear that gets you excited. This in itself can make your workout more fun.

6. **Phone a friend.** Having a workout partner is a great way to keep yourself accountable and keep your workouts fun.

7. **Sign up for a class.** If you are having a tough time convincing yourself to get up and out the door, then maybe the schedule and financial commitment of a class will help you. Workout classes are a great way to meet new people and have fun while being active.

8. **Consider finding a coach or trainer.** A personal trainer can be a great first step for people who are trying to be more active, and you don't have to commit to using one forever. Having someone to cheer you on during those first couple of weeks can make all the difference.

9. **Track your progress.** Remember those awesome sticker charts we had when we were kids to keep track of good behavior? Tracking positive progress feels equally as rewarding in adult life! Make a chart or log and track your accomplishments. It is really motivating! Focus on progress instead of perfection. If you run a mile one day and only feel up to a walk the next day, congratulate yourself just the same because you got your body moving!

Blueberry Yogurt Lemon Bars p. 233
Hibiscus, Citrus, and Berry Cooler p. 236

understanding macronutrients

The scientific facts surrounding a diabetes diagnosis may not seem very exciting, but it is important to understand how your body works. This chapter should help you get a grasp on the basic science behind eating with diabetes. Even if the concepts are a bit difficult to understand, you can at least find some wonder in the fact that everything going on in your body is pretty miraculous. Keep that in mind as you read this book, and you'll appreciate how complex and amazing your body is by the end!

We have already covered the basics of blood glucose and the role that insulin plays to make blood glucose accessible to cells (see Living with Diabetes on page 8). But where exactly does glucose come from in the first place? The short answer is that it is derived from the nutrients in the foods we eat—more specifically from the macronutrient known as carbohydrate. The liver also produces glucose when our blood glucose levels dip below a certain point. While carbohydrate is especially important in relation to our blood glucose levels, we need all of the macronutrients in order to survive and each has its own, relevant role in our overall heath and the management of diabetes. There are three macronutrients: carbohydrate, protein, and fat. Every time we eat, our bodies break down the food into easily digestible carbohydrates, fats, and proteins and extract micronutrients such as

vitamins and minerals to nourish and fuel our bodies. Each macronutrient has many functions once digested. This chapter gives a general overview of each macronutrient and explains why they are so important.

carbohydrate

Carbohydrate is the body's quick-fire source of energy. Carbohydrate-rich foods—made up of starches, sugars, and fiber—are broken down into glucose, which is absorbed through the walls of the small intestine and then into the bloodstream. With the help of insulin, the glucose can fuel the cells throughout the body, keeping you energized and feeling sharp. Excess glucose is either stored in the liver to be distributed later (between meals or during rigorous exercise), or converted into fat for long-term storage. If you eat too much carbohydrate, though, or have a condition like diabetes, which affects insulin productivity, your body won't be able to process the glucose in an efficient way. This will result in excessive amounts of glucose left in the bloodstream. Over time, high blood glucose levels can negatively impact your heart, kidneys, nerves and more. (See Living with Diabetes on page 8 for more information about insulin and diabetes.)

Carbohydrates are found in many different types of food. Starch and fiber, or complex carbohydrates, are found in breads, pastas, grains, and many different fruits and vegetables. These compounds have larger molecular structures than simple carbohydrates and therefore take longer for the body to digest and convert to glucose.

Fiber is an indigestible component of many unrefined sources of carbohydrate such as fruits, vegetables, whole grains, and beans. It plays an important role in overall health and the treatment of diabetes. A diet that is high in dietary fiber has many benefits. High-fiber diets:

- **Promote digestive health.** Dietary fiber plays an important role in bowel health. A high-fiber diet decreases your risk of constipation as the fiber adds bulk to your stool, allowing it to pass more easily. Prebiotic fibers, found in many fruits and vegetables, also support the healthy bacteria (probiotics) in your gut.

- **May lower cholesterol levels.** The soluble fiber found in beans, oats, flaxseed, and oat bran may help lower total blood cholesterol levels by lowering low-density lipoprotein ("bad") cholesterol levels. A diet rich in fiber has also been linked to decreased inflammation and blood pressure.

- **Promote weight management.** High-fiber foods are filling so they leave your feeling satisfied longer than refined, low-fiber foods.

Nourishing, high-fiber carbohydrates include:

- Beans and legumes
- Fruits and vegetables with edible skins (apples, pears, corn, beans, etc.) and edible seeds (berries)
- Whole-grain pastas, cereals, and breads
- Whole grains like barley, spelt, and wheat berries

Less healthy sources of carbohydrates include refined grains (such as white breads, crackers, and pastries), desserts, sweetened beverages like sodas, and other highly processed or refined foods—especially those with added sugars.

protein

While carbohydrate provides energy to your cells and brain, protein makes sure everything runs smoothly. Think of protein as your body's maintenance crew—it builds, strengthens, and repairs tissue; produces antibodies, hormones, and enzymes; aids in muscle movement; transports oxygen throughout the body; and facilitates communication between cells. In other words, protein regulates the intricate processes and chemical reactions that keep us alive.

Proteins such as meat, poultry, and fish do not affect blood glucose levels, though plant-based proteins (beans, lentils, and tofu, for example) do contain some carbohydrate. Balancing and even reducing the amount of starchy carbohydrates on your plate in favor of some healthy protein sources may help to decrease the amount of carbohydrate you consume and may improve your blood glucose levels, but more research is needed. Just make sure that you are mindful of what proteins you introduce into your diet. Meats and other protein-rich foods that are battered, fried, or sauced contain extra carbohydrates that will negatively affect blood glucose levels. Note that some protein-containing foods like beans, legumes, milk, and other dairy products also contain carbohydrate.

Healthy proteins include:

- Chicken and turkey
- Eggs
- Fish and seafood
- Lean meats
- Legumes
- Nuts
- Seeds
- Tofu

fat

Though fat is often villainized as a cause of weight gain and other health conditions, it's actually a vital nutrient that we need to survive. It promotes healthy hormone function, helps our bodies absorb nutrients, and supplies us with energy. While the overconsumption of saturated fats, like those found in most animal products, has been linked to disease, consuming unsaturated fats (including those found in olive oil, nuts, seeds, fish, and avocado) is satisfying and can actually help protect you from disease. Similarly to proteins, replacing some of the carbohydrates on your plate with a healthy fat is nice way to increase the nutrient density of your meal and potentially improve glycemic control. But keep in mind that fats are calorically dense, so it is important to be mindful of portion sizes.

Fat alone has little to no effect on blood glucose but it may help balance overall blood glucose levels when eaten along with carbohydrates. It can be very beneficial to swap some of the carbohydrates on your plate for healthy fats. According to researchers, fats may help slow down the digestion and absorption of the carbohydrates, but more research is needed on this.

Healthy fats include:

- **Olive oil.** Predominantly comprised of healthy, monounsaturated fats, olive oil is also rich in antioxidants that prevent atherosclerosis. Use cold-pressed, unrefined olive oil as part of a salad dressing. Drizzle extra-virgin olive oil onto grains, vegetables, or other healthy foods as a finishing oil. Olive oil can also be used with low- to medium-temperature cooking methods, including baking.

- **Avocado and avocado oil.** Avocados are a satisfying fruit rich in vitamin E, monounsaturated fats, vitamin K, and folate. Avocado oil has a high smoke point and can be used for cooking, baking, and grilling. Try replacing corn oil, vegetable oil, and canola oil with avocado oil when cooking. If you like avocados, you can cut a slice of avocado and sprinkle it with a little sea salt and olive oil for a quick and satisfying healthy snack. Avocados can also be used in place of mayo; thinly slice an avocado and use it as a spread on your next sandwich. You can even add avocado to smoothies to increase the healthy fat content. Avocados are great at breakfast with eggs or smashed onto toast. Just keep in mind that the serving size for these delicious fruits is 1/5 of a medium avocado.

- **Nuts and nut oils.** Rich in protein, fiber, antioxidants, and (of course) healthy fats, nuts also contain minerals including iron, zinc, calcium, and vitamin E. Nut oils, like walnut oil, are packed with anti-inflammatory omega-3 fatty acids. You can use nut oils for dressings, pesto, or as a finishing oil. Do not heat nut oils; when heated, they can burn easily. Add nuts to vegetable and/or grain salads, smoothies, and cereals. Or you can grind them up and make your own nut flours or butters (see the recipes on pages 71 and 72). Eat raw nuts as a snack or throw them into a trail mix.

- **Eggs.** Forget about your egg-white omelet and start using the yolk as well! Some studies have shown that consuming dietary cholesterol (found in egg yolks) does not negatively impact serum or blood cholesterol levels. The yolk houses the majority of the egg's nutrients—other than the protein found in the whites. Choose grass-fed, pastured eggs and enjoy the whole thing—yolk and all! But make sure you limit your egg consumption to no more than one whole egg per day. A hard-boiled egg is a great, make-ahead snack or breakfast. Note: many foods that contain cholesterol, such as eggs, beef, and full-fat dairy, may also contain saturated fats, so they should be consumed in moderation.

- **Seeds.** Rich in magnesium, a nutrient that is commonly lacking in the American diet,

seeds also contain calcium, fiber, protein, and healthy fats. Add seeds such as pumpkin seeds, sunflower seeds, hemp seeds, sesame seeds, and chia seeds to yogurts, smoothies, salads, and cereals (hot or cold). Make your own nut/seed butters by blending whole nuts and seeds together with a pinch of salt in a food processor (see the recipes on pages 71 and 72).

rearrange your plate

Changing your lifestyle and the way you eat can seem like a daunting task. Not sure where to begin? Start with your plate. By adjusting the proportions of your meals to reflect a more plant-centric approach to eating, you can make serious strides toward reducing blood glucose levels and insulin resistance and boosting your overall health.

At each meal, fill half of your plate with non-starchy vegetables, then fill one-quarter of your plate with whole grains or starchy vegetables and fill the remaining one-quarter of the plate with lean protein. To complete the meal, pour yourself a glass of water, unsweetened tea, or milk, include a serving of fruit (if it fits with your meal plan), and enjoy! Remember to include some healthy fats as well; but keep an eye on portion sizes. Pause before you eat to feel grateful and empowered by the nourishing plate of food you have created.

6 ways to decrease your animal protein intake... and still feel satisfied

Decreasing your consumption of animal proteins is an amazing way to reduce your carbon footprint, save money, and make room on your plate for more vegetables! Here are some tips to get you started:

1. **Find inspiration:** Let's be honest, when it comes to meal planning the first thing many people choose is which animal protein will headline the meal. Challenge yourself to plan a meal around a vegetable that inspires you instead. A picture on social media, a trip to the farmers' market, and a few moments in the produce aisle at your grocery store are all great places to find inspiration. You can even ask your family which vegetables they love! Creating a more plant-centric plate can be as easy as roasting, sautéing, or grilling your favorite veggies—though you can get more creative as well. You can cook a plant-based recipe to take center stage on your plate and then choose a complementary animal protein to add to it. Or, be brave and skip the animal protein altogether (even if it's just a few times a week)!

2. **Rearrange your plate:** If you choose to incorporate an animal protein, visualize your rearranged plate for guidance on the correct portion size. Aim for at least half of your plate to be filled with colorful vegetables and then try to fill in the gaps with other plant-based foods like whole grains, fruits, nuts, seeds, and beans. If you include animal proteins, limit the serving size to 1/4 of your plate or a few ounces of protein.

3. **Experiment with plant proteins:** It's easy to omit animal proteins from your meals once you are familiar with their plant-based counterparts—think nuts, seeds, beans, and even whole grains! You can make homemade bean burgers, sprinkle nuts onto vegetables (walnuts and green beans, for example), or incorporate seeds into protein-rich grains like quinoa. Nut butters and seed pastes (like tahini—sesame paste) are amazing additions to marinades and salad dressings. Speaking of salads, you can simply add nuts, seeds, and/or beans to your favorite greens.

4. **Eat real foods:** Aim to be a purist when it comes to your food choices. It is not necessarily healthier to replace animal proteins with highly processed "fake meat" plant-based foods. The quality of the foods you eat is just as important as the breakdown of your plate! Whole foods are more nutrient dense than highly processed and refined versions of the same foods. Use this "real food" test: choose items that have ingredients that you could purchase at the grocery store if you wanted to make them yourself. Try to choose plant and animal ingredients that are free of pesticides, hormones, antibiotics, and chemicals. Buy local when possible to maximize the nutrient density of your ingredients.

5. **Plan ahead:** This is paramount when it comes to making behavior changes because old habits are hard to break. It will be easier to incorporate more vegetables and other plant-based foods into your diet if you have a strategy in place. Choosing recipes, planning weekly menus, and shopping for corresponding ingredients can help keep you on track. By planning your menus you can mindfully choose to incorporate animal proteins in smaller quantities or into fewer meals. Precut fruits and vegetables so they are easily accessible for snacking or recipe creations. Cook large batches of grains, beans, and vegetables and store them in the fridge for easy inclusion in meals throughout the week. For example, a batch of cooked millet can become a part of your breakfast cereal, grain salad, pilaf, or veggie-rich chili.

6. **Get creative:** Don't feel limited to the literal concept of a vegetable-centric plate. There are so many creative ways to eat more vegetables and include more plant-based foods in your diet—even if you're an omnivore. Start your day with a whole-grain breakfast cereal fortified with fruit, nuts, and seeds or enjoy a vegetable-based smoothie. Cook up a frittata that is overflowing with vegetables and light on the eggs. Snack on raw or roasted vegetables dipped into bean purées that are enhanced with roasted sweet potatoes or winter squash. Add vegetables to sauces; try the Zucchini Salsa Verde (page 86) and Walnut Arugula Pesto (page 81) recipes in this book, and couple them with a smaller portion of an animal protein. Create mouthwatering flavors with herbs and spices and explore different cooking methods (like grilling and roasting) that can help bolster any ingredient's natural goodness.

Almond, Wild Blueberry, and Flax Smoothie p. 92

85 everyday superfoods

Just as plants rely on nutrients from the soil to thrive, our bodies rely on nutrients from our daily meals. Whenever I give nutrition consultations, I ask my clients to think about why they eat and to visualize the way certain foods work in their bodies. For example, take those shiitake mushrooms you just threw into your stir-fry. With each bite of the mushrooms, picture them releasing an army of vitamins and minerals into your body that will defend your immune system and boost your heart health. Or how about that green tea you just ordered at the café? Imagine how each sip works to possibly reduce your risk of disease.

For more than 2,000 years—before the discovery of morphine in 1805 and the birth of modern pharmaceuticals—Greek, European, and Asian medicinal practices relied on nothing more than plants and other natural substances to maintain wellness and prevent disease. Somewhere along the line, as modern medicine evolved, the culinary treatments that had been used for centuries fell into the category "alternative medicine," but that doesn't mean these foods ever lost their health benefits. In fact, with the amazing variety of ingredients available to modern-day shoppers— new specialty markets and artisanal growers and producers are cropping up each year—it's easier than ever to use amazing, healing ingredients in your everyday meals. To help you maximize the nourishing power of your food, I've included a list of 85 superfoods that you can keep on hand or add to your shopping list and incorporate into your meals.

herbs and spices

BASIL

Basil contains vitamin A, which is important for good vision and has antioxidant properties. Its many essential oils may play a role in antibacterial, antifungal, and anti-inflammatory properties. Some people consume basil to aid digestion and soothe sore throats. According to a 2012 study published in *Toxicology and Industrial Health*, basil extract may help control diabetes by reducing free radicals in the body.

CARDAMOM

Cardamom, a spice that originated in India, provides a nutty yet sweet flavor that is perfect in hot-and-spicy dishes but also complements sweet flavors. Just 1 teaspoon of ground cardamom seeds provides the body with a healthy amount of manganese, which aids in fat and carbohydrate metabolism, may play a role in blood glucose regulation (though more research is needed), and is a key player in brain and nerve function. Cardamom also contains vitamins A and C, calcium, copper, magnesium, and iron. Studies have found that the flavonoid levels in cardamom can boost antioxidant activity.

CILANTRO AND CORIANDER

Coriander, the seed of the cilantro plant, has a citrusy, sage-like flavor. Studies have also shown that coriander seeds may reduce cholesterol and blood glucose levels. Cilantro, also known as Chinese parsley, contains vitamins A, C, and K and small amounts of potassium, folate, and the antioxidant beta-carotene. It is also a natural breath freshener and digestif, and has been lauded by researchers for its antibacterial properties.

CINNAMON

Cinnamon is a common household spice that provides some unique health benefits. One compound found in cinnamon, cinnamaldehyde, is an anti-inflammatory agent that might prevent blood clotting. Cinnamon's essential oils demonstrate antimicrobial properties, and scientists have also reported that this warming spice has the potential to help inhibit the growth of cervical cancer. Its smell alone, studies suggest, may improve cognitive functioning. Cinnamon could potentially help ease indigestion, flatulence, heartburn, nausea, and stomach cramps.

CLOVE

Ground clove has a unique and sweet, yet earthy and warming flavor profile. It contains essential oils, which have been found to possess antioxidant, antimicrobial, anti-inflammatory, antiviral, and antifungal properties. Cloves also contain flavonoids, which may give this spice immune-boosting potential.

CUMIN

Cumin seeds come from a flowering plant that closely resembles dill, and their nutty, peppery, citrusy flavor is a key component in Indian, Middle Eastern, Mexican, and Tex-Mex cuisines (think curries and other spicy stews like chili). Cumin contains iron, a mineral that helps distribute oxygen through the bloodstream, is a key component in energy production and metabolism, and helps keep your immune system going strong. Studies have also suggested that cumin may promote stress relief and memory retention.

MINT

Mint is perhaps best known as an ingredient in toothpaste, and for good reason. According to various studies, peppermint extract and oil can help promote oral health and prevent dental cavities. This fresh-tasting herb also contains the antioxidant rosmarinic acid, which has been shown to reduce inflammation in the body and relieve symptoms of seasonal allergies.

MUSTARD SEEDS

Mustard seeds contain selenium and magnesium as well as phytonutrients, and may decrease the risk of certain cancers, according to some research. There are about 40 different varieties of mustard plants (a relative of broccoli, Brussels sprouts, and cabbage), but the three types most commonly used for their seeds are black, white, and brown mustard plants. Black mustard seeds have the strongest flavor. White mustard seeds (actually more yellow in color) are the mildest; they're used to make American yellow mustard. And brown mustard seeds (dark yellow in color) are used to make Dijon mustard.

OREGANO

Oregano is a culinary herb that contains antioxidants and vitamin C. In a 2009 study published in the journal *Nutrition and Cancer,* scientists reported that oregano extract may help reduce the risk of colon cancer. Oregano also contains beta-caryophyllene, which, according to various studies, can reduce inflammation in the body, among other possible benefits.

PAPRIKA

Paprika, a spice made from ground chilies, adds a vibrant punch of flavor and color to any dish. Its heat comes from the chemical capsaicin, which has been studied for its anti-inflammatory and anticancer benefits.

PARSLEY

Parsley may be best known as a popular garnish for restaurant dishes, but it's much more than just a pretty decoration. Containing antioxidants, essential oils, vitamins, and minerals—and lots of verdant, zingy flavor—this common herb deserves a spot in your regular cooking routine! It provides vitamins A, C, and K, as well as iron, copper, and manganese. Parsley is grown year-round in different parts of the country, but you'll find the freshest bunches at your farmers' market in early spring.

ROSEMARY

Rosemary is an evergreen herb native to the Mediterranean. It contains iron, calcium, vitamin B6, and antioxidants. According to scientific research, compounds found in rosemary can reduce inflammation and the growth of tumors in the body, help slow the progression of certain cancers, and enhance mood and brain function.

TARRAGON

Tarragon is a delicate herb with a unique, anise-like flavor and peppery notes. Tarragon contains iron, flavonoids, and other antioxidants, and trace amounts of calcium, potassium, and vitamin A. Studies have found that Mexican tarragon has antibacterial and antifungal characteristics, and tarragon in general may help reduce inflammation and prevent damage to the liver.

THYME

Recent studies have shown that extracts found in thyme may have significant anti-inflammatory, antioxidant, and antibacterial properties. Luteolin, the primary phenolic compound in thyme, may have significant anticancer properties.

TURMERIC

Turmeric is a spice that packs a huge punch both in color and in health benefits. According to some studies, curcumin—the yellow or orange pigment in turmeric—might help reduce inflammation and provide relief for patients with inflammatory bowel disease and rheumatoid arthritis. Researchers have also examined curcumin for its antioxidant properties; it has been reported to demonstrate positive effects on arthritis, allergies, asthma, atherosclerosis, heart disease, Alzheimer's disease, diabetes, and cancer.

vegetables

ARTICHOKES

Artichokes, though considered a vegetable, are actually part of the thistle family. The edible parts of the artichoke are the bud and heart, which is located near the top of the stem right below the bud. Artichokes are commonly grown in America, Europe, and in Mediterranean regions. Artichokes are considered a superfood according to various studies, as they have the highest antioxidant content compared to other vegetables.

ARUGULA

Arugula is one of the healthiest salad greens out there. It contains calcium, iron, and vitamins A, C, and K. And like its other cruciferous relatives (broccoli, cauliflower, and cabbage), this peppery green contains glucosinolates, compounds that may help stave off certain forms of cancer, according to some studies.

ASPARAGUS

Asparagus is one of the first vegetables to signify the beginning of spring in most regions across the U.S. Appropriately javelin-shaped, this superfood contains nutrients, antioxidants, and glutathione, a compound thought to help eliminate carcinogens and free radicals. Asparagus also contains vitamins A, C, E, and K; dietary fiber; and chromium.

BELL PEPPERS

Bell peppers come in a variety of colors— green, red, orange, and yellow—and contain antioxidants, vitamins, and minerals that the body needs to stay healthy. One medium red bell pepper provides about twice the recommended daily intake of vitamin C (more than an orange!), and contains B vitamins. And with a healthy dose of dietary fiber, only 5 grams of natural sugar, and about 37 calories per medium pepper, they're the perfect ingredient for adding a burst of flavor to any meal without adding excess calories, fat, or cholesterol. When buying bell peppers, opt for brightly colored peppers with firm, taut skin.

BOK CHOY

Bok choy is a type of Chinese cabbage with thick white stalks and dark green leaves. It contains vitamins A and C, which act as antioxidants and may help stave off and prevent disease, as well as magnesium, calcium, and vitamin K, which promote strong bones and teeth. Bok choy is also a source of folate, vitamin B6, and potassium, all of which may reduce the risk of heart disease according to some studies. And bok choy provides a healthy dose of glucosinolates, unique compounds that may help to prevent certain types of cancer.

BROCCOLI

Broccoli is a member of the cabbage family (*Brassica oleracea*). It has a unique mix of textures (crunchy, fibrous stems and soft, delicate florets) and a ton of potential health benefits to boot. This tree-shaped superfood is brimming with nutrients and compounds that help promote many of the body's vital functions and help stave off disease. Broccoli contains calcium; vitamins A, C, and K; fiber; and chromium.

BRUSSELS SPROUTS

Brussels sprouts, an often under-hyped member of the cabbage family (*Brassica oleracea*), are a source of protein, iron, potassium, and a host of other nutrients that can help keep you healthy and kick disease to the curb. Like their cabbage-family relatives, Brussels sprouts contain glucosinolates, a compound that has been said to reduce the risk of certain types of cancer, and folate, which may reduce the risk of heart disease. Plus, these little gems contain vitamin C and fiber.

CABBAGE

Cabbage plays a starring role in almost every traditional cuisine worldwide, and for good reason. It contains antioxidant phytochemicals, vitamin C, manganese, and polyphenols. Like its fellow members of the cabbage family (*Brassica oleracea*), cabbage also contains glucosinolates—sulfur-containing compounds that scientists have found inhibit the development of certain cancers. While all types of cabbage (white, green, red, savoy, etc.) are incredibly good for you, red cabbage stands above the rest; it has a bolder flavor and contains more polyphenols and other phytonutrients per serving than other types of cabbage.

CARROTS

Carrots have long been associated with promoting healthy eyesight (due to their high concentrations of vitamin A and beta-carotene), but that's just one example of their potential health benefits. These sweet root vegetables—ranging in color from white to yellow, orange, and purple—are also packed with fiber, vitamin K, and phytonutrients, which make them a healthy choice for people with diabetes.

CAULIFLOWER

Cauliflower, broccoli's pale, mild-flavored cousin, shares many of the same health benefits as broccoli. It contains fiber; antioxidants like manganese and vitamin C; anti-inflammatory vitamin K and omega-3 fatty acids; and anticancer glucosinolate compounds.

CHILIES

Chile peppers come in a wide variety of shapes, sizes, and colors, and vary in terms of heat, from mild (cherry peppers and pimentos) to medium (jalapeños and long hots) to extreme (Scotch bonnets and ghost peppers). The heat in chilies comes from the chemical capsaicin, which has been studied for its anti-inflammatory and anticancer benefits (at least with some forms of cancer). And what's more, these powerful little firecrackers have also been shown to contain high amounts of vitamins A and C, and they are a source of folic acid, potassium, and vitamin E.

CUCUMBERS

Cucumbers come in many varieties and belong to the same family as melons. They are typically consumed either pickled or in raw form. Cucumbers contain a variety of nutrients including vitamin A and vitamin C as well as other phytochemicals, which may have antioxidant and anti-inflammatory properties. Researchers are currently looking at compounds in cucumbers called cucurbitacins, which may be helpful in the development of anticancer drugs.

EGGPLANT

Eggplant is a member of the nightshade family, and therefore exhibits health benefits similar to those of its cousins: tomatoes, bell peppers, and potatoes. Eggplant has a good amount of fiber and also contains healthy doses of copper, manganese, B vitamins, vitamin K, potassium, and folate. Eggplant contains polyphenols, which some scientists believe may play a role in preventing cancer and diabetes. Nasunin, an antioxidant compound found in eggplant skin, has been shown to reduce the risk of cell damage caused by free radicals.

GARLIC

Garlic is the most pungent member of the *Allium* family, which also includes onions, scallions, shallots, and leeks. The sulfur compounds that produce garlic's strong odor do much more than ward off vampires and evil spirits (according to folklore); scientific studies suggest that these compounds may also prevent blood clots, fight bacteria in the body, and reduce the risk of cancer. Cured (dried) garlic can be found year-round at the grocery store, and fresh garlic is available at farmers' markets from mid to late summer. Keep your eyes open for garlic scallions (also known as spring garlic) when temperatures begin to climb in March or April, and pick up a bunch or two of garlic scapes (the curly, above-ground stalks of the garlic plant) when they appear at the farmers' market in early summer. Though mature garlic has the most nutritional value, these other parts of the plant also contain sulfur compounds and other powerful phytonutrients.

GINGER

Ginger has been researched extensively as a potential treatment for nausea, pain relief, and symptoms of the common cold. Classified as an herb, this knobby rhizome (root) has a strong, spicy-sweet flavor that is common in Asian and Indian cuisines. Mature ginger can be found in grocery stores year-round, and young ginger (though difficult to find) is harvested in various regions of the U.S. from spring to midsummer. When buying ginger, look for smooth skin and bright yellow flesh.

KALE

Kale is a non-head-forming member of the cabbage family (*Brassica oleracea*), with hearty leaves that range from green to purple in color, and ruffled to poker-straight in shape. Its high concentration of vitamins A, C, and K make it an antioxidant powerhouse, which is great because its peak season spans from early fall to late winter, the time of year when all of our immune systems could use an extra boost. When shopping for kale, look for small to medium bunches of perky, richly colored leaves.

MUSHROOMS

Mushrooms are especially known for their powerful antioxidant properties, which can both boost and suppress the body's immune response as needed. Scientific studies have found that mushrooms are nutritious and may boost your immune system. Most mushrooms also contain high amounts of vitamin D. When shopping for mushrooms, look for smooth, plump caps and avoid those with bruises or soft brown spots. Though you can always find cremini, white, shiitake, and portobello mushrooms at the grocery store, there are many other varieties, both wild and cultivated, that crop up at farmers' markets throughout the year. Look out for brain-like morels in early spring; hefty, orange Chicken of the Woods mushrooms in summer and early fall; and fan-shaped oyster mushrooms in the winter.

MUSTARD GREENS

Mustard greens (the leaves of the mustard plant) have a peppery flavor that is almost as strong as the arsenal of nutrients they contain. A member of the *Brassica* family, these frilly greens are full of antioxidants that may help reduce inflammation in the body. Most grocery stores carry mustard greens all year long, but they are best from mid-fall to early spring, when you'll find them in heaps at the farmers' market, ranging in color from neon green to blood red. Look for

vibrant, small- to medium-sized bunches, and avoid greens that look wilted or spotty.

ONIONS

Onions are a universal ingredient of most traditional cuisines throughout the world. Like their fellow *Alliums* (garlic, scallions, shallots, etc.), onions contain sulfur compounds that may play a role in reducing inflammation in the body and lowering the risk of cancer. Plus, onions contain the flavanoid quercitin, which has been shown to have antibacterial properties. Cured (dried) onions can be found at the grocery store year-round, but it's worth the trip to the farmers' market in spring and summer for spring onions (also known as scallions) and fresh onions. These have the highest concentration of nutrients and a bright, slightly mellow flavor. When shopping for onions, look for firm bulbs without any discoloration.

POTATOES

Potatoes are one of the most popular vegetables on the planet, though they get a bad rap due to the fact that they're often prepared using popular, but less-than-healthy cooking methods like frying. Be sure not to judge the humble spud on its color alone; white vegetables, including potatoes, provide significant amounts of key shortfall nutrients (nutrients that Americans usually don't consume enough of) including potassium and fiber. After all, potatoes are tubers—swollen roots that provide food for the above-ground plants. You may be surprised that to learn that one medium potato with the skin is an excellent source of vitamin C; contains as much or more potassium than bananas, spinach, or broccoli; and contains vitamin B6 and various other important vitamins and minerals such as thiamin, riboflavin, folate, magnesium, phosphorus, iron, and zinc—all for around 170 calories and minimal fat. Potatoes are grown year-round in the U.S., and there are seven different types: white, red, russet, fingerling, yellow, petites, and blue/purple.

SEAWEED

Seaweed is a mineral powerhouse that also contains unique flavonoids with antioxidant properties. Seaweed contains protein and B vitamins—an unlikely combination for a vegetable. Some scientists have looked at seaweed and its role in preventing cancer, reducing the risk of blood clots, and fighting viruses, but more research is needed. The sulfate polysaccharides found in seaweed may also play a role in cardiovascular benefits as they have anticoagulation properties. Sea veggies are rich in iodine and contain vitamin C and iron.

SPINACH

Spinach belongs to the same family as Swiss chard and beets, and contains phytochemicals, vitamins, and minerals that may show promise in preventing certain cancers and reducing inflammation in the body. It is also one of the best plant-based sources of iron, which contributes to our energy level. Spinach boasts especially high levels of potassium, too. Look for spinach at the farmers' market in the spring and fall, and pick bunches or bags full of firm, richly colored leaves.

SUMMER SQUASH

Summer squash comes in many different varieties—from the familiar zucchini, to yellow crookneck squash, globe-shaped eight-ball squash, and scalloped pattypan squash. Like their fellow gourds (cucumber, pumpkin, and melon), their flesh is tender and sweet, and they are packed with antioxidants and other essential nutrients. Look for summer squash at the farmers' market from June to late August, when squash harvests are so plentiful that farmers practically give them away. The best summer squash are firm, smooth, and evenly colored.

SWEET POTATOES

Sweet potatoes are one of the best plant sources of vitamin A and an excellent starch choice for people with diabetes. Though the orange-fleshed varieties are the most common, you'll also find sweet potatoes in varying shades of white and purple at the farmers' market during their peak season, mid- to late fall. Look for firm, smooth tubers with even coloring. In order to get the most nutritional bang for your buck, make sure you eat the skins of the sweet potatoes, which are rich in antioxidant phytochemicals.

SWISS CHARD

Swiss chard's vibrant green leaves and colorful stalks make it one of the prettiest vegetables at the farmers' market and also one of the most nutritious. That's because those same pigments that make Swiss chard so eye-catching are actually indications of a plethora of polyphenols and phytonutrients such as kaempferol, betalains, syringic acid—which, according to scientific research, *may* aid in heart health, exhibit antioxidant, anti-inflammatory, and anticancer properties, and play a role in blood glucose regulation. Look for chard at the farmers' market throughout the summer, and choose the brightest bunches with rainbow-colored stems.

TOMATOES

Tomatoes are actually a fruit, but I include them in the vegetable category because they're typically used in savory rather than sweet applications. Like their fellow nightshades (such as eggplant and bell peppers), tomatoes contain antioxidants like vitamins C and E. But where they really shine is in their unique concentration of phytonutrients, which are most prevalent in vibrantly hued heirloom varieties of tomatoes. You'll find a rainbow of colored tomatoes at the farmers' market in the peak of summer, including green-and-yellow zebra tomatoes, aubergine-colored Cherokee purple tomatoes, tangerine sun gold tomatoes, and, of course, giant, wrinkly beefsteak tomatoes. Though you might think tomatoes are at their most nutritious when eaten raw, some research has suggested that cooking actually enhances this fruit's antioxidant activity. One study also looked at the glucose-controlling benefits of tomatoes and found that people who consume tomatoes on a regular basis are 66% less likely to have elevated A1C levels, but more research is needed on this topic.

WINTER SQUASH

Winter squash, relatives of melon and cucumber, is a variety of vegetables that includes pumpkins,

local love

Sure, a plate full of vegetables is a great place to start, but it's also important to think about where those vegetables come from and how far they need to travel from the farm to your kitchen. Think about it like this: a tomato grows on a vine thousands of miles away, receiving nutrients from the soil through the plant's leaves and stem, but as soon as that tomato is picked from the plant, it no longer has a nutrient source. With each mile it is transported and with each day it sits—first in the grocery store and then on your kitchen counter—it loses more nutritional value and becomes a little more bland in flavor and dull in color. If you eat a tomato right off the vine, however, you'll notice the difference immediately, as the sweet, tangy juices dribble down your chin. Not only are fresh-picked veggies more vibrant in color and flavor, but because there's much less of a disconnect between their source (the soil and the plants) and your plate, they also contain higher concentrations of nutrients. Plus, each time you choose to buy your produce directly from local producers—at farmers' markets or farm stands—you help their businesses and boost the local food economy, making it possible for farmers to diversify their crops and grow more plants—which will, in turn, benefit you in the future.

buying organic

My clients often ask me if they should buy organic and my answer is always the same: it is a personal decision. It is difficult to eat a 100% organic diet, so remember, perfection does not exist. If you can afford organic foods, then by all means purchase them when you can. But remember, "organic" does not equal "healthy;" the term simply means that there are regulations around the chemicals and growing practices that are used. For example, an organic cookie will have just as much sugar as a conventional cookie! Instead of focusing on buying organic, keep your focus on providing as much nourishment for your body as possible. Remember that a plate full of whole foods is a nourishing plate no matter what!

butternut squash, acorn squash, delicata squash, spaghetti squash, and Hubbard squash, many of which are native to North America. Though they vary widely in color, shape, size, and flavor, each variety of winter squash has a tough shell, mildly sweet flesh, and a hollow center containing its seeds, which are also edible (and delicious!). Swing by the farmers' market in mid- to late fall to see the many different types of winter squash that are grown in your region. And don't worry about buying too many; some of the thicker-skinned varieties of winter squash will keep for up to 6 months in a cool, dry place. Winter squash contain vitamin A, vitamin C, potassium, manganese, and an assortment of antioxidants, including beta-carotene, which, according to research, may help reduce the risk of breast cancer. And don't forget about the seeds: winter squash seeds contain fiber, omega-3 fatty acids, protein, minerals, and vitamins.

fruits

APPLES

As the saying goes, apples might actually help to keep the doctor away with their various nutritional benefits. The antioxidants found in apples may potentially help neutralize free radicals in the body, specifically protecting against heart disease. The particular combination of nutrients, antioxidants, and soluble fiber in apples has also been shown to lower total and low-density lipoprotein, or LDL ("bad"), cholesterol with regular intake. Studies have shown that the flavonoids in apples, such as

quercetin, might slow down the development of cancers of the colon, lung, and breast in several stages of cancer development. To get the most nutrients from this fruit, choose firm, blemish-free apples and eat the skin as well as the flesh.

AVOCADOS

Avocados contain a wide range of carotenoids, such as beta-carotene, alpha-carotene, and lutein, as well as monounsaturated fats, which can reduce LDL ("bad") cholesterol levels. In fact, avocados have an impressive nutrient profile, containing nearly 20 different vitamins and minerals. Though about 80% of an avocado's calories come from fat, the type of fat contained in this creamy-textured fruit includes anti-inflammatory phytosterols, polyhydroxylated fatty alcohols (PFAs), and oleic acid, which can help with the absorption of fat-soluble nutrients and may reduce the risk of heart disease. These fats increase satiety and energy. Avocado falls very low on the glycemic index, and the sugars it does contain may help regulate the metabolism of blood glucose in the body, though scientific studies are still ongoing. Avocados *may* also help control post-meal insulin levels; when pairing avocados with carbohydrate, some studies show that initial post-meal blood glucose levels are lower than the post-meal levels in people who don't eat the avocado. But more research is needed on this potential benefit.

BLACKBERRIES

Blackberries are one of the most antioxidant-rich fruits available. Brimming with vitamin C and phytonutrients, they also contain tannins that have been shown to reduce inflammation in the body. And since they're very low in calories and high in fiber, these little jewels make a great snack to hold you over between meals. Look for them at the farmers' market in the peak of summer, and choose the deepest-colored berries for the best flavor and the most nutritional benefit.

BLUEBERRIES

Blueberries are one of the few fruits native to North America, and their cultivation is relatively recent, dating back to the early 1900s. Now, the U.S. is one of the largest producers of these blue-black shrub berries, with growers located primarily in New Jersey, Michigan, Indiana, North Carolina, Washington, and Oregon. Rich in fiber, phytonutrients, and other antioxidants—and very low in calories per serving—blueberries have been studied for their possible connection to a lowered risk of heart disease, age-related cognitive decline, and some cancers. Look for them at the farmers' market from summer to early fall, and choose berries that are taut, smooth, and vibrant in color. For an added boost of nutrients, choose wild blueberries, which are commonly found in Maine and Canada and have a higher concentration of flavonoids and phytochemicals.

CANTALOUPE

Cantaloupe has more beta-carotene, an antioxidant, than oranges and is a great source of vitamin C, vitamin A, potassium, copper, folate, and B vitamins. Plus, its seeds contain heart-healthy omega-3 fatty acids.

CHERRIES

Cherries have a very short season, from May to July (weather permitting), and though they are most commonly used in summer pies, both the tart and sweet varieties are delicious in savory recipes, too. Containing a plethora of antioxidants, such as vitamin C, anthocyanins, carotenoids, and possibly some melatonin, these stone fruits—especially the tart varieties—may help increase the quality of your sleep, reduce inflammation in the body, decrease the risk of gout attacks, and protect against heart disease and diabetes. And as an added bonus, they provide the body with a healthy dose of fiber. When shopping for cherries, look for shiny, taut skin and deep, vibrant color.

CRANBERRIES

Cranberries are most well-known for their prevention of urinary tract infections. This benefit is due to their proanthocyanidin (PAC) content, which prevents bacteria from adhering to the urinary tract lining. Some studies suggest that extracts and compounds found in cranberries may help prevent not only urinary tract infections but possibly even cancer. However, consumers should be cautious when choosing cranberry products because many cranberry juices contain a large amount of added sugar.

GRAPEFRUIT

Grapefruit is grown throughout the year in the warmer U.S. states, with harvests coming from the west (Arizona and California) in spring and summer and from the south (Florida and

Texas) from fall through spring. Though they are available in three different colors—white, pink, and ruby red—I recommend opting for the boldest hue, since richer pigments suggest higher concentrations of phytonutrients. Along with a healthy dose of vitamin C, grapefruit's unique combination of phytonutrients has been shown in some studies to relieve symptoms of the common cold and may prevent certain types of cancer. Studies have also found that eating fresh grapefruit may help improve insulin resistance and contribute to weight loss.

GRAPES

Grapes are one of the most universal fruits, as they are cultivated on every continent except Antarctica. They are an excellent source of flavonoid compounds and other antioxidants, which have been studied in connection to a decreased risk of heart disease, cancer, neurodegenerative disease, and age-related cognitive decline. In addition, grapes are also a good source of vitamin K, copper, and vitamin B2, and they fall very low on the glycemic index, making them a good choice for people who are monitoring their blood glucose.

KIWI

Kiwi, also known as kiwifruit, may be small, but they are mighty. Don't let this fruit fool you, it is packed with nutritional benefits; kiwi contains vitamin A, vitamin K, and potassium. Research has shown that kiwi has the ability to protect the DNA in the nucleus from oxygen-related damages. Kiwi is a good source of fiber that may help to reduce the risk of heart disease.

LEMONS

Lemons originated in Southeast Asia and have been used for millennia in all sorts of applications, from culinary to medicinal to purely pragmatic (as a bleaching agent). Depending on the variety and where they are grown, lemons can be as small as eggs or as large as grapefruits. But no matter their size, fruits rich in vitamin C and phytonutrients have been shown to potentially reduce inflammation and may help prevent certain types of cancer.

LIMES

Limes are very similar to lemons in terms of nutritional value, boasting high amounts of vitamin C (in the whole fruit), a healthy dose of folate, and lots of antioxidant flavonoid compounds. Some studies have shown that limes may have antibacterial and antiseptic properties. Though limes are available year-round in the U.S., their peak season is from spring to late summer.

MANGO

The mango, a universally popular fruit, is rich in vitamin C, beta-carotene, and fiber. The polyphenols found in the edible parts of the mango have been shown to have antioxidant and anticancer properties.

ORANGES

Oranges are known for their high vitamin C and fiber content. They also contain a variety of minerals such as calcium, potassium, and copper.

Orange zest contains essential oils that are rich in antioxidants, which may help to prevent cancer.

PEARS

Pears provide fiber, copper, vitamin C, and vitamin K, but it's the phytonutrient content of pears that make this fruit a true superfood. Between the flesh and the skin, pears contain a unique mix of antioxidant and anti-inflammatory phenolic phytonutrients and flavonoids. The fiber in pears helps control satiety, keeping people fuller for a longer period of time. Because the majority of pears' phytonutrients and about half of their dietary fiber are found in the skin, you should resist the urge to peel pears before cooking or eating them. You can find pears in most farmers' markets across the country from late summer through the end of fall, and sometimes into early spring.

POMEGRANATES

Pomegranates are one of the most labor-intensive fruits to eat, but trust me, they're well worth the effort. The juicy, sweet yet tart arils (seeds), which are clustered in web-like membranes beneath the fruit's outer skin, contain a powerhouse of vitamin C, phytochemicals, and fiber—all key nutrients for fighting disease and maintaining a healthy heart. Pomegranates are grown throughout Asia, the Mediterranean, Africa, and California and are available in the U.S. from August to December.

RASPBERRIES

Raspberries may be small, but they are mighty. A relatively low-sugar fruit, not only do raspberries contain vitamin C, manganese, and a great deal of fiber, but they also provide a diverse number of phytonutrients that work as antioxidant and anti-inflammatory agents in the body. According to scientific research, the phytochemicals found in raspberries may have potential to lower the risk of cardiovascular disease and cancer, and raspberry ketone, an aromatic compound found in red raspberries, may aid in healthy metabolism and the prevention of obesity. Raspberries are in season from May to September (weather permitting), and in three different varieties: red, golden, and black.

STRAWBERRIES

Strawberries are very low in calories and high in fiber, vitamin C, manganese, and phytonutrients that may potentially benefit heart health and protect the body from disease. According to some scientific research, consuming strawberries on a regular basis may reduce certain risk factors for and complications of diabetes.

WATERMELON

Watermelon's red, juicy flesh is rich in lycopene, and its white rind is an excellent source of vitamin C, both of which boost the anti-inflammatory properties of this fruit. The antioxidant content of watermelon increases as the fruit ripens, so choose a ripe and juicy melon for the most nutritional benefits. Studies have suggested that watermelon may relieve muscle soreness, and help lower blood pressure.

nuts and seeds

ALMONDS

Almonds have been cultivated since prehistoric times and are now grown predominately in California, Spain, and Italy. Though they are stone fruits, related to apricots, peaches, and cherries, the fruit that grows around the almond nut (or pit) is generally too tough to enjoy and can only be eaten when immature. Almonds, however, are one of the most nutrient-rich of all nuts, containing high amounts of calcium, fiber, folic acid, magnesium, potassium, riboflavin, and vitamin E, plus a healthy dose of monounsaturated fats, which, according to some research, may help reduce the risk of heart disease.

BRAZIL NUTS

The Brazil nut, a tree nut, is unique for its high selenium content. Just one nut contains around 137% of your daily value of selenium, which works as an antioxidant in the body and plays an important role in metabolism. Aside from their high selenium content, Brazil nuts are also rich in healthy fats, protein, and fiber. This chewy yet firm nut is perfect for snacking or making nut butter or milk. Brazil nuts also contain important minerals including calcium, magnesium, and zinc.

CASHEWS

Cashews contain less fat than many other varieties of nuts, and the type of fat they do contain, monounsaturated fat, may potentially provide protective benefits for cardiovascular health. The benefits of cashews are also tied to their copper content; copper has been shown to promote bone health, and it *may* help prevent osteoporosis according to some studies, though more research is needed. The magnesium content of cashews also aids in building and maintaining strong bones. Nut intake in general is linked to a lower risk of weight gain, but be sure to keep an eye on serving sizes when enjoying nuts.

CHIA SEEDS

Chia seeds resemble poppy seeds in both texture and size and come from the chia plant. These seeds can be sprinkled onto salads or into yogurt, smoothies, or drinks. Chia seeds have a very impressive nutrient profile as they contain heart-healthy fats, fiber, protein, and a variety of vitamins and minerals in just a small serving. Chia seeds contain a high concentration of the omega-3 fat alpha-linolenic acid which has been associated with health benefits including lowering triglyceride levels, producing anti-inflammatory activity, lowering blood pressure, and protecting overall heart health. At a serving of only 1 ounce, chia seeds also give us about 18% of the recommended daily allowance of calcium and about 24% of the recommended daily allowance of magnesium.

FLAXSEED

Flaxseed contains high amounts of alpha-linolenic acid, a type of omega-3 fatty acid that may be beneficial in the prevention of heart disease, inflammatory bowel disease, and arthritis, according to some research. Flaxseeds also contain lignans, fiber-like antioxidants that decrease inflammation, and mucilage, a gel-like substance that may provide digestive health benefits, including increasing digestion time to allow for more nutrient absorption.

HEMP SEEDS

Hemp seeds (or hemp hearts) have about a 3:1 ratio of omega-3 to omega-6 fatty acids, making this nutty-tasting seed optimal for heart health. The seeds contain nine essential amino acids, and just one serving of hemp seeds provides us with 10 grams of protein. Hemp seeds help with digestion as they have both soluble and insoluble fiber. Hemp is also rich in magnesium. You can eat hemp seeds for all of these benefits, or purchase hemp oil which gives you all of the heart-healthy fats and packs anti-inflammatory properties. Ditch protein powder and try using these seeds in your next smoothie or shake!

PECANS

Pecans contain high amounts of antioxidants as well as essential minerals like manganese, copper, magnesium, and zinc. Some research has shown that the monounsaturated fats found in pecans may aid in heart health, and that consuming pecans on a regular basis could potentially help protect your nervous system from degenerative diseases such as ALS (Lou Gehrig's disease).

PISTACHIOS

Per serving, pistachios are lower in calories and higher in potassium and vitamin K than most other nuts, making them a good midday snack that will fill you up between meals. They have also been shown to help lower cholesterol. That beautiful green-ish purple hue pistachios have comes from antioxidants, which aid in removing free radicals from the body. Compared to most other nuts, pistachios are lower in fat and calories. At about 49 nuts per serving, they'll keep you satisfied. They also contain fiber and protein. Pistachios (and other nuts with shells), are a great mindful eating snack; they take time to eat due to the shell, which helps prevent people from overeating. Native to the Middle East, the pistachio tree thrives in warm climates, producing olive-like fruits that encase the green nut or kernel.

POPPY SEEDS

Poppy seeds, also referred to as khus khus, are normally thought of as a bagel topping. But these little seeds can be enjoyed on many things other than bagels, as they have a nutty yet mild taste and pack a lot of health benefits. They contain fiber, essential fatty acids, and good amounts of calcium, potassium, and iron. Poppy seeds also contain essential essential oils including oleic acids, which may play a role in reducing LDL ("bad") cholesterol.

PUMPKIN SEEDS

Pumpkin seeds are a good source of zinc, an essential nutrient that affects many cellular functions and may positively impact both prostate and bone health. These seeds may decrease the risk of some cancers according to studies. Pumpkin seeds contain phytosterols, which, according to some research, may help regulate cholesterol levels. Additionally, pumpkin seeds contain a wide variety of minerals, including magnesium.

SESAME SEEDS

These nutty seeds, which range in color from cream and brown to red and black, are used prolifically in Asian, African, and Middle Eastern cuisines. For their miniscule size, they pack a major nutritional punch. Not only are they a good source of copper,

10 everyday uses for nuts and seeds

Packed with fats, protein, and nutrients galore, nuts and seeds are incredibly good for us—and it's easy to fit them in our everyday routines. Including nuts and seeds in a meal or enjoying them as a snack can improve satiety, satisfaction, and the overall nutrient density of your plate!

Here are some simple ways to include more nuts and seed in your diet:

- Substitute ground flaxseed for eggs when baking: Use 1 tablespoon finely ground chia seeds or flaxseed (grind them dry in a blender, food processor, or coffee grinder) mixed with 3 tablespoons of water. This ratio will replace 1 egg.

- Use them to thicken soups and stews. Just stir in a couple of tablespoons of ground or whole chia seeds to hot soup or stews until you reach your desired thickness. Wait 10–15 minutes for the chia to thicken to its full capacity.

- Use ground nuts, nut flours (see the recipe on page 72), or seeds as a breading or topping: A mix of ground seeds, like sunflower, pumpkin, flax, sesame, and/or chia seeds, makes a great, crunchy topping either used alone or tossed with some herbs and spices. Coat fish or chicken with egg or mustard and then press the protein into the ground mixture. Then bake or pan sear.

- Add whole or ground seeds, such as chia, sesame, poppy, or pumpkin seeds, to the batter of muffins, breads, cakes, waffles, or pancakes for a nutrition boost and extra crunch.

- Mix ground flaxseed or chia seeds into yogurt and smoothies.

- Add a few tablespoons of whole chia seeds to iced tea or fresh juice. Allow the seeds to sit in the liquid overnight so the seeds plump up.

- Top vegetable or grain salads, cooked or raw veggies, or hot cereal with pumpkin, sunflower, chia, or poppy seeds.

- Grind sunflower or pumpkin seeds together with garlic, parsley, and cilantro, and then mix in some lemon juice and olive oil to make a flavorful and healthy dressing for greens.

- Roast sunflower seeds or pumpkin seeds with a dash of salt, pepper, and olive oil for a tasty and healthy snack.

- Make a nut-free "nut" butter: grind sunflower seeds in a food processor on high speed until a paste forms (you may need to add a touch of vegetable oil to thin it out).

which helps boost the immune system and reduce inflammation, but they also provide healthy amounts of manganese, calcium, magnesium, iron, phosphorous, vitamin B1, zinc, molybdenum, selenium, and fiber. One ounce of sesame seeds has about as much calcium as a glass of milk!

SUNFLOWER SEEDS

Sunflower seeds are one of my favorite snacks. They help curb hunger in between meals and provide the body with a good boost of vitamin E, magnesium, and selenium. Plus, they contain phytosterols, which, according to some research, may help regulate cholesterol. You will find both shelled and unshelled sunflower seeds in the bulk sections of most health-food stores.

WALNUTS

Walnuts are a heart-healthy nut! They have been shown to lower both total cholesterol and LDL ("bad") cholesterol, and they are a good source of vitamin E, which acts as an antioxidant in the body. Walnuts also contain the minerals calcium, magnesium, and potassium, which may help protect against hypertension. Walnuts are a good source of alpha-linolenic acid (ALA), a type of omega-3 fatty acid that aids in cardiovascular health, may help ease the symptoms of asthma, and may help reduce inflammation in the body.

whole grains, beans, and legumes

AMARANTH

Amaranth is a gluten-free seed that is commonly categorized as a grain. This "grain" looks similar to couscous and can be cooked much like pasta. Amaranth contains iron, calcium, protein, and carotenoids. It also contains phytochemicals and peptides that some research has linked to a potential reduction in the risks of hypertension and cancer. The phytochemical content of this seed has been associated with lower incidence of heart disease.

BARLEY

Barley looks similar to wheat berries but has a pasta-like consistency and a rich, nutty flavor. The high fiber content of barley supports digestive health and promotes healthy gut bacteria. The insoluble fiber in barley produces a short-chain fatty acid that helps maintain a healthy colon and may help to lower total cholesterol. Barley contains selenium, which may prevent inflammation, improve immune response, and detoxify some cancer-causing compounds in the body. Barley also contains magnesium, which acts as a co-factor to enzymes that are involved in the body's use of insulin secretion.

BEANS

Beans—like black, navy, and cannellini beans, for example—are a digestive health powerhouse, with 1 cup containing roughly 10–15 grams of protein and around 15 grams of fiber. They are especially beneficial to colon health, and as with all beans, they may promote cardiovascular health and help you maintain a healthy weight. Beans are also a good source of magnesium and potassium.

BROWN RICE

Brown rice is a more nutritious choice than white rice because it has not been stripped of its nutrient-dense bran and germ the way that white rice has. Brown rice is a good source of manganese, magnesium, selenium, and fiber. Selenium and fiber may reduce the risk of colon cancer, and the rice bran oil naturally found in brown rice has been shown to help lower blood cholesterol. Additionally, brown rice is a whole grain and is associated with all the benefits that may accompany the consumption of whole grains, including increased cardiovascular health, a lower risk of weight gain, and much more.

BUCKWHEAT

Buckwheat, surprisingly enough, is not related to wheat but is rather a gluten-free seed related to rhubarb. It can be served hot in cereals or stews or cold in salads, and it is comparable in size and texture to rice. Buckwheat contains high amounts of dietary fiber and magnesium, which some studies suggest may decrease the risk of developing type 2 diabetes. It also contains protein, B vitamins, manganese, copper, and phosphorous.

LENTILS

Lentils are a heart-healthy legume and, like beans, they have a smooth exterior with a starchy-soft interior. Lentils are often sold dried and can be prepared much like beans—though, unlike beans, most of the dried varieties of lentils do not need to be soaked prior to cooking. Lentils are glorified for their fiber content, which may play a role in lowering cholesterol levels and promoting overall heart health. These legumes also contain a significant amount of folate and magnesium, a calcium-channel blocker that allows veins and arteries to relax. Lentils are a complex carbohydrate that digests slowly and

they are a good source of iron, a mineral that is responsible for increasing our energy. Add lentils into soups and stews or eat them cold in a salad; they provide protein and healthy carbohydrate!

MILLET

Millet may be best known for its use in birdseed, but this ancient grain has been cultivated since prehistoric times. There are many different varieties, but the most common type of millet (Indian millet or broomcorn) is sweet and nutty in flavor and is a staple food in many cuisines across the world. Millet is a good source of dietary fiber, copper, phosphorous, magnesium, manganese, and phytonutrients, which have been shown to help regulate blood pressure, potentially prevent certain types of cancer, and promote overall good health.

OATS

Enjoying oats is truly one of the best ways to start off the day. Oats contain a specific type of fiber called beta-glucans that have been shown to lower total blood cholesterol levels. Oats contain unique antioxidants—avenanthramides—that may help to protect against free radicals from LDL ("bad") cholesterol. Because of these antioxidants and its total fiber content, this whole grain helps protect against cardiovascular disease, according to research. Studies have shown that consuming oats may help to improve carbohydrate metabolism. Oats are naturally gluten-free, so they're safe for people with celiac disease; but look for "gluten-free" on the label when shopping for oats to ensure that they have not been cross-contaminated with gluten-containing products during processing and packaging.

QUINOA

Quinoa (pronounced "keen-wah") is a seed—though we often refer to it as a grain—that originated in the Andes mountains thousands of years ago. It has been called "the gold of the Incas" because of its nutritive value. Quinoa is a good source of complete protein (it has the highest protein content of any grain/seed), which means it contains all the essential amino acids our bodies cannot make on their own. It is a good source of calcium, lysine, B vitamins, and iron. Quinoa is also easy to digest, gluten-free, and extremely tasty. When cooked, quinoa has a feathery look, an almost crunchy texture, and a delicate, nutty flavor. The most commonly found variety of quinoa is tan or yellow in color (other varieties can be orange, red, pink, purple, or black) and can be found at health-food stores and many grocery stores. It is cheapest when purchased in bulk. Store quinoa in an airtight container; it will keep in its uncooked form for several months if refrigerated.

SORGHUM

Sorghum is an ancient, gluten-free grain that, when cooked, has a consistency similar to rice. Sorghum has an impressive nutrient profile; it contains high levels of protein, fiber, calcium, and antioxidants. The phytochemicals in sorghum are associated with a reduced risk of colon and skin cancer.

WHEAT

Like other whole grains, wheat is rich in fiber, protein, and magnesium, which may aid in blood pressure regulation, digestion, and overall good health. Farro, a type of wheat, is especially popular in Italy for its chewy texture and nutty flavor, and is a common substitute for Arborio rice in traditional risotto. For maximum health benefits, look for whole-grain varieties of wheat (farro, bulgur, wheat berries, freekeh, etc.) in the bulk aisle of health-food stores. Wheat berries are whole, unprocessed kernels of wheat that are packed with fiber, protein, manganese, and magnesium. When cooked (see the recipe for Wheat Berries with Pesto, Kale, and White Beans on page 168), their nutty, slightly sweet flavor complements just about anything, from sweet puddings to herbaceous salads to hearty stews. Look for wheat berries in the bulk food section of any major health-food store, and use them wherever you would use rice or other grains.

beneficial beta-glucans

A popular topic of discussion as of late, beta-glucans are a type of fiber that have been studied for their beneficial role in lowering insulin resistance and blood cholesterol, their potential for reducing the risk of obesity, and their ability to boost the immune system to fight cancer.

Beta-glucans are found in the cell walls of certain grains (such as oats and barley), certain types of mushrooms (such as reishi, shiitake, and maitake), and yeasts, seaweed, and algae. A lesser amount of beta-glucans can be found in wheat, rye, and sorghum. Among these sources, barley and oats contains the highest quantities.

Grilled Fish Tacos with Strawberry-Mango Salsa p. 193

prepping for success
tips and tricks for everyday cooking

I have a confession to make: while I cook for a living, I don't usually have the time or the energy to whip up elaborate meals for myself. After spending years working in the homes of my clients, helping them improve their cooking know-how, I have learned that approachability is the key to nutritious cooking. What my clients and I crave are delicious-yet-simple meals that can be whipped up in a cinch, without the stress of fussy ingredients or difficult techniques. This chapter is full of tips to help you make your shopping, meal planning, and cooking experiences fun and easy!

Cooking at home is one of the best ways to improve your eating habits and adapt to a healthier lifestyle. The more confident you are in the kitchen, the more likely you are to incorporate nourishing foods into your meals. Studies have shown that establishing a regular cooking routine can reduce stress and improve longevity, too.

Need some motivation? Here are five ways to embrace cooking at home:

1. **Find your motivation.** Check in with yourself and figure out what inspires you to cook at home. Is it the money you'll save by eating in? The pounds you'll shed and the sense of overall well-being you'll feel? Or is it simply the joy that cooking brings you? Whatever gets you into the kitchen, harness it, write it down, and draw from it when you need to.

2. **Turn inspiration into excitement.** Sure, cooking is good for your health, but it can also be fun! Make it a group activity by including friends and loved ones, or challenge yourself to create an entire meal around an ingredient you find at the farmers' market. Maybe a new, funky apron or baking bandana would liven up the event. Some people love cooking to their favorite playlist, and others enjoy the sound of the sizzling sauté pan. There are so many ways to find joy in even the most basic tasks as you whip up a meal that will nourish your body and spirit.

3. **Feeling overwhelmed? Start small.** It is important to manage your expectations. The last thing you want is to set out to make an elaborate meal and end up feeling overwhelmed, exasperated, and frustrated. Engaging with your kitchen can be as simple as making yourself breakfast or packing your lunch. If you are new to cooking, then choosing just a recipe or two to try is a great place to start. Cooking is meant to make you feel good, so keep it simple and don't take yourself too seriously. We all mess up a meal from time to time—if it happens to you, find humor in the experience! All of the recipes in this book are written to help build your

overcoming kitchen fears

If you're new to cooking, the idea of creating meals from scratch can be downright frightening. Here are a few tips to help you quell those fears and gain confidence in the kitchen:

- **Keep it simple.** You don't have to spend hours in the kitchen to make a delicious meal. Look for recipes that have five ingredients or less, and only a few, easy-to-follow steps.

- **Go easy on yourself.** Approach meal preparation with curiosity and a sense of humor—don't worry about crafting the perfect meal. It takes time to hone your cooking skills, and it's much easier if you embrace the process.

- **Be prepared.** Before you start cooking, prep all of the ingredients in your recipe and look up any terms or techniques you don't understand.

- **Call for support.** Sign up for a group cooking class or invite friends and family to help you tackle a new recipe. Once you create a meal for the first time with a little help, you'll feel much more confident on your own.

- **Use quality ingredients.** Locally grown, in-season fruits and vegetables and grass-fed meats have more nutrients and flavor than their lower-quality counterparts. When you choose high-quality ingredients, you don't need to worry as much about adding extra flavor to the dish.

confidence in the kitchen and inspire you to make cooking a part of your everyday routine.

4. **Ask for help.** Asking for help can mean inviting a friend over for cooking support or engaging with your butcher or fishmonger at the grocery store. I love swapping kitchen tips and advice with my friends—it's great to discuss their favorite kitchen hacks and or the gadgets they can't live without.

5. **Be patient.** Rome wasn't built in a day, and I doubt that your first attempt at cooking will yield a perfect Thanksgiving dinner. Your first few meals may not be pretty— they may not even taste that great—but with every meal cooked you will build confidence and skill. Don't let your fears get in your way. We all have to start somewhere!

healthy cooking 101: creating flavor

If you think that eating nutritious food means sacrificing taste, think again! Healthy, home-cooked meals made with quality ingredients are packed with vibrant flavors. Whether you're new to cooking or you're an experienced chef looking to include more nourishing foods in your meals, these easy tips will help you make healthy dishes even more delicious:

1. **Add acids.** Citrus fruits, such as lemons and limes, and vinegars play an important role in healthy cooking. Acids act a little like salt in that they help bring out the natural brightness of foods and work to meld flavors together. Try making a quick salad dressing

with lemon juice and zest or red wine vinegar and a smidge of oil, or toss veggies and grains with citrus or vinegar to brighten them up. With this added pop of flavor, you'll think it's summer all year long.

2. **Texture, texture, texture.** A healthy meal doesn't have to mean mushy baby food or raw veggies. Add texture to your meal and mix and match your textures for a little smoothness here and a nice surprise crunch or pop there. For example, make a fall grain salad using quinoa to experience the little pop of the kernels, then add some crunch with raw veggies like kale or peppers, add beans or avocado for a silky, buttery feel, and add some dried cranberries for something to chew on.

3. **Herb it up.** When the summer months fade, they leave an abundance of fresh garden herbs in their wake. Nothing brings a little extra life to a meal or dish like some fresh herbs, and they don't add any extra fat or calories. Next time you harvest or buy fresh herbs (such as basil, cilantro, rosemary, or thyme), give them a good chop and mix them with a little oil (see Everyday Herb Oil recipe on page 60). Add some of the herb-infused oil to veggies or meats before grilling, and store the rest in ice-cube trays in the freezer so you have a ready-to-use marinade or seasoning oil on hand all winter long!

4. **Spice and everything nice.** While herbs are often used fresh, spices tend to be dried and jarred, enabling you build a diverse collection over time. Spices are another great way to add flavor and character to a dish without adding calories and fat from sauces. Try the Moroccan Spice Blend recipe on page 73 or experiment with a new spice you're been wanting to try.

5. **Taste the rainbow.** Summer isn't the only time for rainbows. How can you tell a healthy meal by looking at it? Just count the colors! Think of foods as a color wheel; we should draw nutrients from the whole spectrum—reds and oranges, dark greens, blues and purples, and lighter colors. To harness the colors of the rainbow (even in the winter months), roast some fall harvest vegetables or whip up a colorful grain salad (like Curried Quinoa with Butternut Squash and Chickpeas on page 158). A well-rounded, healthy meal is not only scrumptious to eat but also beautiful to look at.

meal planning 101

It's common knowledge that a little planning goes a long way— and this concept certainly applies to most healthy living habits. When you plan time for exercise, cooking, and self-care, you are more likely to prioritize these activities. That being said, taking the time to plan out your weekly meals ahead of time is an excellent way to ensure you will stay on track with your healthy eating goals. All you need is 30 minutes each weekend to take stock of your kitchen, plan your meals for the week, and tackle any prep work in advance. Here are some plan-ahead tips and techniques that will make your life easier during the week:

1. **Look at your calendar.** It's important to have a good idea of your weekly schedule

before you dive into menu planning. This way you can take into consideration any commitments you may have that will influence the number of meals you eat at home and the amount of food you need to purchase for the week. A calendar can help you be more efficient with your planning, save your money, and cut down on food waste. It can also help you plan for busy days by cooking ahead so that a healthy meal is prepared even if you won't have the time to cook.

2. **Check the weather.** Maybe it's going to be blazing hot on Wednesday and there is no way you will want to turn on your stove or oven. Conversely, on a chilly winter evening, you may prefer a soup or stew over a more refreshing salad. This may sound silly, but the weather often influences our food preferences so it is something to consider when planning!

3. **Choose your recipes.** This can be as basic as just choosing the main component of each meal you intend on preparing or as specific as picking out the individual recipes that will be the most efficient use of your time and ingredients. Keep it simple and choose two or three breakfast and lunch options you can use throughout the week. Plan on cooking larger portions of dinner as well so you can save the leftovers for your lunches. If you are cooking for your family or a loved one, make sure to ask them to weigh in on their favorite meals and recipes so that everyone is happy at dinnertime!

4. **Inventory your kitchen.** Save money at the grocery store by taking an inventory of your pantry, fridge, and freezer and planning your meals around items you have on hand (like beans, grains, and excess produce). If you store fruits, vegetables, and animal proteins in the freezer, plan to use a few of those items each week, as frozen foods do not have an unlimited shelf life.

5. **Prep.** I have found that the best time to prep is right when I get home from the grocery store. Cut and store melon so that it is easy to eat. You can dramatically cut down on weeknight prep by precutting frequently used vegetables (onions, peppers, broccoli, zucchini, and more). You can even take things a step further and roast a batch of vegetables or brown some sausage ahead of time so that it is ready to go when you need it. This is a great time to make sure your fridge and pantry are stocked with any of the do-it-yourself (DIY) pantry essentials you will need for the week like sauces, nut milks, and more. (See Chapter 1 beginning on page 59, for some great DIY recipes.)

6. **Portion it out.** Portion out smoothie ingredients into individual bags to be stored in the freezer for morning ease (see Chapter 2 beginning on page 91, for some great smoothie recipes). Or count out individual serving sizes of nuts, seeds, grapes, or berries and store them in plastic sandwich bags so you can grab a healthy snack when you need one.

7. **Batch cook.** At the beginning of each week, I choose a bean and a grain, such as wild

rice, quinoa, millet, or farro, and make a large batch for use later in the week. Cooked whole grains can be used for every meal. To make a breakfast cereal, just reheat the grain with your milk of choice and some cinnamon, then add fruits, nuts, seeds, etc. For lunch or a snack, you can use the precooked grains to whip up one of the grain salads in Chapter 5. Come dinnertime, you can substitute cooked grains for breadcrumbs in a meatball or meat loaf recipe or use them to create a simple side dish.

8. **Boil eggs.** Hard-boiled eggs are an easy, on-the-go protein source. You can enjoy them as a snack or as part of your breakfast. Once you have cooked hard-boiled eggs on hand, you can even whip up a batch of "Everything" Deviled Eggs (page 117) at a moment's notice. Hardboiled eggs also make for a tasty addition to a sandwich or salad.

9. **Whisk up a dressing.** I like to keep homemade vinaigrettes on hand to use on salads, as a marinade, or as a dip for raw and cooked vegetables. Try the Everyday Vinaigrette recipe on page 62 or play around with one of the other dressing recipes in this book. Olive oil is one of the healthiest fats available, but it can be difficult to find a store-bought salad dressing that contains it. Most store-bought dressings (even the organic varieties) contain less healthy, less expensive oils (like soybean oil, for example) as well as added sugars and loads of sodium. So making your own dressings is a healthy option.

10. **DIY lunch meat.** Fresh chicken or turkey is always a healthier option than even the best processed lunch meats available. Store-bought lunch meats are loaded with sodium (even the organic versions). Over the weekend, grill or cook a few chicken breasts for use in salads and on sandwiches, or roast a fresh turkey breast and slice it thinly like lunch meat. You can even roast a whole chicken and use the meat for chicken salad.

11. **Stock up on snacks.** By making your own baked goods and snacks, you can control the ingredients and keep added fats and sugars in check. Make a batch of Zucchini and Carrot Mini Muffins (page 234) or some Curry Roasted Chickpeas (page 120). Remember that you can freeze certain items for later use. It is as important to plan your snacks as it is to plan your meals!

12. **Make friends with your freezer.** Speaking of freezing, you can prep simple, one-pot meals like African Peanut Stew (page 178) or Chipotle-Chocolate Chicken and Root Vegetable Chili (page 183), portion them out, and pop them in the freezer for future use. Having a few freezer meals on hand will prevent you from ordering less-healthy, last-minute takeout!

eating healthy on a budget

Contrary to popular belief, a lifestyle that focuses on whole, nutrient-dense ingredients can work with even the tightest of budgets. Here are some tips and tricks to help you save money at home and in the grocery store:

AT HOME:

- **Do your homework.** Read up on weekly sales and search for healthy recipes that include discounted whole ingredients.

- **Plan it out.** Make a meal plan for the week, factoring in extra servings you'll need to make of certain dishes if you plan to save some for lunch the next day or another dinner later in the week.

- **Inventory.** Take a kitchen inventory of your pantry, fridge, and freezer before you go shopping. This is a great way to reduce waste as you can plan meals around the ingredients you already have that are going bad or that are excessively stocked. This little trick also prevents you from buying double as you will know what you have!

- **Make your own condiments.** Why spend your hard-earned money on store-bought condiments and salad dressings when you can make them at home in minutes and at a fraction of the cost? In Chapter 1 (page 59) you'll find an arsenal of easy recipes for ketchup, salad dressings, tapenade, and other everyday condiments that will add flavor to your meals without a lot of added sugars and preservatives. Keep homemade condiments in jars in the door of your fridge, and you'll never crave the plastic-bottled kind again.

- **Plant a garden.** I promise, you don't have to be a green thumb or have a huge backyard to grow your own produce and herbs. Place pots of basil, chives, oregano, parsley, rosemary, sage, tarragon, or thyme in a sunny window and watch them thrive. Or, if you want to be more adventurous (and have the space to play with), experiment with different vegetable and fruit plants, either in-ground or in containers. You can find detailed information online about which plants grow best in your region.

- **Use it all.** When you plan meals for the week, find ways to utilize the same ingredients in different recipes. That way, you won't waste money on things you only need half of (like bunches of herbs or carrots). Whenever possible, buy beets, turnips, and radishes with tops and cook the greens just as you would kale or spinach. Use fruit scraps to make refreshing infused water.

AT THE MARKET:

- **Don't shop hungry.** Grab a snack before you go to the grocery store. If you go when you're even a little hungry, you'll be tempted to buy things you don't need.

- **Stick to your list.** Grocery stores are designed to tempt you with shiny new promotions, bright packaging, and racks of impulse buys. Let your shopping list act as a blinder to these ploys, and you'll get the last laugh—and you'll have a much lower total at the checkout.

- **Buy in bulk.** If your grocery store has a bulk section, head there for grains, flours, nuts, beans, and pastas. But only buy what you need—sometimes bulk foods can end up being wasted. Also, don't assume that all bulk prices are cheaper than the packaged versions. Check the prices before you buy.

- **Compare prices.** Organic foods and more obscure ingredients are often less expensive at large health-food stores because of supply and demand, and seasonal produce is usually cheaper at the farmers' market than at the grocery store. Do your homework; at many large grocery stores the same food items can be available in different sections at different prices. For example, I once found quinoa in my local grocery store in five different places with prices ranging from $5 to more than $10 a pound.

- **Think in seasons.** Fruits and vegetables that are in-season do not require expensive growing methods and are generally sourced closer to home. Because of their shorter travel time from the farm to the grocery store, they contain more nutrients than exotic and out-of-season produce, and they tend to be cheaper, too.

- **Embrace the frozen section.** Buy frozen fruits and vegetables when they're not in-season. Not only are frozen fruits and vegetables more cost effective, but studies have shown that they can also be more nutrient dense than some of their fresh counterparts because they are picked ripe and then flash frozen. I always have frozen raspberries, wild blueberries, kale, broccoli, quinoa, beans, and rice in my freezer. You can also find great deals on seafood in the frozen aisle; the seafood in the "fresh" case is often frozen and thawed anyway, and frozen seafood has the same health benefits as fresh.

- **Skip convenience foods.** You pay extra when you buy prechopped fruits and vegetables or prepared salads, dips, and other items. Instead, buy whole ingredients and set aside an hour at the beginning of each week to prep them for recipes.

- **Stay away from the drink and junk food aisles.** There's no need to spend money on packaged beverages or bottled water when the ingredients needed to make your own beverages—like Summer Melon Aqua Fresca (page 235), Hibiscus, Citrus, and Berry Cooler (page 236), or smoothies (see Breakfast chapter, page 91)—are much better for you and your wallet. If you are concerned about the quality of your tap water, invest in a filtered pitcher.

- **Buy animal proteins in healthy portion sizes.** When buying meat and other animal proteins, plan for only 2–3 ounces per serving. This way, you will save money and be inspired to fill your plate with more vegetables. Another way to save money on animal protein is to buy whole chickens and larger cuts of meat (like roasts) instead of the pricier, smaller cuts. As soon as you get home, cut the meat into individual portions for the week ahead and stash any extras in the freezer for future weeks.

- **Know when to splurge.** Don't waste money on foods that don't necessarily need to be organic. Study the Environmental Working Group's (EWG) "Clean Fifteen," a list of the safest conventionally grown produce in terms of pesticide contamination. There's no need to spring for the organic versions of these fruits and vegetables. However, you should always choose organic versions when buying produce on the EWG's "Dirty Dozen" list; conventional farms typically use high amounts of pesticides and other chemicals when growing these fruits and vegetables. (Visit www.ewg.org for the full lists.)

- **Maximize your nutrients per dollar.** Sure, potato chips may be inexpensive, but so is a potato—and the whole vegetable is far more nutrient dense and healthy, pound for pound, than processed chips. If you start thinking less in terms of quantity and more in terms of quality when you shop, calculating how many nutrients you can get for your dollar, you'll end up paying less overall and enjoying your food much more.

everyday pantry essentials

By now you've learned the basics of healthy, mindful eating, found new motivations to get you cooking, and armed yourself with tips and techniques that will empower you in the kitchen and beyond. You're almost ready to whip up some delicious, nourishing meals and get started with your new lifestyle. But there's one more thing we need to do before moving forward: it's time to roll up your sleeves, purge all those sugary snacks, processed foods, and refined grains from your kitchen, and restock your pantry and fridge with the nutritious, whole foods that will help you succeed on your journey to better health.

While you may want to have a variety of healthy ingredients on hand—too many options can lead to clutter, spoilage, and food waste. Follow these rules of thumb for stocking your pantry and storing foods to maximize their shelf life:

BEANS AND LENTILS

- **Stock:** 2–3 varieties of dried beans and lentils and/or BPA-free, low-sodium canned beans, such as black beans, chickpeas, and navy beans. (BPA—bisphenol A—is a synthetic compound used in the packaging of many foods and beverages; look for BPA-free products when possible.)

- **Store it:** Legumes can be stored at room temperature though they thrive in a cool, dark place with minimal moisture. Store dried beans in glass jars or canisters.

- **Shelf life:** 1 year.

NUTS, NUT FLOURS, AND SEEDS

- **Stock:** Purchase 2–3 varieties of raw, organic nuts and seeds whenever possible. Raw nuts and seeds are less likely to go rancid then their roasted counterparts. You can make your own nut flours and nut butter (see the DIY recipes listed on page 59) or purchase them from the store. Read the ingredients and look for varieties that only use the ingredients you would use to make it yourself. For example, a nut butter should contain nuts and possibly some sea salt. Period.

- **Store it:** Though nuts can be stored at room temperature it is better to store them in your refrigerator or freezer to protect the natural fats from going rancid. Mason jars and glass canisters work well for storage. I often blend a variety of nuts and seeds together in a jar and keep them in my refrigerator to add to smoothies, yogurt, cereals, grains, salads, and more.
- **Shelf life:** 1 year maximum.

OILS AND BUTTER

- **Stock:** Healthy fats are an important part of a nutritious diet but they are not all created equal. Avoid refined oils and processed vegetable oils like soy, cottonseed, and corn oils—even the organic varieties. The best options are cold-pressed olive oil, walnut oil, and avocado oil. Olive oil is best used cold or for low- to medium-heat cooking. Walnut oil can only be used cold. Avocado oil is good for higher-heat cooking. I also use organic, grass-fed and pastured butter from time to time and I always avoid margarines and vegetable oil spreads that contain hydrogenated fats—I would rather eat the real thing, just less of it.
- **Store it:** Oils can be stored in a cool, dark place, though I recommended storing lesser-used oils in your refrigerators to prevent the fats from going rancid.
- **Shelf life:** 6 months maximum.

VINEGAR

- **Stock:** Balsamic, champagne, and red vinegars, apple cider vinegar, white wine vinegar, etc.
- **Store it:** Store vinegars in a cool, dark place.
- **Shelf life:** Indefinite.

GRAINS

- **Stock:** 2–3 varieties of whole grains such as farro, quinoa, and brown or wild rice, for example.
- **Store it:** Store grains in a cool, dark place with minimal moisture. I also store precooked grains in my freezer for anytime use. Mason jars and glass canisters work well for grain storage.
- **Shelf life:** Up to 3 months in the pantry; up to 6 months in the freezer.

SALT AND SPICES

- **Stock:** Purchase good quality sea salt and small containers of dried herbs and spices to ensure freshness.
- **Store it:** Salt can be stored at room temperature and is not light sensitive. Spices and dried herbs should be stored in tightly covered containers in a cool, dry, and dark environment.
- **Shelf life:** 6 months to 1 year maximum.

SWEETENERS

- **Stock:** Even natural sweeteners should be used in moderation and limited whenever possible. Raw honey, pure maple syrup, dates, and coconut sugar are less refined than white sugar and contain trace amounts of vitamins and minerals.

- **Store it:** Store unrefined, natural sweeteners at room temperature in closed containers away from light, heat, and moisture. Honey will crystallize as it ages and can be warmed slightly to make it pourable again.
- **Shelf life:** Indefinite.

whole foods pantry checklist

Keep these things in your kitchen at all times and you'll never lack options for a healthy meal:

OILS
- Avocado oil
- Extra-virgin olive oil

VINEGARS
- Apple cider vinegar
- Red wine vinegar
- Rice wine vinegar
- White or regular balsamic vinegar
- White wine vinegar

DRIED HERBS AND SPICES
- Basil
- Black peppercorns
- Cardamom
- Chili powder
- Cilantro
- Cinnamon
- Coriander
- Crushed red pepper
- Cumin
- Ginger
- Oregano
- Rosemary
- Sea salt
- Smoked paprika
- Thyme

CONDIMENTS AND SWEETENERS
- Baking powder (aluminum free)
- Cocoa powder
- Dijon mustard
- Maple syrup
- Raw honey
- Whole-grain mustard

NUTS AND SEEDS
- Almonds
- Cashews
- Chia seeds
- Flax
- Hemp seeds
- Nut butter
- Nut flours
- Pistachios
- Pumpkin seeds
- Sesame seeds
- Sunflower seeds
- Walnuts

GRAINS AND BEANS
- Barley
- Black beans
- Brown or wild rice
- Bulgur
- Farro
- Garbanzo beans
- Lentils
- Millet
- Navy beans
- Oats
- Quinoa
- Sorghum
- Spelt

STAPLE PRODUCE
- Avocado
- Carrots
- Cucumbers
- Fresh herbs:
  —Oregano
  —Basil
  —Parsley
  —Thyme
  —Cilantro
- Garlic
- Lemons
- Limes
- Onions
- Oranges
- Shallots
- Tomatoes

kitchen tools checklist

Stocking your kitchen with the right equipment is almost as important as keeping healthy ingredients on hand! However, you don't need a million kitchen tools and gizmos to make healthy meals at home. (I actually love using my hands and have very few gadgets in my kitchen.) Here are the tools that will make your life easier, without creating too much kitchen clutter:

POTS AND PANS

(Note: These are the pots and pans that I use most often in *my* kitchen, but you probably don't need all of them at once. Build your collection of pots and pans slowly over time, based on how and what you like to cook.)

- 8-inch and 12-inch stainless steel skillets or ceramic-lined nonstick skillet
- 10-inch cast-iron skillet
- 16-quart stock pot
- 4-quart saucepan (stainless, cast iron, or ceramic)
- 5–6-quart Dutch oven
- Slow cooker/crock pot
- 9 × 9-inch baking dish
- 9 × 13-inch baking dish
- Bread loaf pan
- Muffin tins (regular and mini)
- Rimmed baking sheet
- Grill pan

ACCESSORIES

- 8-inch kitchen knife
- Box grater
- Can opener
- Cooking thermometer
- Cutting board
- Glass mixing bowls
- Mandolin
- Small grater/zester
- Measuring cups and spoons
- Paring knife
- Vegetable peeler
- Whisk

OTHER

- Blender
- Food processor
- Glass storage containers
- Tea kettle

skip traditional nonstick cookware

Traditional nonstick cookware, which has been coated with polytetrafluoroethylene (PTFE)—a synthetic polymer—is incredibly easy to use and clean. But when heated to high temperatures, experts believe that these pots and pans emit toxic fumes that can cause flu-like symptoms in humans, increase air pollution, and even kill small animals.

The next time you find yourself shopping for new cookware, avoid those that are made with PTFE, and opt for "not nonstick" versions instead. Or, better yet, ditch nonstick all together and go with cast-iron or stainless steel cookware. Both of these alternatives are extremely durable and provide a more even cooking surface than nonstick cookware.

Shrimp Saganaki p. 200

part 2
recipes

pantry staples, condiments, and sauces

Everyone knows that a well-used condiment or seasoning can transform the simplest dish into an exceptional bite. (Think of roasted potato wedges with chipotle ketchup, cucumbers with hummus and roasted red peppers, almond butter on apples, and Moroccan spiced nuts.) However, the store-bought versions of these condiments and seasonings tend to be loaded with excess sugar or artificial sweeteners, salt, preservatives, dyes, and artificial flavor and texture enhancers, all of which we should strive to minimize in our diet.

In this chapter, I will arm you with recipes for all the whole food–based pantry staples, condiments, and sauces you could ever need to spice up your meals. It's time to evict those half-used jars and bottles of processed mayo, ketchup, salad dressings, and sauces from the refrigerator door. Once you discover how easy and rewarding it is to whip up a batch of homemade nut milk, ketchup, pesto, or exotic spice blends, there's no turning back! The dynamic flavors of the fresh, whole ingredients in these recipes will blow you away and make you wonder why you ever used that fake stuff from the grocery store.

Everyday Herb Oil

SERVES: 32 | SERVING SIZE: 1 TABLESPOON | PREP TIME: 5 MINUTES | COOKING TIME: 5 MINUTES

Herb oil makes a great base for vinaigrettes or a simple seasoning for fish, chicken, or vegetables. For this recipe, I use a combination of parsley, oregano, rosemary, and thyme, but you should feel free to experiment with whatever herbs you have growing in your herb garden (or beginning to wilt in the fridge). I keep a variety of infused oils on hand for all my sautéing, roasting, and stir-frying needs. Try on Everyday Grilled Chicken Breasts (page 220). Just remember: a little goes a long way!

1 cup fresh flat-leaf parsley leaves

4 sprigs fresh oregano, stems removed and discarded

2 sprigs fresh rosemary, stems removed and discarded

6 sprigs fresh thyme, stems removed and discarded

2 cups extra-virgin olive oil

1. Bring a medium pot of water to a boil. Fill a medium bowl with ice water and set it nearby.

2. Add the parsley, oregano, rosemary, and thyme leaves to the boiling water, blanch the herbs for 10–15 seconds, then immediately remove the herbs with a slotted spoon and transfer them to the ice water. After a few seconds, remove the herbs from the ice water with a slotted spoon and pat them dry with paper towels.

3. In a blender or food processor, purée the blanched herbs with the olive oil.

4. Pour the herb oil into a dark-colored glass bottle or jar with a tight-fitting lid, seal the container, and set it in a cool, dark place (such as your pantry) to infuse for at least 5 days. After it has been fully infused, keep the oil in the refrigerator for up to 1–2 weeks. Or freeze the herb oil in ice cube trays for future use. (Note that each ice cube is 2 tablespoons of oil.)

EXCHANGES/CHOICES	3 Fat
CALORIES	120
CALORIES FROM FAT	125
TOTAL FAT	14.0 g
SATURATED FAT	1.9 g
TRANS FAT	0.0 g
CHOLESTEROL	0 mg
SODIUM	0 mg
POTASSIUM	5 mg
TOTAL CARBOHYDRATE	0 g
DIETARY FIBER	0 g
SUGARS	0 g
PROTEIN	0 g
PHOSPHORUS	0 mg

maximize your herb use

Fresh herbs are simple and tasty ways to add flavor, color, and a boost of antioxidants and other essential nutrients to your cuisine. Here are some ideas for sneaking fresh herbs into everyday meals, snacks, and even beverages:

- **Herbed Salad Greens:** Toss sprigs of parsley, basil, dill, or rosemary into a salad to add some extra pizzazz.

- **Herbed Ice Cubes:** When freezing ice cubes, add mint or basil leaves to freshen up an ordinary glass of water or iced tea.

- **Fresh Herb Pizza:** Whether you make your pizza from scratch or buy it, there's always room to add a few fresh leaves of basil, rosemary, or oregano to the top before you stick it in the oven.

- **Herb-Infused Honey:** Add lavender, rosemary, thyme, or sage to a jar of honey for delicious flavor and a subtle fragrance. Leave the herbs in the honey jar for at least 5 days prior to use to allow the robust flavors to fully infuse into the honey.

- **Fresh Herbs and Tea:** Add a few leaves of sage or spearmint in with your favorite varieties of tea to spice them up a little!

- **Flavored Salt:** Crush 10–15 leaves of your favorite fresh herb. Place them in a jar with 2 cups of salt. Mix well to combine, pour the mixture into jars, and let it rest for 2–3 weeks to allow the essence of the herbs to infiltrate into the salt. Stir the mixture every 2 days to prevent clumping. Try this with lemon balm, lavender, mint, cilantro, oregano, dill, or rosemary.

While they are available year-round in most markets and grocery stores, like other greens, herbs have the highest nutritional value when picked right from the plant or bought directly from a local farm. To store fresh herbs, wrap the stems in a moist paper towel and place them in a ventilated plastic bag in the refrigerator.

Everyday Vinaigrette

SERVES: 16 | SERVING SIZE: 1 TABLESPOON | PREP TIME: 5 MINUTES | COOKING TIME: NONE

Wash out a glass salad dressing bottle, condiment jar, or a mason jar with a lid and keep it in the pantry for shaking up a quick batch of this homemade vinaigrette. If you have some Everyday Herb Oil (page 60) on hand, use it instead of the regular olive oil. This vinaigrette tastes great on the Kale and Brussels Sprout Salad with Cashews, Pears, and Pomegranate on page 130. This vinaigrette will keep in an airtight container in the refrigerator for up to 1 week.

1/2 cup extra-virgin olive oil

1 teaspoon freshly grated lemon zest

2 tablespoons freshly squeezed lemon juice

1/4 cup white wine vinegar

1 teaspoon Dijon mustard

1/2 teaspoon whole-grain mustard

1/4 teaspoon fine sea salt

1/4 teaspoon freshly ground black pepper

1. In a glass bottle or jar, or in a small bowl, combine the olive oil, lemon zest, lemon juice, vinegar, both mustards, salt, and pepper. If you are using a bottle or jar, seal the container and shake until all of the ingredients are well incorporated. If you are using a bowl, whisk vigorously.

EXCHANGES/CHOICES	1 1/2 Fat
CALORIES	60
CALORIES FROM FAT	70
TOTAL FAT	7.0 g
SATURATED FAT	0.9 g
TRANS FAT	0.0 g
CHOLESTEROL	0 mg
SODIUM	45 mg
POTASSIUM	0 mg
TOTAL CARBOHYDRATE	0 g
DIETARY FIBER	0 g
SUGARS	0 g
PROTEIN	0 g
PHOSPHORUS	0 mg

Everyday Marinara Sauce

SERVES: 20 | SERVING SIZE: 1/2 CUP | PREP TIME: 5 MINUTES | COOKING TIME: 1 HOUR

Growing up in an Italian family, the smell of marinara on the stove was the equivalent of an air freshener in my house. Every few weekends my mom would make a fresh batch and freeze the leftovers for later use. I didn't try a jarred tomato sauce until I was in my twenties. To this day, nothing beats the real deal—homemade marinara—and the memories that are evoked when I make a batch. When I make this sauce, I love to crush the tomatoes by squeezing them through my fingers; it is a wonderful way to channel my Italian grandparents and to feel really engaged in the cooking process. You can whip up this simple sauce any day of the week; not only is it much more flavorful than the jarred stuff you get at the store, but it's also completely free of added sugar, cheap oils, additives, and preservatives.

1/4 cup extra-virgin olive oil

2 cups diced yellow onion

1/2 teaspoon fine sea salt, divided

6 cloves garlic, halved lengthwise

3 (28-ounce) jars or cans whole tomatoes, chopped or crushed with your hands, juices reserved

2 cups water

1 cup chiffonade fresh basil (see Technique Tip)

1 tablespoon fresh oregano

1/4 teaspoon freshly ground black pepper

1. Add the oil, onion, and 1/4 teaspoon salt to a large nonreactive saucepan. Sauté over medium heat for 5–6 minutes or until onions are softened and browned. Add the garlic and sauté for 1 minute.

2. Add the crushed tomatoes, reserved juice, and water. Bring the sauce to a boil then decrease the heat and simmer for at least 1 hour. Stir in the herbs and season with remaining salt and pepper.

3. Purée gently in blender if you want a less chunky consistency.

tip: Chiffonade is a fancy word that refers to the technique of cutting basil or some other delicate herb or green into ribbons. To do this, simply stack the leaves, roll them into a long cigar shape, and then thinly slice the cigar crosswise.

EXCHANGES/CHOICES	1/2 Starch
	1/2 Fat
CALORIES	60
CALORIES FROM FAT	25
TOTAL FAT	3.0 g
SATURATED FAT	0.4 g
TRANS FAT	0.0 g
CHOLESTEROL	0 mg
SODIUM	400 mg
POTASSIUM	260 mg
TOTAL CARBOHYDRATE	8 g
DIETARY FIBER	1 g
SUGARS	4 g
PROTEIN	1 g
PHOSPHORUS	30 mg

Everyday Roasted Garlic

SERVES: 10 | SERVING SIZE: 1 CLOVE | PREP TIME: 5 MINUTES | COOKING TIME: 30–45 MINUTES

Once you experience the amazing aroma of garlic roasting in your oven, you will want to make it all the time. Roasted garlic is buttery, soft, and much sweeter than its raw counterpart. It can be spread on crackers for an easy snack, whisked into vinaigrettes, sauces, and dips, and swapped for fresh garlic in soups and baked dishes. It also adds amazing flavor to the Garlicky Grilled Pork Chops with Navy Beans recipe on page 214.

1 large head garlic

2 tablespoons extra-virgin olive oil, divided

1. Preheat the oven to 350°F.
2. Trim the top 1/4 off the head of garlic to expose the garlic cloves. Place the head of garlic on a sheet of aluminum foil, cut-side up. Drizzle 1 tablespoon of the olive oil on top and enclose the garlic in the foil, making a pouch.
3. Place the aluminum pouch directly on a rack in the top third of the oven and roast for 30–45 minutes or until the cloves are tender and the garlic skins are golden brown.
4. Remove the aluminum pouch from the oven and carefully open the pouch, making sure not to get burned when the steam escapes. Let the garlic cool. When the garlic is cool enough to handle, squeeze the cloves out of their skins.
5. Transfer the roasted garlic cloves to an airtight container and drizzle the remaining tablespoon of olive oil on top. They will keep in the refrigerator for up to 2 weeks.

EXCHANGES/CHOICES	1/2 Fat
CALORIES	30
CALORIES FROM FAT	20
TOTAL FAT	2.5 g
SATURATED FAT	0.4 g
TRANS FAT	0.0 g
CHOLESTEROL	0 mg
SODIUM	0 mg
POTASSIUM	10 mg
TOTAL CARBOHYDRATE	1 g
DIETARY FIBER	0 g
SUGARS	0 g
PROTEIN	0 g
PHOSPHORUS	0 mg

Everyday Roasted Tomatoes

SERVES: 8 | SERVING SIZE: 2 TABLESPOONS | PREP TIME: 5 MINUTES | COOKING TIME: 30 MINUTES

Roasted tomatoes are sweet, caramelized, and completely drool worthy. When I have a batch in the house, I literally slather them onto everything! I love to add these tomatoes to the Socca with Poached Eggs, Roasted Tomatoes, and Fresh Basil recipe on page 101. They are a delicious addition to fish and chicken, sauces and salads or you can enjoy them alone—they are like candy! For best results, make these in the summertime with ripe, juicy tomatoes right off the vine. While the cooking process can reduce the nutritional value of some fruits and vegetables, it actually intensifies the antioxidant properties of tomatoes—particularly their concentration of the phytochemical lycopene.

1 pint grape tomatoes

1 tablespoon extra-virgin olive oil

3 cloves garlic, halved

1 tablespoon chopped fresh herbs (thyme, rosemary, oregano, etc.)

1/4 teaspoon fine sea salt

1/4 teaspoon freshly ground black pepper

1 teaspoon freshly grated lemon zest

1 tablespoon freshly squeezed lemon juice

1. Preheat the oven to 425°F.

2. On a rimmed baking sheet, toss the tomatoes with the olive oil, garlic, herbs, salt, and pepper. Transfer the baking dish to the oven and roast for 25–30 minutes or until the tomatoes burst open and begin to brown.

3. Remove the dish from the oven and toss the roasted tomatoes with the lemon zest and lemon juice before serving.

4. Roasted tomatoes will keep in an airtight container in the refrigerator for up to 1 week.

EXCHANGES/CHOICES	1/2 Fat
CALORIES	25
CALORIES FROM FAT	20
TOTAL FAT	2.0 g
SATURATED FAT	0.2 g
TRANS FAT	0.0 g
CHOLESTEROL	0 mg
SODIUM	70 mg
POTASSIUM	100 mg
TOTAL CARBOHYDRATE	2 g
DIETARY FIBER	1 g
SUGARS	1 g
PROTEIN	0 g
PHOSPHORUS	10 mg

Everyday Roasted Bell Peppers

SERVES: 8 | SERVING SIZE: 1/2 CUP | PREP TIME: 5 MINUTES | COOKING TIME: 30 MINUTES

The smoky, tangy flavor of roasted bell peppers is a welcome addition to all kinds of dishes and you may be surprised at how easy they are to make at home. Chop them up and stir them into homemade hummus, fold them into pasta or cooked grains, blend them into marinara sauce, or simply toss them into your favorite salad. I like to make a Roasted Red Pepper Sauce (page 82) with them. Feeling adventurous? If you have a gas stove you can char the peppers over an open flame (rather than oven roasting them) before steaming and peeling.

5 large red bell peppers

2 tablespoons extra-virgin olive oil

1/4 teaspoon fine sea salt

1/4 teaspoon freshly ground black pepper

1. Preheat the oven to 500°F.

2. Place whole peppers on a rimmed baking dish and roast them in the oven for 30–40 minutes, turning them after 20 minutes, until the skins are completely wrinkled and the peppers are charred and tender.

3. Remove peppers from the oven and transfer them to a bowl. Cover the bowl with aluminum foil or plastic wrap and let the peppers steam for 10 minutes.

4. Remove the foil from the bowl. Peel off pepper skins, cut peppers in half lengthwise, and scoop out the seeds. Cut peppers into strips and place in an airtight container, along with any reserved juices from the bowl, the olive oil, and the salt and pepper. Toss gently to combine.

5. The peppers will keep in an airtight container in the refrigerator for up to 1 week.

EXCHANGES/CHOICES	1 Nonstarchy Vegetable
	1 Fat
CALORIES	70
CALORIES FROM FAT	30
TOTAL FAT	3.5 g
SATURATED FAT	0.5 g
TRANS FAT	0.0 g
CHOLESTEROL	0 mg
SODIUM	70 mg
POTASSIUM	245 mg
TOTAL CARBOHYDRATE	7 g
DIETARY FIBER	2 g
SUGARS	5 g
PROTEIN	1 g
PHOSPHORUS	30 mg

Everyday Applesauce

SERVES: 6 | SERVING SIZE: 1/2 CUP | PREP TIME: 15 MINUTES | COOKING TIME: 40 MINUTES

Sure, you can purchase some no-sugar-added applesauce at the grocery store, but I guarantee this recipe will be far tastier than a store-bought version. Experiment with different kinds of apples according to your taste. If you like your applesauce on the sweeter side, try using Fuji, gala, or Honeycrisp varieties of apples. If you like tart flavors mix in Granny Smiths, Ida Reds, or Gold Rushes. The result is a spoonful of fall goodness the whole family will love. This applesauce is also great for baking; try it in the Oat and Quinoa Breafast Bars with Raisins and Tahini (page 99).

2 pounds apples, peeled, cored, and chopped

1 cup water

2 tablespoons freshly squeezed lemon juice

1 teaspoon ground cinnamon

1. In a medium saucepan, combine the apples, water, lemon juice, and cinnamon. Cover the pan and bring the mixture to a boil over high heat. Then reduce heat to medium-low and simmer for about 30 minutes, stirring occasionally, until the apples are broken down completely.

2. Remove pan from heat and let applesauce cool for 10 minutes. Then transfer the applesauce to a food processor or blender and purée until smooth.

3. Transfer applesauce to an airtight container and store in the refrigerator for up to 1 week.

EXCHANGES/CHOICES	1 Fruit
CALORIES	70
CALORIES FROM FAT	0
TOTAL FAT	0.0 g
SATURATED FAT	0.0 g
TRANS FAT	0.0 g
CHOLESTEROL	0 mg
SODIUM	0 mg
POTASSIUM	120 mg
TOTAL CARBOHYDRATE	17 g
DIETARY FIBER	2 g
SUGARS	13 g
PROTEIN	0 g
PHOSPHORUS	15 mg

Everyday Cinnamon Walnut Crumble

SERVES: 12 | SERVING SIZE: 1 TABLESPOON | PREP TIME: 3 MINUTES | COOKING TIME: NONE

As simple as this combination of nuts and cinnamon may be, it is wildly versatile and great to have on hand for everyday use. By combining nutrient-dense walnuts with fragrant cinnamon, you create the perfect, no-sugar-added topping for just about anything! Sprinkle it onto yogurt, cereal, fruit, or even a salad. Or use it to top warm, delicious Oven-Roasted Figs (page 240). The possibilities are endless.

1 cup chopped walnuts

2 teaspoons ground cinnamon

1. Combine the ingredients in a food processor, pulsing to form a "crumble" texture.
2. Store in the refrigerator in an airtight container for up to 1 month.

EXCHANGES/CHOICES	1 1/2 Fat
CALORIES	70
CALORIES FROM FAT	60
TOTAL FAT	7.0 g
SATURATED FAT	0.6 g
TRANS FAT	0.0 g
CHOLESTEROL	0 mg
SODIUM	0 mg
POTASSIUM	45 mg
TOTAL CARBOHYDRATE	2 g
DIETARY FIBER	1 g
SUGARS	0 g
PROTEIN	2 g
PHOSPHORUS	35 mg

DIY Nut Milk

SERVES: 4 | SERVING SIZE: 1 CUP | PREP TIME: 6 HOURS | COOKING TIME: 5 MINUTES

With fewer calories and less fat than whole cow's milk, and a variety of essential nutrients and minerals, nut milk is a great milk alternative for people with dairy allergies or lactose intolerance or for those who are simply looking for an interesting alternative to milk. This recipe works well using hazelnuts, cashews, walnuts, almonds, or even sesame seeds, and is delicious both plain and with the optional additions of cinnamon, vanilla, or maple syrup. Make a double or triple batch of this recipe on Sunday and use it throughout the week with whole-grain cereal or oatmeal, in smoothies (on pages 92–94) and soups, or to drink straight from a glass.

Seeds make great milks as well! Follow the instructions below but try swapping nuts for sesame, hemp, pumpkin, or sunflower seeds!

1 cup raw, unsalted hazelnuts, Brazil nuts, cashews, walnuts, or almonds

4 cups water, divided

1/4 teaspoon ground cinnamon (optional)

1/2 teaspoon pure vanilla extract (optional)

1 tablespoon pure maple syrup (preferably grade B; optional)

Cheesecloth

1. In an airtight container, combine nuts with 1 cup water. Seal the container and let the nuts soak in the refrigerator overnight (or for at least 6 hours).

2. In a high-speed blender or food processor, combine soaked nuts and soaking water with the remaining 3 cups water. Blend for 1 minute at the highest speed. Add the cinnamon, vanilla, and maple syrup (if using), and blend to combine.

3. Line a fine-mesh sieve with cheesecloth and strain the milk into an airtight container. Nut milk will keep in the refrigerator for up to 1 week.

EXCHANGES/CHOICES	1/2 Fat
CALORIES	30
CALORIES FROM FAT	20
TOTAL FAT	2.5 g
SATURATED FAT	0.2 g
TRANS FAT	0.0 g
CHOLESTEROL	0 mg
SODIUM	10 mg
POTASSIUM	35 mg
TOTAL CARBOHYDRATE	1 g
DIETARY FIBER	1 g
SUGARS	0 g
PROTEIN	1 g
PHOSPHORUS	25 mg

why soak nuts, grains, and seeds?

Just like that packet of tomato seeds you bought for spring planting, all kinds of edible nuts, grains, and seeds exist in a dormant state, waiting for the right growing conditions to germinate and produce a new plant. The only things keeping them from sprouting spontaneously are their own natural survival mechanisms—nutritional inhibitors and toxic substances that keep them from spoiling or rotting while they wait for their growing season. When it rains and the nuts, seeds, or grains get wet, these nutritional inhibitors and substances are washed away and the nuts, seeds, or grains reach their highest nutritional potential and are able to support new life.

When you soak nuts, grains, and seeds before eating them, you are mimicking this natural process and removing any traces of nutritional inhibitors and toxic substances. Soaking makes them more easily digestible and allows your body to absorb the highest amount of nutrients possible.

DIY Nut/Seed Butter

SERVES: 12 | SERVING SIZE: 2 TABLESPOONS | PREP TIME: 10 MINUTES | COOKING TIME: NONE

Regular, store-bought peanut butter—yes, even the natural and organic kinds—can be laden with added sugar, unhealthy oils, and other preservatives. So give it a go and make your own nut (or seed) butters and you'll never be tempted by the name brands again. You can use any variety of nuts and/or seeds in this recipe; try peanuts, almonds, cashews, Brazil nuts, hazelnuts, walnuts, or sesame seeds. Once you get the hang of it, you can try adding different ground spices to make your own signature recipe or try the Chai Spice Nut Butter recipe on page 77. You may also save some money as some trendier nut butters can be really expensive!

2 cups raw, unsalted nuts and/or seeds

1 teaspoon fine sea salt

1. Place nuts/seeds and salt in a food processor and process for 10 minutes or until they form a butter-like consistency. (Within 1 minute, the nuts will form a flour-like consistency. You can use nut "flours" in many of the recipes in this book.) You do not need to add water or oil to the mixture—simply continue to blend nuts and they will naturally form a butter-like consistency.

2. Transfer nut/seed butter to an airtight container and keep it in the refrigerator for up to 2 months.

tip: Nuts and seeds are great sources of calcium! One cup of whole almonds has around the same amount of calcium as 1 cup of whole milk, and 1 cup of sesame seeds will give you more than 100% of the daily value of calcium intake. Add nuts and seeds to your meals and snacks when you can!

EXCHANGES/CHOICES	1 1/2 Fat
CALORIES	70
CALORIES FROM FAT	50
TOTAL FAT	6.0 g
SATURATED FAT	0.8 g
TRANS FAT	0.0 g
CHOLESTEROL	0 mg
SODIUM	90 mg
POTASSIUM	85 mg
TOTAL CARBOHYDRATE	2 g
DIETARY FIBER	1 g
SUGARS	1 g
PROTEIN	3 g
PHOSPHORUS	45 mg

DIY Nut Flour

SERVES: 4 | SERVING SIZE: 1/2 CUP | PREP TIME: 5 MINUTES | COOKING TIME: NONE

This gluten-free, low-carb "flour" could not be easier to make, and it will add a boost of protein and healthy fats to whatever recipe you use it in. Make sure to use raw, not roasted, nuts for a more mild-flavored flour. Plus, roasted nuts may go rancid more quickly than raw nuts as a result of the destabilization of fats that happens to roasted nuts during the heating or roasting process. Peanuts, almonds, cashews, hazelnuts, and walnuts all work well in this recipe. Nut flour adds great flavor to baked goods like Almond, Millet, and Pear Cake (page 225).

2 cups of raw, unsalted nuts

1. Place nuts in a food processor and pulse 100 times to form a four-like consistency. Transfer flour to an airtight container and keep it in the refrigerator for up to 6 months.

which nut or seed is the healthiest?

This is a common question I receive from my clients. The answer is that variety is the key, as with most foods! Each nut, seed, vegetable, fruit, etc., contains its own unique nutritive properties. Enjoying a variety of healthy foods will expose you to a greater array of nutrients.

tip: Head to the bulk aisle of your local grocery store. Take small scoops of a variety of nuts and seeds such as raw sesame seeds, sunflower seeds, pumpkin seeds, almonds, and cashews. Once you are home, pour them into a jar or container, give them a shake, and store the mix in your fridge. You can add 1–2 tablespoons to your cereal, oatmeal, grains, salads, smoothies, and more. This is a great way to add both protein and healthy fats, along with a multitude of vitamins and minerals, to a meal.

EXCHANGES/CHOICES	1 Carbohydrate
	2 Lean Protein
	6 Fat
CALORIES	420
CALORIES FROM FAT	320
TOTAL FAT	36.0 g
SATURATED FAT	2.7 g
TRANS FAT	0.0 g
CHOLESTEROL	0 mg
SODIUM	0 mg
POTASSIUM	510 mg
TOTAL CARBOHYDRATE	16 g
DIETARY FIBER	9 g
SUGARS	3 g
PROTEIN	15 g
PHOSPHORUS	350 mg

Moroccan Spice Blend

SERVES: 16 | SERVING SIZE: 1 TEASPOON | PREP TIME: 5 MINUTES | COOKING TIME: NONE

Full of vibrant, smoky flavor, this seasoning blend can be rubbed on meat, chicken, or fish before cooking, tossed with roasted squash or potatoes, sprinkled over popcorn or toasted chickpeas, or stirred into stews and soups, like Moroccan Carrot and Red Lentil Soup (page 177). Keep some in a spice shaker jar on the table, and notice how salt loses the spotlight.

2 tablespoons ground cumin

1 tablespoon ground coriander

1 tablespoon ground cinnamon

1 teaspoon ground cardamom

1 teaspoon ground ginger

1 teaspoon paprika

1/4 teaspoon cayenne pepper

1/4 teaspoon fine sea salt

1. In a small bowl, whisk together cumin, coriander, cinnamon, cardamom, ginger, paprika, cayenne pepper, and salt. Transfer the mixture to a small jar or other airtight container and store it in a cool, dry place.

EXCHANGES/CHOICES	Free food
CALORIES	5
CALORIES FROM FAT	0
TOTAL FAT	0.0 g
SATURATED FAT	0.0 g
TRANS FAT	0.0 g
CHOLESTEROL	0 mg
SODIUM	35 mg
POTASSIUM	30 mg
TOTAL CARBOHYDRATE	1 g
DIETARY FIBER	0 g
SUGARS	0 g
PROTEIN	0 g
PHOSPHORUS	5 mg

"Everything" Spice Blend

SERVES: 16 | SERVING SIZE: 1 TEASPOON | PREP TIME: 5 MINUTES | COOKING TIME: NONE

There is so much to love about an everything bagel, especially its blend of seeds and spices that is wildly rich in both flavor and texture. Well, that blend is not just for bagels anymore! I upgraded the traditional blend by adding chia seeds and hemp. Try this "Everything" Spice Blend on yogurt, in savory oatmeal, or as a topping for my "Everything" Deviled Eggs on page 117.

1 tablespoon white sesame seeds

1 tablespoon chia seeds

1 tablespoon poppy seeds

1 tablespoon hemp hearts

1 tablespoon dried onion flakes

2 teaspoons dried garlic flakes

1 teaspoon fine sea salt

1/4 teaspoon freshly ground black pepper

1. Combine all of the ingredients in a sealed glass jar and store the blend in a cool, dark place for up to 3 months.

EXCHANGES/CHOICES Free food

CALORIES	15
CALORIES FROM FAT	10
TOTAL FAT	1.0 g
SATURATED FAT	0.1 g
TRANS FAT	0.0 g
CHOLESTEROL	0 mg
SODIUM	115 mg
POTASSIUM	20 mg
TOTAL CARBOHYDRATE	1 g
DIETARY FIBER	1 g
SUGARS	0 g
PROTEIN	1 g
PHOSPHORUS	15 mg

DIY Tahini

SERVES: 48 | SERVING SIZE: 1 TEASPOON | PREP TIME: 5 MINUTES | COOKING TIME: 10 MINUTES

Did you know that tahini is just sesame seeds that are ground into a paste (just like peanuts are ground into peanut butter)? While tahini is most commonly used as an essential ingredient in hummus, like the Roasted Eggplant Hummus on page 114, I also love using it as a spread, in baked goods, and blended into dressings!

2 cups hulled sesame seeds

1/4 cup avocado oil or extra-virgin
  olive oil

1/4 teaspoon fine sea salt

1. Add sesame seeds to a medium-sized, dry saucepan over medium-low heat. Toast the seeds, stirring constantly, for 3–5 minutes. They will become fragrant. Do not allow them to brown.

2. Add toasted sesame seeds to a food processor and process until a crumbly paste forms, about 1 minute. Add oil then process for 2–3 more minutes, stopping to scrape the bottom and sides of food processor a couple times. Check tahini's consistency; it should be smooth and pourable when finished.

EXCHANGES/CHOICES	1 Fat
CALORIES	45
CALORIES FROM FAT	40
TOTAL FAT	4.5 g
SATURATED FAT	0.6 g
TRANS FAT	0.0 g
CHOLESTEROL	0 mg
SODIUM	15 mg
POTASSIUM	20 mg
TOTAL CARBOHYDRATE	1 g
DIETARY FIBER	1 g
SUGARS	0 g
PROTEIN	1 g
PHOSPHORUS	35 mg

Masala Chai Spice Blend

SERVES: 16 | SERVING SIZE: 1 TEASPOON | PREP TIME: 5 MINUTES | COOKING TIME: NONE

This spice blend brings exotic dimension to simple hot breakfast cereals such as amaranth, grits, or quinoa without even a pinch of sugar. Of course, its most famous use is as a hot tea served with milk, but it is equally enticing stirred into coffee, hot cocoa, almond milk, or nut butter (see Chai Spice Nut Butter recipe on page 77).

2 tablespoons ground cinnamon

3 teaspoons dried ground ginger

3 teaspoons ground cardamom

1 1/2 teaspoons ground cloves

1 1/2 teaspoons ground nutmeg

tip: While many people choose to avoid artificial sweeteners, it's a good idea to think twice before using the natural varieties of sweeteners as well. Like artificial sweeteners, no-calorie, natural sweeteners are very sweet and can train your palate to crave sugar. Plus, the fact that they are calorie free makes some people feel like they can enjoy as much as they want of these products, further adding to their sweet cravings.

1. In a small bowl, whisk together cinnamon, ginger, cardamom, cloves, and nutmeg. Transfer mixture to a small jar or other airtight container and store it in a cool, dry place.

EXCHANGES/CHOICES	Free food
CALORIES	5
CALORIES FROM FAT	0
TOTAL FAT	0.0 g
SATURATED FAT	0.1 g
TRANS FAT	0.0 g
CHOLESTEROL	0 mg
SODIUM	0 mg
POTASSIUM	15 mg
TOTAL CARBOHYDRATE	1 g
DIETARY FIBER	1 g
SUGARS	0 g
PROTEIN	0 g
PHOSPHORUS	0 mg

Chai Spice Nut Butter

SERVES: 72 | SERVING SIZE: 1 TEASPOON | PREP TIME: 5 MINUTES | COOKING TIME: NONE

I am a huge fan of nut butters and I have been ever since I was a child. When I was little, I would crouch down under the counter, then spring up to snag a spoonful of peanut butter from the jar as my mom made me a sandwich. I called myself the peanut butter monster, and now my son has titled himself the same. While there is something quite magical about good 'ole peanut butter, I also love playing around with variations, like this recipe. The warming Masala Chai Spice Blend I whip up (page 76) can be blended into any nut butter to create a cozy flavor that is very, very satisfying.

1 1/2 cups DIY Nut Butter (page 71, try with peanuts)

2 teaspoons Masala Chai Spice Blend (page 76)

1/4 teaspoon pure vanilla extract

1/4 teaspoon fine sea salt

1. In a food processor or large bowl, mix together the nut butter, chai spice blend, vanilla, and salt. Transfer the mixture to an airtight container and store it in the refrigerator for up to 2 months.

EXCHANGES/CHOICES	1/2 Fat
CALORIES	25
CALORIES FROM FAT	20
TOTAL FAT	2.0 g
SATURATED FAT	0.3 g
TRANS FAT	0.0 g
CHOLESTEROL	0 mg
SODIUM	40 mg
POTASSIUM	30 mg
TOTAL CARBOHYDRATE	1 g
DIETARY FIBER	0 g
SUGARS	0 g
PROTEIN	1 g
PHOSPHORUS	15 mg

naturally sweet

When sugars are refined (think cane sugar, brown sugar, confectioners' sugar) all the nutrients are removed and the sugar is left in its purest state. Refined sugar digests very quickly, causing spikes in blood glucose. Natural sweeteners are much less processed (sometimes not at all), and they do contain some nutrients. Processed, artificial sweeteners often boast zero calories, but will still keep your body craving the sweet stuff, which can be dangerous if you have diabetes. My recommendation is to avoid refined and artificial sweeteners completely, and use only natural sweeteners in moderation. And try eating sweet veggies like carrots, sweet potatoes, beets, and squash when cravings strike. Here are a few natural sweeteners that are safe to enjoy in moderation if they fit with your meal plan:

- Honey is one of the oldest, most commonly used sweeteners available. Honey can vary in both taste and color depending on the predominant flower in bloom at the time of the bees' production, and many varieties of honey can be found at local farmers' markets. Honey is also a great natural throat soother and cough suppressant. Opt for raw, local honey when available.

- Pure maple syrup (I recommend grade B) is the boiled down sap of maple trees and is a good source of trace minerals. Syrup labeled "pancake syrup" is not pure maple syrup. Maple syrup can also be dehydrated and sold as maple sugar. They both have strong, sweet, distinctive tastes. Maple syrup contains zinc and manganese, minerals that may help support immune function.

- Molasses is a by-product of the refining process of white sugar and is rich in iron. It also contains calcium, zinc, copper, and chromium. However, because molasses is only 65% as sweet as sugar and has a distinctive flavor, it may not be suitable in all recipes.

- Coconut nectar is a syrup made from boiling down the sap of coconut flowers, and coconut sugar results from dehydrating that nectar. Coconut nectar and sugar are less sweet than white sugar and both have a score of 35 on the glycemic index.

Peach and Mango Chipotle Ketchup

SERVES: 32 | SERVING SIZE: 1 TABLESPOON | PREP TIME: 10 MINUTES | COOKING TIME: 40 MINUTES

While they are much better for you than the processed varieties you get at the grocery store, most homemade ketchup recipes still include large amounts of processed sugar. In this recipe, I've sidestepped the fake sweet stuff by replacing sugar with raw honey and peaches, both of which contribute bold flavors and nutrients of their own. Keep a bottle of this ketchup on hand for burgers, fries, sandwiches, and more, and notice how much of a difference whole-food ingredients can make! Try it with the Rutabaga and Turnip Fries on page 149!

1 tablespoon extra-virgin olive oil

1 medium yellow onion, diced

2 cloves garlic, minced

1 cup peeled and diced peaches (fresh or frozen)

1 1/2 cups (12 ounces) jarred or BPA-free canned tomato paste

1/2 chipotle pepper in adobo sauce, chopped

1/2 cup apple cider vinegar

3/4 cup diced mango

1 tablespoon honey

1 teaspoon Dijon mustard

1 cup water

1/4 teaspoon ground cinnamon

1. In a medium saucepan over medium heat, combine oil, onion, and garlic. Cook for 4–6 minutes or until onions are soft but not yet browned. Add the peaches and cook for another 2–3 minutes.

2. Add the tomato paste, chipotle pepper, apple cider vinegar, mango, honey, mustard, water, and cinnamon and simmer for 30 minutes.

3. Remove pan from the heat and let the mixture cool for a few minutes. Then transfer mixture to a food processor or blender and purée until smooth.

4. Transfer the ketchup to an airtight container and keep it in the refrigerator for up to 2 weeks.

EXCHANGES/CHOICES	1 Nonstarchy Vegetable
CALORIES	20
CALORIES FROM FAT	5
TOTAL FAT	0.5 g
SATURATED FAT	0.1 g
TRANS FAT	0.0 g
CHOLESTEROL	0 mg
SODIUM	90 mg
POTASSIUM	135 mg
TOTAL CARBOHYDRATE	4 g
DIETARY FIBER	1 g
SUGARS	3 g
PROTEIN	1 g
PHOSPHORUS	15 mg

Harissa Paste

SERVES: 16 | SERVING SIZE: 1 TABLESPOON | PREP TIME: 30 MINUTES | COOKING TIME: 10 MINUTES

This garlicky chile paste originally hails from Tunisia, where it has long been used to liven up cooked vegetables and meats. Here, I chose to keep the heat level on the milder side by using ancho chilies. If you want yours fiery hot, use a few chilies de arbol instead and add a pinch of cayenne pepper. For a smoky harissa, use canned chipotle peppers and blend in 2 tablespoons of adobo sauce. You can use this paste as a dip for crudités or a marinade for chicken, meat, fish, or roasted vegetables (like the Harissa-Roasted Root Vegetables with Cilantro Yogurt Sauce on page 141). Stir it into scrambled eggs or cooked couscous. Or simply serve it as a sandwich spread. The possibilities are endless!

4 ounces dried red chilies (ancho, pasillas, guajillo, or chipotle in adobo)

1 teaspoon coriander seeds OR 3/4 teaspoon ground coriander

1 teaspoon cumin seeds OR 1/2 teaspoon ground cumin

1 teaspoon caraway seeds OR 1/2 teaspoon ground caraway

1 1/2 cups Everyday Roasted Bell Peppers (page 66)

1 tablespoon extra-virgin olive oil

3 fresh or roasted cloves garlic, coarsely chopped

1 1/2 teaspoons tomato paste

2 tablespoons freshly squeezed lemon juice

2 tablespoons freshly squeezed orange juice

1/2 teaspoon freshly grated orange zest

2 teaspoons honey

1/2 teaspoon fine sea salt

1/4 teaspoon freshly ground black pepper

1. In a medium bowl, cover the dried chilies with warm water and let them soak at room temperature for 30 minutes or until tender.

2. If using whole spice seeds: In a dry sauté pan over low heat, combine the coriander, cumin, and caraway seeds and toast them, stirring constantly, for 1–2 minutes or until fragrant. Remove the pan from heat and grind toasted spices in a spice grinder or with a mortar and pestle. If using ground spices, proceed to step 3.

3. Drain the chilies and transfer them to the bowl of a food processor, along with ground spices, roasted bell pepper, olive oil, garlic, tomato paste, lemon juice, orange juice, orange zest, and honey. Process the mixture until it forms a smooth paste. Stir in the salt and pepper.

4. Transfer paste to an airtight container and store it in the refrigerator for up to 2 weeks.

EXCHANGES/CHOICES	1 Nonstarchy Vegetable 1/2 Fat
CALORIES	45
CALORIES FROM FAT	20
TOTAL FAT	2.0 g
SATURATED FAT	0.3 g
TRANS FAT	0.0 g
CHOLESTEROL	0 mg
SODIUM	95 mg
POTASSIUM	165 mg
TOTAL CARBOHYDRATE	7 g
DIETARY FIBER	2 g
SUGARS	4 g
PROTEIN	1 g
PHOSPHORUS	20 mg

Walnut Arugula Pesto

SERVES: 16 | SERVING SIZE: 1 TABLESPOON | PREP TIME: 5 MINUTES | COOKING TIME: NONE

Pesto is the kind of condiment you want to keep in the fridge or freezer at all times. It's great on eggs, beans, spaghetti squash (see the recipe on page 148), and whole-wheat pasta, and you can also use it as a marinade or seasoning for all kinds of meats and vegetables. In this recipe, the mixture of basil, arugula, garlic, lemon juice, and walnuts creates a flavor bomb that just happens to be brimming with the antioxidants, vitamins, and minerals your body needs to stay healthy.

2 1/2 cups packed fresh basil leaves

1 1/2 cups packed baby arugula

2 cloves garlic, peeled

1 teaspoon freshly grated lemon zest

2 tablespoons freshly squeezed lemon juice

1/4 cup raw, unsalted walnuts

1/4 cup grated parmesan cheese

1/2 cup extra-virgin olive oil

2 tablespoons water, as needed

1/4 teaspoon fine sea salt

1/4 teaspoon freshly ground black pepper

1. In a food processor, combine basil, arugula, garlic, lemon zest, lemon juice, walnuts, and parmesan cheese. Pulse a few times until the ingredients are coarsely chopped and well incorporated.

2. With food processor running, stream in the oil and process until pesto resembles a smooth paste. Add water a little at a time and process until pesto reaches your desired consistency. Season pesto with salt and pepper.

3. To store the pesto, transfer it to an airtight container. Drizzle a very thin layer of olive oil on the surface of the pesto, seal the container, and keep it in the refrigerator for up to 2 weeks.

tip: Don't feel restricted to the blend of herbs called for in this recipe. When basil is not in season, you can add volume with other herbs like parsley or chives. You can even swap the arugula for baby kale.

EXCHANGES/CHOICES	2 Fat
CALORIES	80
CALORIES FROM FAT	70
TOTAL FAT	8.0 g
SATURATED FAT	1.2 g
TRANS FAT	0.0 g
CHOLESTEROL	0 mg
SODIUM	55 mg
POTASSIUM	70 mg
TOTAL CARBOHYDRATE	1 g
DIETARY FIBER	1 g
SUGARS	0 g
PROTEIN	1 g
PHOSPHORUS	25 mg

Roasted Red Pepper Sauce

SERVES: 16 | SERVING SIZE: 2 TABLESPOONS | PREP TIME: 5 MINUTES | COOKING TIME: NONE

Before you reach for a jar of mayo, consider making a batch of this simple, flavorful sauce instead—you can smear it onto just about anything. Roasted red peppers are a great source of vitamin C, vitamin A, and calcium, and their natural sweetness and smoky flavor can be found in traditional dishes all over the world—from Mexico to the Middle East. Try this sauce spooned over baked potatoes, served with grilled chicken or fish, or as a spread on your favorite sandwich. It's also a great sauce for roasted vegetables; try the Roasted Baby Artichokes with Roasted Red Pepper Sauce recipe on page 134.

1 1/2 cups fat-free, plain strained yogurt (Greek or skyr)

6 cloves Everyday Roasted Garlic (page 64)

1 cup chopped Everyday Roasted Bell Peppers (page 66) or jarred roasted red peppers, drained

1/4 cup chopped fresh basil

1/4 teaspoon fine sea salt

1/4 teaspoon freshly ground black pepper

1. In a food processor or blender, combine yogurt, roasted garlic, roasted peppers, and basil. Purée until smooth and season with salt and pepper.

2. Transfer sauce to an airtight container and keep it in the fridge for up to 1 week.

tip: Make it smoky and rich! You can amp up the flavor of this simple sauce with a 1/4 teaspoon of smoked paprika or a teaspoon or two of adobo sauce.

EXCHANGES/CHOICES	1/2 Fat
CALORIES	35
CALORIES FROM FAT	20
TOTAL FAT	2.0 g
SATURATED FAT	0.5 g
TRANS FAT	0.0 g
CHOLESTEROL	0 mg
SODIUM	50 mg
POTASSIUM	70 mg
TOTAL CARBOHYDRATE	2 g
DIETARY FIBER	0 g
SUGARS	1 g
PROTEIN	2 g
PHOSPHORUS	35 mg

Chive and Lemon Pistou

SERVES: 8 | SERVING SIZE: 2 TABLESPOONS | PREP TIME: 5 MINUTES | COOKING TIME: 15 MINUTES

Pistou is a traditional French sauce typically made with garlic, fresh basil, and olive oil—essentially a pesto without the pine nuts. This sauce is the perfect condiment for simple grilled fish, chicken, or vegetables. For a quick, refreshing entrée, try Oven-Roasted Shrimp with Chive and Lemon Pistou (page 201). For this recipe, I use fresh parsley and chives instead of basil to add a bright, springy flavor and an extra boost of nutrients.

- 2 cups chopped fresh flat-leaf parsley
- 3/4 cup chopped fresh chives
- 1 clove garlic, peeled
- 2 tablespoons freshly squeezed lemon juice
- 1 tablespoon freshly grated lemon zest
- 2 tablespoons extra-virgin olive oil
- 1/4 teaspoon fine sea salt
- 1/4 teaspoon freshly ground black pepper

1. Bring a small pot of water to a boil. Fill a small bowl with ice water and set it nearby. Blanch parsley and chives for 10–15 seconds in boiling water, then remove with a slotted spoon and add to the ice water for a few seconds. Drain the herbs and pat them dry with paper towels.

2. In a food processor, combine blanched herbs, garlic, lemon juice, zest, and olive oil, and process until mixture resembles a smooth paste. Stir in salt and pepper.

3. Transfer pistou to an airtight container and keep it in the refrigerator for up to 1 week.

EXCHANGES/CHOICES	1/2 Fat
CALORIES	35
CALORIES FROM FAT	30
TOTAL FAT	3.5 g
SATURATED FAT	0.5 g
TRANS FAT	0.0 g
CHOLESTEROL	0 mg
SODIUM	75 mg
POTASSIUM	55 mg
TOTAL CARBOHYDRATE	1 g
DIETARY FIBER	0 g
SUGARS	0 g
PROTEIN	0 g
PHOSPHORUS	5 mg

Horseradish Chimichurri

SERVES: 8 | SERVING SIZE: 2 TABLESPOONS | PREP TIME: 5 MINUTES | COOKING TIME: 5 MINUTES

In Argentina, this thick, herbaceous sauce is a must-have condiment for any grilled meat. It is traditionally made with parsley, garlic, olive oil, oregano, and vinegar, but I find that slipping in some grated fresh horseradish takes the flavors (and nutritional value) to a whole new level, and makes it a natural addition to fish and shrimp dishes, too. Try it with the Seared Flank Steak recipe on page 219.

1 cup packed fresh flat-leaf parsley leaves

1/2 cup chopped scallions (white and light green parts)

1/4 cup packed fresh cilantro leaves

2 tablespoons extra-virgin olive oil

1/3 cup red wine vinegar

2 cloves garlic, peeled

1/2 teaspoon ground cumin

2 teaspoons grated fresh horseradish

1/4 teaspoon fine sea salt

1/4 teaspoon freshly ground black pepper

1. In a blender or food processor, combine all ingredients. Process until smooth.

2. Transfer chimichurri to an airtight container and store it in the refrigerator for up to 1 week.

EXCHANGES/CHOICES	1 Fat
CALORIES	40
CALORIES FROM FAT	30
TOTAL FAT	3.5 g
SATURATED FAT	0.5 g
TRANS FAT	0.0 g
CHOLESTEROL	0 mg
SODIUM	75 mg
POTASSIUM	70 mg
TOTAL CARBOHYDRATE	1 g
DIETARY FIBER	0 g
SUGARS	0 g
PROTEIN	0 g
PHOSPHORUS	10 mg

Saffron-Walnut Romesco Sauce

SERVES: 12 | SERVING SIZE: 2 TABLESPOONS | PREP TIME: 6 MINUTES | COOKING TIME: NONE

This incredibly versatile Spanish sauce is delicious with any kind of seafood or poultry dish. Though saffron is an expensive spice, just a few threads will impart a deep orange color and a floral, slightly bitter flavor to the sauce. It pairs well with the Grilled Halibut recipe on page 189.

1 teaspoon saffron threads

1 tablespoon warm water

2 cups chopped Everyday Roasted Bell Peppers (page 66) or jarred roasted red peppers, drained

1 clove garlic, peeled OR 2 cloves Everyday Roasted Garlic (page 64)

1/2 cup raw, unsalted walnuts

1/4 cup chopped fresh flat-leaf parsley

2 tablespoons sherry vinegar

1 teaspoon smoked paprika

1/4 cup extra-virgin olive oil

1/4 teaspoon fine sea salt

1/4 teaspoon freshly ground black pepper

1. In a small bowl, combine the saffron and water, and let saffron steep for 1 minute.

2. In a food processor or blender, combine saffron/water mixture, peppers, garlic, walnuts, parsley, vinegar, paprika, and olive oil. Purée mixture until it forms a smooth sauce, then stir in salt and pepper.

3. Transfer sauce to an airtight container and store it in the refrigerator for up to 1 week.

tip: Switch it up and try different colored roasted peppers, like yellow or orange, to create a new variation on this sauce! If you don't have time to roast peppers yourself, you can substitute the jarred variety of roasted peppers. Make sure you drain the jarred peppers. You can also make a large batch of Everyday Roasted Bell Peppers (page 66) and freeze them for later use in sauces and condiments.

EXCHANGES/CHOICES	2 Fat
CALORIES	100
CALORIES FROM FAT	80
TOTAL FAT	9.0 g
SATURATED FAT	1.1 g
TRANS FAT	0.0 g
CHOLESTEROL	0 mg
SODIUM	75 mg
POTASSIUM	115 mg
TOTAL CARBOHYDRATE	3 g
DIETARY FIBER	1 g
SUGARS	2 g
PROTEIN	1 g
PHOSPHORUS	30 mg

Zucchini Salsa Verde

SERVES: 16 | SERVING SIZE: 1 TABLESPOON | PREP TIME: 5 MINUTES | COOKING TIME: 5 MINUTES

Not to be confused with the Mexican tomatillo salsa of the same name, this classic Italian salsa verde is typically made with fresh herbs, capers, anchovies, lemon, and garlic. In my version, I swap the anchovies for zucchini to give it an extra boost of nutrition and lighter texture. It's delicious spooned over grilled and roasted meats, poultry, and fish, or as a dip for shrimp and crudités. Try it over lamb with the Grilled Lamb Chops and Lemony Barley Pilaf recipe on page 217.

1/2 large zucchini, cubed

2 cups chopped fresh flat-leaf parsley

1/2 cup extra-virgin olive oil

1 small shallot, chopped

3 tablespoons capers

1 teaspoon freshly grated lemon zest

1/4 cup freshly squeezed lemon juice

1/4 cup white wine vinegar

3 cloves garlic, peeled

1. In a food processor or blender, combine all ingredients and process until smooth.

2. Transfer salsa to an airtight container and store it in the refrigerator for up to 1 week.

EXCHANGES/CHOICES	1 1/2 Fat
CALORIES	70
CALORIES FROM FAT	60
TOTAL FAT	7.0 g
SATURATED FAT	0.9 g
TRANS FAT	0.0 g
CHOLESTEROL	0 mg
SODIUM	50 mg
POTASSIUM	55 mg
TOTAL CARBOHYDRATE	1 g
DIETARY FIBER	0 g
SUGARS	0 g
PROTEIN	0 g
PHOSPHORUS	10 mg

Greek Dressing

SERVES: 12 | SERVING SIZE: 1 TABLESPOON | PREP TIME: 5 MINUTES | COOKING TIME: NONE

There is something about the combination of lemon juice, olive oil, and dill that makes me so happy. Refreshing and bright, this is a beautiful summer dressing you can use as a marinade or as a dressing for vegetables like green beans or zucchini, or you can toss it into the Super Green Greek-Style Salad on page 126.

1/4 cup freshly squeezed lemon juice

1 teaspoon freshly grated lemon zest

1/4 cup extra-virgin olive oil

1 ounce light feta cheese, crumbled

1 tablespoon Olive Tapenade (page 113) or store-bought tapenade

1 tablespoon Everyday Herb Oil (page 60)

1 tablespoon chopped fresh dill

1/4 teaspoon freshly ground black pepper

1. Combine all dressing ingredients in a blender or food processor and purée until smooth. Store in an airtight jar in the refrigerator for up to 1 week.

tip: Does dairy upset your stomach? No problem. You can skip the cheese in this recipe! The tapenade is so flavorful you won't even miss it. I promise.

EXCHANGES/CHOICES	1 Fat
CALORIES	60
CALORIES FROM FAT	50
TOTAL FAT	6.0 g
SATURATED FAT	1.0 g
TRANS FAT	0.0 g
CHOLESTEROL	0 mg
SODIUM	40 mg
POTASSIUM	10 mg
TOTAL CARBOHYDRATE	0 g
DIETARY FIBER	0 g
SUGARS	0 g
PROTEIN	1 g
PHOSPHORUS	10 mg

Creamy Avocado Dressing

SERVES: 12 | SERVING SIZE: 1 TABLESPOON | PREP TIME: 5 MINUTES | COOKING TIME: NONE

1/4 ripe avocado

3 tablespoons extra-virgin olive oil

1 tablespoon apple cider vinegar

2 tablespoons freshly squeezed lime juice

1/4 teaspoon crushed red pepper flakes

2 tablespoons chopped fresh cilantro

1/4 teaspoon ground cumin

1/2 teaspoon Dijon mustard

1/4 teaspoon fine sea salt

1/4 teaspoon freshly ground black pepper

1. Combine avocado, olive oil, apple cider vinegar, lime juice, red pepper flakes, cilantro, cumin, and mustard, salt, and pepper in a blender and purée until smooth. Store in a sealed container in the refrigerator for up to 1 week.

tip: Has your avocado started to brown? Don't toss it! Scoop out the flesh and freeze it for use in smoothies and dressings like this one.

EXCHANGES/CHOICES	1 Fat
CALORIES	35
CALORIES FROM FAT	35
TOTAL FAT	4.0 g
SATURATED FAT	0.5 g
TRANS FAT	0.0 g
CHOLESTEROL	0 mg
SODIUM	50 mg
POTASSIUM	20 mg
TOTAL CARBOHYDRATE	1 g
DIETARY FIBER	0 g
SUGARS	0 g
PROTEIN	0 g
PHOSPHORUS	5 mg

Cilantro Ginger Vinaigrette

SERVES: 4 | SERVING SIZE: 2 TABLESPOONS | PREP TIME: 5 MINUTES | COOKING TIME: NONE

1 clove garlic, grated

1 teaspoon grated fresh ginger

1 tablespoon freshly squeezed lime juice

1 teaspoon freshly grated lime zest

3 tablespoons rice wine vinegar

3 tablespoons extra-virgin olive oil

1/2 cup chopped fresh cilantro

1/4 teaspoon fine sea salt

1/4 teaspoon freshly ground black pepper

1. In a small bowl, whisk together the garlic, ginger, lime juice, lime zest, vinegar, olive oil, cilantro, salt, and pepper. Vinaigrette can be refrigerated in an airtight container for up to 1 week.

tip: Buy a big piece of ginger then peel it with a spoon. Freeze it whole for up to 1 month—you will always have fresh ginger on hand. Grate it into teas, dressings, and other recipes with a small grater.

EXCHANGES/CHOICES	2 Fat
CALORIES	100
CALORIES FROM FAT	90
TOTAL FAT	10.0 g
SATURATED FAT	1.4 g
TRANS FAT	0.0 g
CHOLESTEROL	0 mg
SODIUM	140 mg
POTASSIUM	25 mg
TOTAL CARBOHYDRATE	1 g
DIETARY FIBER	0 g
SUGARS	0 g
PROTEIN	0 g
PHOSPHORUS	0 mg

Tomatillo Salsa

SERVES: 8 | SERVING SIZE: 2 TABLESPOONS | PREP TIME: 3 MINUTES | COOKING TIME: NONE

Tart and tangy, tomatillos are one of my favorite summer fruits. What is a tomatillo? It looks like a small green tomato that grows encased in a paper-like husk. Tomatillos are more tart than sweet and they make for a killer salsa! Try this salsa in the Chorizo Chicken Sausage, Sweet Potato, and Mushroom Tostadas on page 213 or simply grab some vegetables or chips and start dipping!

6 tomatillos, husks removed

1/2 jalapeño pepper, seeded

1/4 cup chopped fresh cilantro

1 small shallot, peeled

1 teaspoon freshly grated lime zest

1 tablespoon freshly squeezed lime juice

1/4 teaspoon fine sea salt

1/4 teaspoon freshly ground black pepper

1. Combine all ingredients in a blender or food processor and pulse to your desired consistency.

tip: Concentrate the sweetness of the fruit by tossing halved tomatillos in 1 teaspoon of olive oil and then broiling them for a few minutes before blending them with the other ingredients.

EXCHANGES/CHOICES	Free food
CALORIES	10
CALORIES FROM FAT	0
TOTAL FAT	0.0 g
SATURATED FAT	0.0 g
TRANS FAT	0.0 g
CHOLESTEROL	0 mg
SODIUM	70 mg
POTASSIUM	90 mg
TOTAL CARBOHYDRATE	2 g
DIETARY FIBER	1 g
SUGARS	1 g
PROTEIN	0 g
PHOSPHORUS	15 mg

Socca with Poached Eggs, Roasted Tomatoes, and Fresh Basil p. 101

breakfast

It might be an easy meal to skip, especially amidst the chaos of busy weekday mornings, but there's nothing like a good, healthy breakfast to energize your body and set a positive tone for the rest of the day. Think about it: the period of time between last night's dinner and this morning's meal is the longest your body goes without food on a daily basis, so what you choose to eat can affect you in a big way. A breakfast packed with protein, fiber, and lots of vitamins and minerals will keep you feeling satisfied for hours. And you'll be much less likely to overindulge on unhealthy snacks throughout the day if you eat breakfast.

Whether you're looking for a portable meal or a brunch-worthy dish, the following recipes will keep you inspired with their vibrant flavors and unexpected ingredient pairings. With recipes for chewy bars that can be made ahead of time and smoothies that can be whipped up in just 5 minutes, you've got no excuse for skipping the most important meal of the day!

Almond, Wild Blueberry, and Flax Smoothie

SERVES: 3 | SERVING SIZE: 1 CUP | PREP TIME: 5 MINUTES | COOKING TIME: NONE

This quick-and-easy breakfast has everything you need to wake up and keep going all morning long. Blueberries provide an almost unmatched amount of antioxidants—especially wild blueberries; freshly squeezed lime juice helps detoxify the body and brighten the flavors; mint promotes digestion and stimulates the senses; and flax meal and almond flour offer a double dose of fiber. If you don't have blueberries on hand, feel free to swap in the same amount of strawberries, raspberries, or blackberries instead.

1 1/2 cups fresh or frozen wild blueberries

1 1/2 cups DIY Nut Milk (page 69, using almonds) or organic, unsweetened almond milk

2 tablespoons almond flour

3 tablespoons ground flax meal

1 tablespoon packed fresh mint leaves

2 teaspoons freshly squeezed lime juice

2 teaspoons raw honey

1 cup ice

1. In a blender, combine all ingredients and purée until smooth.

2. Divide smoothie among 3 glasses and enjoy immediately.

tip: Did you know that wild blueberries have more antioxidants than traditional blueberries? Make sure to use ground flax seeds in this recipe. Whole flax seeds are not digestible, so you will benefit from added fiber if you eat the whole seeds but will not reap the benefits of all the good-for-you nutrients that live inside.

EXCHANGES/CHOICES	1/2 Fruit
	1 Carbohydrate
	1 1/2 Fat

CALORIES	160
CALORIES FROM FAT	70
TOTAL FAT	8.0 g
SATURATED FAT	0.7 g
TRANS FAT	0.0 g
CHOLESTEROL	0 mg
SODIUM	15 mg
POTASSIUM	210 mg
TOTAL CARBOHYDRATE	21 g
DIETARY FIBER	6 g
SUGARS	12 g
PROTEIN	5 g
PHOSPHORUS	110 mg

Peach, Vanilla, and Chai Spice Smoothie

SERVES: 3 | SERVING SIZE: 1 CUP | PREP TIME: 5 MINUTES | COOKING TIME: 5 MINUTES

Once you try this smoothie, you'll never go back to those calorie-laden, chai spice lattes again. If you are using fresh peaches, make sure to keep the skins on. You will barely notice them after everything has been blended together, but they will infuse the smoothie with even more antioxidants. The chai spice pairs perfectly with the flavor of the peaches for a sweet and savory treat that really satisfies.

1 1/2 cups fresh or frozen sliced peaches

3/4 cup fat-free plain strained yogurt (Greek or skyr) or kefir

1 cup DIY Nut Milk (page 69, using almonds or coconut) or organic, unsweetened almond or coconut milk

3 tablespoons hemp seeds

2 tablespoons Masala Chai Spice Blend (page 76)

1 teaspoon pure vanilla extract

2 teaspoons raw honey

1/2 cup cold water

1. In a blender, combine all ingredients and purée until smooth.
2. Divide the smoothie among 3 glasses and enjoy immediately.

EXCHANGES/CHOICES	1/2 Fruit
	1/2 Carbohydrate
	1 Lean Protein
	1/2 Fat
CALORIES	150
CALORIES FROM FAT	40
TOTAL FAT	4.5 g
SATURATED FAT	0.8 g
TRANS FAT	0.0 g
CHOLESTEROL	5 mg
SODIUM	25 mg
POTASSIUM	270 mg
TOTAL CARBOHYDRATE	17 g
DIETARY FIBER	4 g
SUGARS	11 g
PROTEIN	9 g
PHOSPHORUS	105 mg

Kale-Chia Orange Cream Smoothie

SERVES: 2 | SERVING SIZE: 1 CUP | PREP TIME: 5 MINUTES | COOKING TIME: 5 MINUTES

Remember those orange cream popsicles you loved to eat as a kid? Well, consider this smoothie the grownup version. While its sweet orange flavor will remind you of the good old days, the more sophisticated—and nutrient-rich—additions of kale, chia, and nut milk will make you feel energized and ready for whatever comes your way.

3/4 cup DIY Nut Milk (page 69, using almonds or coconut) or organic, unsweetened almond or coconut milk

1 small banana, peeled

1 large navel orange, peeled

2 cups chopped green kale

1/2 teaspoon pure vanilla extract

2 teaspoons chia seeds

1. In a blender, combine nut milk, banana, orange, kale, and vanilla, and purée until smooth.

2. Divide the smoothie between 2 glasses, top each with 1 teaspoon of the chia seeds, and enjoy immediately.

EXCHANGES/CHOICES	1 1/2 Fruit
	1/2 Fat
CALORIES	130
CALORIES FROM FAT	20
TOTAL FAT	2.5 g
SATURATED FAT	0.3 g
TRANS FAT	0.0 g
CHOLESTEROL	0 mg
SODIUM	15 mg
POTASSIUM	465 mg
TOTAL CARBOHYDRATE	25 g
DIETARY FIBER	6 g
SUGARS	15 g
PROTEIN	3 g
PHOSPHORUS	90 mg

benefits of eating in season

Think about this: what adjectives come to mind when you think of winter squash and sweet potatoes? Warm, cozy, and rich, right? That makes sense because these foods are in season during the winter months when the air is cool and your body craves warm, grounding foods. Conversely, a cucumber is refreshing and cooling, which makes it the perfect ingredient for a hot summer day! This is a great example of why we should try to eat foods that are in season. Here are a few more reasons to embrace in-season eating:

- **Save money.** Seasonal produce is usually less expensive because it is locally abundant, which means there are no added costs for shipping from distant places.

- **More nutrients.** When produce is picked it is removed from its nutrient source. The longer it remains in transit, at your grocery store, or on your counter, the more nutrients are lost. In-season, local produce is picked when ripe and consumed more quickly than produce that has to travel long distances or those varieties that are held in storage. The fresher the produce, the more nutrient dense!

- **Great taste.** Local, in-season produce tastes delicious! Why? Because it is allowed to ripen prior to being picked. When it comes to creating a healthy dish, the quality and taste of the ingredients is so important. Using in-season produce is a great way to maximize the flavors of your meal.

tip: Frozen produce rocks! These fruits and vegetables are allowed to ripen naturally, which maximizes nutrient density. Then they are picked and quickly frozen to lock in most of the good-for-you nutrients. Plus, frozen produce is often less expensive than its fresh counterparts. If you can't buy a certain fruit or vegetable fresh, frozen is a good alternative.

Sweet Potato Oats

SERVES: 4 | SERVING SIZE: 1/2 CUP | PREP TIME: 5 MINUTES | COOKING TIME: 5 MINUTES

What's better than a steaming bowl of oatmeal on a crisp fall morning? In this recipe, sweet potato purée works double time, infusing the oatmeal with sweet, autumnal flavor and amping up the nutritional profile of the dish with an extra boost of vitamin A, potassium, and fiber. With the crunch of the pecans, hints of vanilla and cinnamon, and a touch of maple syrup, this recipe is sure to become a new favorite in your breakfast rotation.

3/4 cup gluten-free rolled oats (not instant)

3/4 cup unsweetened vanilla almond milk

3/4 cup water

1/4 teaspoon pure vanilla extract

1/4 teaspoon ground cinnamon

1/4 teaspoon fine sea salt

1/2 cup BPA-free canned sweet potato purée

1 tablespoon pure maple syrup (preferably grade B)

3 tablespoons chopped raw, unsalted pecans

1. In a small saucepan, combine oats, almond milk, water, vanilla, cinnamon, and salt. Bring mixture to a boil over medium-high heat, then reduce heat to low and simmer uncovered until oatmeal has thickened, about 5 minutes.

2. Remove pan from the heat and stir in sweet potato purée, maple syrup, and pecans. Serve hot.

EXCHANGES/CHOICES	1 1/2 Starch
	1/2 Carbohydrate
	1 Fat
CALORIES	180
CALORIES FROM FAT	50
TOTAL FAT	6.0 g
SATURATED FAT	0.7 g
TRANS FAT	0.0 g
CHOLESTEROL	0 mg
SODIUM	180 mg
POTASSIUM	245 mg
TOTAL CARBOHYDRATE	28 g
DIETARY FIBER	4 g
SUGARS	5 g
PROTEIN	5 g
PHOSPHORUS	185 mg

Tahini-Banana Buckwheat Porridge

SERVES: 4 | SERVING SIZE: 1 CUP | PREP TIME: 5 MINUTES | COOKING TIME: 15 MINUTES

Buckwheat is one of my favorite grains, as it has a beautifully nutty flavor and earthy aroma that calms the senses and warms the soul. Contrary to its name, it is actually a gluten-free grain. The savory, rich taste of this grain pairs perfectly with tahini and warming spices such as cinnamon and slightly sweet cardamom. Add to that the creaminess of banana and this breakfast porridge becomes the ultimate morning comfort food. Buckwheat groats (the hulled seeds of a plant related to rhubarb) can be found online and at many specialty grocers and health-food stores throughout the country.

2 cups water

1 cup buckwheat groats

1/2 teaspoon cinnamon

1/4 teaspoon cardamom

1 teaspoon vanilla extract

1 tablespoon maple syrup

2 tablespoons tahini

1/4 cup unsweetened almond milk

4 tablespoons ground flax meal, divided

1 banana, sliced, divided

1. In a small saucepan, combine water, buckwheat groats, cinnamon, cardamom, and vanilla. Bring mixture to a boil over medium-high heat, then reduce heat to low and simmer, covered, for 10–15 minutes or until the groats are tender and have absorbed most of the liquid.

2. Remove pan from the heat and stir in maple syrup, tahini, and almond milk. Divide the porridge among 4 bowls and top each with 1 tablespoon ground flax meal and 1/4 of the sliced banana.

EXCHANGES/CHOICES	2 Starch
	1/2 Fruit
	1/2 Carbohydrate
	1 Lean Protein
	1 Fat
CALORIES	300
CALORIES FROM FAT	90
TOTAL FAT	10.0 g
SATURATED FAT	1.3 g
TRANS FAT	0.0 g
CHOLESTEROL	0 mg
SODIUM	20 mg
POTASSIUM	380 mg
TOTAL CARBOHYDRATE	46 g
DIETARY FIBER	6 g
SUGARS	8 g
PROTEIN	10 g
PHOSPHORUS	260 mg

Single-Serve Golden Chai Overnight Oats with Pear and Flax

SERVES: 1 | SERVING SIZE: 3/4 CUP OATS, 1/4 CUP DICED PEAR, 1 TABLESPOON CHOPPED WALNUTS
PREP TIME: 5 MINUTES | REFRIGERATION TIME: AT LEAST 4 HOURS (OR OVERNIGHT)

1/3 cup rolled oats

1 tablespoon ground flax seed

1/2 cup DIY Nut Milk (page 69; using almonds) or organic, unsweetened almond milk

1 teaspoon maple syrup

1/2 teaspoon Masala Chai Spice Blend (page 76)

1/4 teaspoon ground turmeric

1/4 cup diced fresh pear

1 tablespoon walnuts

1. In a storage jar, like a 16-ounce mason jar, combine oats, flax seed, almond milk, maple syrup, spice blend, and turmeric. Stir well to combine.

2. Refrigerate, covered, for at least 4 hours or overnight. Serve topped with fresh pear and walnuts.

tip: No Masala Chai Spice Blend on hand? Try a pinch of cinnamon, cardamom, or ginger to add flavor!

EXCHANGES/CHOICES	1 1/2 Starch
	1/2 Fruit
	1/2 Carbohydrate
	2 Fat
CALORIES	270
CALORIES FROM FAT	120
TOTAL FAT	13.0 g
SATURATED FAT	1.3 g
TRANS FAT	0.0 g
CHOLESTEROL	0 mg
SODIUM	15 mg
POTASSIUM	320 mg
TOTAL CARBOHYDRATE	36 g
DIETARY FIBER	9 g
SUGARS	9 g
PROTEIN	8 g
PHOSPHORUS	220 mg

Oat and Quinoa Breakfast Bars with Raisins and Tahini

SERVES: 12 | SERVING SIZE: 1 BAR | PREP TIME: 10 MINUTES | COOKING TIME: 30 MINUTES

Make a batch of these bars over the weekend and keep them on hand for energy-packed, on-the-fly breakfasts throughout the week. Their sweet, nutty flavor and crunchy-yet-chewy texture will give those grocery store breakfast bars a run for their money. And these delicious bars don't contain all the unhealthy preservatives and added sugars of store-bought varieties.

Nonstick cooking spray

1 cup DIY Nut Flour (page 72, using almonds) or store-bought almond flour

1/2 teaspoon aluminum-free baking powder

1/2 teaspoon baking soda

2 cups gluten-free rolled oats (not instant)

1/3 cup raw, unsalted sunflower seeds

1/3 cup raw, unsalted pumpkin seeds

1/2 cup raw, unsalted sliced almonds

1 teaspoon ground cinnamon

1/4 cup tahini

1/3 cup pure maple syrup (preferably grade B)

1 large egg

1 egg white

1/2 cup Everyday Applesauce (page 67) or organic, unsweetened applesauce

1 teaspoon pure vanilla extract

2 cups cooked quinoa

2/3 cup raisins

1. Preheat the oven to 375°F. Spray a 9 x 13-inch baking pan with nonstick cooking spray.

2. In a medium bowl, whisk together almond flour, baking powder, baking soda, oats, sunflower seeds, pumpkin seeds, almonds, and cinnamon.

3. In a large bowl, combine tahini, maple syrup, egg, egg white, applesauce, and vanilla. Slowly add the flour mixture to the bowl of wet ingredients and stir with a wooden spoon until fully incorporated. Fold in the quinoa and raisins.

4. Spoon batter into the prepared pan and bake for 20 minutes, or until bars are golden brown and a toothpick poked into the center comes out clean.

5. Remove pan from the oven and let it cool completely, about 30 minutes. Then cut into 12 bars. Store any leftovers in an airtight container in the refrigerator for up to 1 week.

EXCHANGES/CHOICES 1 Starch
1/2 Fruit
1 Carbohydrate
1 Lean Protein
2 1/2 Fat

CALORIES	330
CALORIES FROM FAT	150
TOTAL FAT	17.0 g
SATURATED FAT	1.9 g
TRANS FAT	0.0 g
CHOLESTEROL	15 mg
SODIUM	90 mg
POTASSIUM	400 mg
TOTAL CARBOHYDRATE	37 g
DIETARY FIBER	6 g
SUGARS	13 g
PROTEIN	11 g
PHOSPHORUS	350 mg

Asparagus, Mushroom, and Kale Frittata

SERVES: 6 | SERVING SIZE: 1 SLICE | PREP TIME: 5 MINUTES | COOKING TIME: ABOUT 35 MINUTES

Frittatas are the perfect "clean out the fridge" meal, as you can add almost any vegetable to the mix! Enjoy a frittata for breakfast, lunch, or dinner—hot or cold—and wrap the wedges individually for easy, grab-and-go meals throughout the week. This recipe is best to use in the spring, when tender asparagus abounds at the farmers' market. For the best flavor and texture, look for firm, slender asparagus spears that are not dried or split at the ends.

6 large eggs

8 egg whites

1/2 cup 1% milk or DIY Nut Milk (page 69)

1/4 teaspoon fine sea salt

1/4 teaspoon freshly ground black pepper

1 tablespoon extra-virgin olive oil

1 cup halved lengthwise and thinly sliced leeks (white and light green parts)

1 cup sliced cremini mushrooms

6 ounces roughly chopped asparagus (ends trimmed and cut into 1-inch pieces)

1 cup chopped kale

2 tablespoons crumbled soft goat cheese

1. Preheat the oven to 400°F.

2. In a medium bowl, whisk together eggs, egg whites, and milk. Season with salt and pepper. Set aside.

3. Heat oil in a 10–12-inch cast-iron skillet (or another nonstick *ovenproof* skillet) over medium-high heat. Add leeks and sauté for 2–3 minutes or until tender, then add mushrooms and cook for another 3–4 minutes until mushrooms begin to brown. Add asparagus and kale to the skillet and cook for 1–2 minutes, stirring constantly, until the asparagus is bright green and the kale is wilted.

4. Add egg mixture to the skillet, reduce the heat to medium, and cook without stirring for 3–4 minutes, or until the sides are set.

5. Sprinkle the goat cheese on top and transfer the skillet to the oven. Bake the frittata for 15–20 minutes, or until it is firm.

6. Remove frittata from the oven, let it rest for 5 minutes, and then cut it into 6 slices. Serve immediately.

EXCHANGES/CHOICES	1 Nonstarchy Vegetable
	2 Lean Protein
	1 Fat
CALORIES	150
CALORIES FROM FAT	70
TOTAL FAT	8.0 g
SATURATED FAT	2.6 g
TRANS FAT	0.0 g
CHOLESTEROL	190 mg
SODIUM	260 mg
POTASSIUM	295 mg
TOTAL CARBOHYDRATE	5 g
DIETARY FIBER	1 g
SUGARS	2 g
PROTEIN	13 g
PHOSPHORUS	155 mg

Socca with Poached Eggs, Roasted Tomatoes, and Fresh Basil

SERVES: 8 | SERVING SIZE: 1 SLICE OF SOCCA, 1 POACHED EGG, 2 TABLESPOONS ROASTED TOMATOES, AND 2 TABLESPOONS BASIL
PREP TIME: 1 HOUR (INCLUDING BATTER RESTING TIME) | COOKING TIME: 10 MINUTES

Socca, also known as *farinata,* is a thin chickpea flour pancake commonly found in both Italian and French cuisines. In this recipe, I top wedges of the warm chickpea crepe with roasted tomatoes, poached eggs, and fresh basil. For an easy, make-ahead brunch or weekday breakfast, make the batter and poach the eggs the night before. To store the poached eggs overnight, plunge them into an airtight container filled with cold water and place them in the fridge.

1 cup chickpea flour

1/2 teaspoon cumin

1/4 teaspoon fine sea salt

1 cup warm water

2 tablespoons extra-virgin olive oil, divided

1 tablespoon white wine vinegar

8 large eggs

1 cup Everyday Roasted Tomatoes (page 65)

1 cup chopped fresh basil

1/4 teaspoon freshly ground black pepper

1. Place a 10-inch cast-iron skillet about 12 inches from your oven's heating element and set the oven to "Broil."

2. In a small bowl, whisk together chickpea flour, cumin, and salt. Slowly stream in water, whisking quickly to eliminate lumps, then stir in 1 tablespoon of the olive oil. Cover the bowl and set aside for at least 15 minutes. (Or store it in the refrigerator for up to 12 hours.) The batter should be a thin, pancake batter–like consistency.

3. After the batter has rested, carefully remove the hot skillet from the oven. Add the remaining 1 tablespoon of olive oil to the skillet and pour in the socca batter. Broil for 8–10 minutes, or until the edges of the socca are browned and the center is set.

4. Meanwhile, set a metal strainer in the bottom of a large pot, fill the pot 2/3 full with water, and add the vinegar. Crack each egg into a small prep bowl. Place the pot over medium-high heat and bring the vinegar and water to a simmer. Using a long-handled spoon, stir the water in a wide, circular motion to create a whirlpool. Quickly, while the whirlpool is still going, slide in the eggs, one by one. Once all the eggs are in the water, poach them without stirring until the whites are set and the yolks are no longer runny, about 4–6 minutes. Using tongs, carefully lift the strainer out of the water with the eggs.

5. Remove socca from the oven and cut it into 8 wedges. To serve, place a socca wedge on each of 8 plates and top each serving with 1 poached egg, 2 tablespoons roasted tomatoes, and 2 tablespoons chopped basil. Season servings with pepper.

EXCHANGES/CHOICES	1/2 Starch
	1 Medium-Fat Protein
	1 Fat
CALORIES	170
CALORIES FROM FAT	100
TOTAL FAT	11.0 g
SATURATED FAT	2.4 g
TRANS FAT	0.0 g
CHOLESTEROL	185 mg
SODIUM	220 mg
POTASSIUM	290 mg
TOTAL CARBOHYDRATE	9 g
DIETARY FIBER	2 g
SUGARS	3 g
PROTEIN	9 g
PHOSPHORUS	150 mg

healthy cooking techniques for eggs

Eggs get a bad reputation for their fat and cholesterol content, but studies have shown that, when cooked using healthy methods, eggs are actually one of the best sources of protein available, and research has shown that consuming moderate amounts of dietary cholesterol does not negatively affect serum cholesterol as much as was once thought.

- **Hard or Soft Boiled:** Place the eggs in a saucepan or pot large enough to accommodate them in a single later, and cover them by one inch with cold water. Set the pan over medium-high heat. As soon as the water begins to boil, cover the pan, remove it from the heat, and let the eggs sit in the hot water for 3–5 minutes (for soft-boiled eggs) or 10–13 minutes (for hard-boiled eggs).

- **Scrambled:** Heat 2 teaspoons of extra-virgin olive oil in a medium nonstick or cast-iron skillet over medium-high heat. In a large bowl, whisk the eggs with some 1% milk or unsweetened almond milk (about 1 tablespoon of liquid per egg). Pour the egg mixture into the skillet and turn and fold the eggs just until they are set.

- **Poached:** Set a metal strainer in the bottom of a deep saucepan. Fill the pan 2/3 full with water and add in 1 tablespoon of vinegar. Crack each egg into a small prep bowl. Place the pan over medium-high heat and bring the vinegar and water to a simmer. Using a long-handled spoon, stir the water in a wide, circular motion to create a whirlpool. Quickly, while the whirlpool is still going, slide in the eggs, one by one. Once all the eggs are in the water, poach them without stirring until the whites are set and the yolks are no longer runny, 4–6 minutes. Using tongs, carefully lift the strainer out of the water with the eggs.

- **Baked:** Preheat the oven to 325°F and coat a few ramekins lightly with nonstick cooking spray. Crack 2 eggs into each ramekin, and spoon in some seasoning ingredients—such as Everyday Roasted Tomatoes (page 65), Everyday Roasted Bell Peppers (page 66), Harissa Paste (page 80), or Walnut Arugula Pesto (page 81). Stir gently, making sure not to break the yolks. Bake the eggs for 12–15 minutes, or until the whites have set and the yolks are still a little jiggly.

Garden Vegetable Shakshuka

SERVES: 8 | SERVING SIZE: 1 WEDGE | PREP TIME: 15 MINUTES | COOKING TIME: 35 MINUTES

Though the name might sound intimidating (I think it sounds fun!), this Tunisian one-pan wonder simply consists of eggs poached in a spicy tomato–bell pepper sauce seasoned with cumin and paprika. It's a common breakfast staple in North Africa and the Middle East, but it also makes for an ideal eggs-for-dinner dish, if the mood strikes you. Looking to spice up this recipe a little more? Consider serving it with a tablespoon of Harissa Paste (page 80).

2 tablespoons extra-virgin olive oil

1 medium yellow onion, finely chopped

1 large green bell pepper, cored, seeded, and chopped

1 large red bell pepper, cored, seeded, and chopped

1 zucchini, quartered lengthwise and cut into 1-inch chunks

2 cloves garlic, minced

1/4 cup tomato paste

1 (28-ounce) can whole peeled tomatoes, drained and crushed by hand

1/2 teaspoon fine sea salt

1 tablespoon ground cumin

1/2 teaspoon smoked paprika

1/4 teaspoon red pepper flakes

1 teaspoon freshly ground black pepper

1 tablespoon chopped fresh oregano

8 large eggs

1/4 cup chopped fresh flat-leaf parsley

1. Heat olive oil in a large cast-iron skillet over medium heat. Add onions and sauté for 5–10 minutes, or until onions are translucent. Add bell peppers, zucchini, and garlic and cook just until softened, 3–5 minutes. Add tomato paste and sauté for another 2 minutes.

2. Add tomatoes, salt, cumin, paprika, red pepper flakes, pepper, and oregano and let the mixture simmer for 20 minutes, or until it thickens.

3. Crack the eggs into the tomato mixture one by one. Cover and simmer for approximately 5–8 minutes, or until the whites of the eggs are no longer translucent and the yolks are no longer runny. Garnish with fresh parsley and serve immediately.

EXCHANGES/CHOICES	2 Nonstarchy Vegetable
	1 Medium-Fat Protein
	1/2 Fat
CALORIES	150
CALORIES FROM FAT	80
TOTAL FAT	9.0 g
SATURATED FAT	2.1 g
TRANS FAT	0.0 g
CHOLESTEROL	185 mg
SODIUM	300 mg
POTASSIUM	490 mg
TOTAL CARBOHYDRATE	10 g
DIETARY FIBER	2 g
SUGARS	5 g
PROTEIN	8 g
PHOSPHORUS	155 mg

Pesto Scramble with Fresh Tomatoes

SERVES: 1 | SERVING SIZE: 3/4 CUP SCRAMBLED EGG, 1/4 CUP TOMATO | PREP TIME: 5 MINUTES | COOKING TIME: 5 MINUTES

We call these "green eggs" in our house where they are a morning staple. I keep pesto in the freezer and simply scrape off 1 teaspoon to add to my scramble. Serve the scramble with fresh tomatoes that are sprinkled with citrus zest and you'll be in heaven.

1 whole egg

1/2 cup egg whites

1 teaspoon pesto

1/8 teaspoon freshly ground black pepper

1 teaspoon extra-virgin olive oil

1/4 cup chopped fresh tomatoes

1/4 teaspoon freshly grated lemon zest

1 tablespoon fresh basil

1/16 teaspoon fine sea salt

1. In a small bowl, whisk together eggs, egg whites, pesto, and pepper. Set aside.

2. Heat olive oil in a small, ceramic-coated skillet over medium heat. Add the egg mixture and scramble until cooked through, about 3 minutes.

3. In a small bowl, toss the tomatoes with the lemon zest, fresh basil, and salt.

4. Top eggs with the tomato and serve.

EXCHANGES/CHOICES	3 Lean Protein
	1 Fat
CALORIES	200
CALORIES FROM FAT	100
TOTAL FAT	11.0 g
SATURATED FAT	2.4 g
TRANS FAT	0.0 g
CHOLESTEROL	185 mg
SODIUM	470 mg
POTASSIUM	390 mg
TOTAL CARBOHYDRATE	4 g
DIETARY FIBER	1 g
SUGARS	2 g
PROTEIN	20 g
PHOSPHORUS	130 mg

Spiced Raspberries
with Cottage Cheese and Walnuts

SERVES: 4 | SERVING SIZE: 1/2 CUP COTTAGE CHEESE, 1/4 CUP BERRIES, 1 TABLESPOON CHOPPED WALNUTS
PREP TIME: 15 MINUTES (TO ALLOW RASPBERRIES TO DEFROST) | COOKING TIME: NONE

I think cottage cheese gets a bad rep. Creamy and packed with satisfying protein, this is not your grandmother's breakfast bowl. By the way, you don't have to break the bank on fresh berries for this recipe. Frozen berries rock! Why? They are just as rich in fiber and antioxidants as fresh varieties, and when they defrost, they create their own naturally sweet syrup. I added a few savory spices to play with the flavor profiles and topped the recipe off with crunchy walnuts. I sometimes defrost a bag of frozen berries and store them in the fridge for recipes just like this.

1 cup frozen raspberries

1/4 teaspoon freshly grated
   orange zest

1/8 teaspoon cardamom

1/8 teaspoon cinnamon

2 cups low-fat cottage cheese

1/4 cup walnuts, chopped

1. Place raspberries in a small bowl and allow them to defrost for 15 minutes. Add orange zest, cardamom, and cinnamon, and mix to combine.

2. Divide cottage cheese evenly among 4 bowls. Top each bowl with 2 tablespoons of the fruit mixture and 1 tablespoon walnuts.

EXCHANGES/CHOICES	3 Lean Protein
	1 Fat
CALORIES	200
CALORIES FROM FAT	100
TOTAL FAT	11.0 g
SATURATED FAT	2.4 g
TRANS FAT	0.0 g
CHOLESTEROL	185 mg
SODIUM	470 mg
POTASSIUM	390 mg
TOTAL CARBOHYDRATE	4 g
DIETARY FIBER	1 g
SUGARS	2 g
PROTEIN	20 g
PHOSPHORUS	130 mg

Broiled Grapefruit with Yogurt and Granola

SERVES: 4 | SERVING SIZE: 1/2 GRAPEFRUIT, 1/4 CUP YOGURT, AND 2 TABLESPOONS GRANOLA
PREP TIME: 5 MINUTES | COOKING TIME: 5 MINUTES

If the tartness of grapefruit usually turns you away, this recipe will welcome you back. Broiling grapefruit helps to concentrate its natural sweetness. Add the creaminess of yogurt and some crunchy granola, and you've created a magical breakfast!

2 grapefruit, halved

1 cup fat-free, plain strained yogurt
   (Greek or skyr)

1/2 cup Maple-Tahini Oat and
   Amaranth Granola (page 107)

1. Preheat broiler. Place grapefruit halves on a parchment paper–lined baking sheet.

2. Broil grapefruit halves for 3–5 minutes, until the natural sugars caramelize and begin to brown. Let grapefruit cool for a few minutes; serve warm or at room temperature, each topped with 1/4 cup yogurt and 2 tablespoons granola.

EXCHANGES/CHOICES	1 Fruit
	1/2 Carbohydrate
	1 Lean Protein
	1/2 Fat
CALORIES	180
CALORIES FROM FAT	45
TOTAL FAT	5.0 g
SATURATED FAT	0.7 g
TRANS FAT	0.0 g
CHOLESTEROL	5 mg
SODIUM	45 mg
POTASSIUM	375 mg
TOTAL CARBOHYDRATE	26 g
DIETARY FIBER	3 g
SUGARS	15 g
PROTEIN	9 g
PHOSPHORUS	165 mg

Maple-Tahini Oat and Amaranth Granola

SERVES: 12 | SERVING SIZE: 1/4 CUP | PREP TIME: 8 MINUTES | COOKING TIME: 40 MINUTES

Granola tends to be thought of as one of those "unhealthy health foods" because the sugar and fat content of store-bought granola is often through the roof. I like to think of granola as more of a condiment than a cereal, which helps keep portions in check. By making it yourself, you can really control the ingredients that go into the granola! Once you master this homemade granola recipe, you can make your own variations. For instance, try swapping sunflower seeds for the pumpkin seeds or raisins for the cherries, and experiment with different ground spices like cinnamon, cardamom, and ginger.

Nonstick cooking spray

1/2 cup uncooked amaranth

1 1/2 cups gluten-free rolled oats (not instant)

1 1/4 cups raw, unsalted pumpkin seeds

1/4 cup raw, unsalted sliced almonds

1/2 cup unsweetened dried cherries

14 cup pure maple syrup (preferably grade B)

1 teaspoon pure vanilla extract

1/4 cup avocado oil

1 tablespoon DIY Tahini (page 75)

1/4 teaspoon fine sea salt

1. Preheat the oven to 325°F.

2. Line a rimmed baking sheet with parchment paper and spray with nonstick cooking spray.

3. In a large bowl, mix together amaranth, oats, pumpkin seeds, almonds, and dried cherries. In a separate small bowl, whisk together the maple syrup, vanilla, olive oil, tahini, and salt. Add maple syrup mixture to the amaranth mixture and stir to combine.

4. Spread mixture out on the prepared baking sheet and bake for 30–40 minutes, rotating the baking sheet halfway through cooking time, until granola is slightly golden.

5. Remove baking sheet from the oven and let it cool completely. Break granola into clusters.

6. Store granola in an airtight container at room temperature for up to 1 week.

EXCHANGES/CHOICES	1 Starch
	1/2 Carbohydrate
	1 1/2 Fat
CALORIES	190
CALORIES FROM FAT	80
TOTAL FAT	9.0 g
SATURATED FAT	1.2 g
TRANS FAT	0.0 g
CHOLESTEROL	0 mg
SODIUM	50 mg
POTASSIUM	160 mg
TOTAL CARBOHYDRATE	23 g
DIETARY FIBER	3 g
SUGARS	6 g
PROTEIN	4 g
PHOSPHORUS	155 mg

Kale and Brussels Sprout Salad with Cashews, Pears, and Pomegranate p. 130
Roasted Beet and Apple Soup p. 175

light bites and salads

Repeat after me: *Every bite of food I take is an opportunity to nourish and fuel my body.* It's easy enough to say, but what do you do around 3:00 p.m., when your stomach gurgles and the most convenient food source is a vending machine full of candy bars? It's the ultimate test of your willpower, for sure—but with a little planning, you can pass this test every time.

In the pages that follow, you'll find a slew of super yummy, easy-to-make recipes that will satisfy those sudden cravings, round out your meals, and help you thrive throughout the day. Are you prone to snack attacks during your morning or evening commute? Store single-serving bags of Curry Roasted Chickpeas (page 120) in your car's center console. Need a midday pick-me-up that won't weigh you down? Apples with Tahini, Honey, and Sunflower Seeds (page 116) are just the thing to keep you going.

In this chapter, I've also included a few salads that are great either on their own or as part of a larger meal. Not only do these vegetable-centric recipes come together in record time, but they can also help you stave off hunger and prevent overeating. Pack salads in a jar or container for a perfectly portable lunch, and enjoy the benefits of all-natural, longer-lasting energy. That vending machine has got nothing on you!

Herby Brazil Nut Cheese

SERVES: 16 | SERVING SIZE: 1 TABLESPOON | PREP TIME: 8 HOURS | COOKING TIME: 5 MINUTES

Even if you don't get along with dairy, you can still enjoy the savory goodness of cheese! By combining nutrient-dense Brazil nuts with nutritional yeast, I created an earthy, cheesy blend that works well as a dip or even a spread on a sandwich or apple. Nutritional yeast, nicknamed "nooch," is a denatured yeast, and a mere 2 tablespoons of nooch boasts 3 grams of protein and 2 grams of fiber. Plus, it is a good source of minerals and B vitamins.

1 cup Brazil nuts

2 cups water

2 tablespoons nutritional yeast

1/4 cup freshly squeezed lemon juice

1 clove garlic

1 teaspoon Everyday Herb Oil (page 60)

1/4 teaspoon fine sea salt

1. Combine the Brazil nuts and water in a bowl. Cover and refrigerate to soak for at least 8 hours.
2. Strain the water from the nuts. Purée the soaked nuts with the remaining ingredients in a food processor and blend until smooth.

tip: You can also sprinkle nutritional yeast on popcorn for a "cheesy," savory snack.

EXCHANGES/CHOICES	1 Fat
CALORIES	60
CALORIES FROM FAT	50
TOTAL FAT	6.0 g
SATURATED FAT	1.4 g
TRANS FAT	0.0 g
CHOLESTEROL	0 mg
SODIUM	35 mg
POTASSIUM	75 mg
TOTAL CARBOHYDRATE	2 g
DIETARY FIBER	1 g
SUGARS	0 g
PROTEIN	2 g
PHOSPHORUS	70 mg

Fresh Figs with Herby Brazil Nut Cheese

SERVES: 4 | SERVING SIZE: 1 FIG AND 1 TABLESPOON NUT CHEESE | PREP TIME: 5 MINUTES | COOKING TIME: NONE

I like to think of this recipe as a fun play on figs with goat cheese; instead of using cheese we are using savory Herby Brazil Nut Cheese (see recipe on page 110). The sweetness of the figs pairs perfectly with the savory cheese and the punch of freshly ground black pepper that finishes off this dish, making it an event-friendly appetizer or a snack worth savoring.

4 fresh figs, halved

1/4 cup Herby Brazil Nut Cheese
  (page 110)

1/4 teaspoon freshly ground black
  pepper

1. Place 1/2 tablespoon nut cheese on each fig half. Garnish with pepper and serve.

EXCHANGES/CHOICES	1 Fruit
	1 Fat
CALORIES	100
CALORIES FROM FAT	50
TOTAL FAT	6.0 g
SATURATED FAT	1.4 g
TRANS FAT	0.0 g
CHOLESTEROL	0 mg
SODIUM	35 mg
POTASSIUM	190 mg
TOTAL CARBOHYDRATE	11 g
DIETARY FIBER	2 g
SUGARS	9 g
PROTEIN	2 g
PHOSPHORUS	75 mg

no-fuss snack ideas

For the days when preparing a snack feels out of the question, here are a few ideas that are easy to eat almost any time or place—even when you are on the run.

- Apple slices with 1 tablespoon of regular nut butter or Chai Spice Nut Butter (page 77)

- Pear with 1 tablespoon Herby Brazil Nut Cheese (page 110)

- Cut-up vegetables with 1/4 cup hummus

- Low-fat, plain strained yogurt with 1/2 cup berries

- 1/5 avocado with sea salt and lime zest

- Hardboiled egg with a small piece of fruit

- 1/2 banana with 1 tablespoon of tahini

- 5 raspberries stuffed with dark chocolate chips (1 chip per berry)

- 1/4 cup mixed nuts, seeds, and unsweetened dried fruits

- 1 cup papaya with lime juice and sea salt

Olive Tapenade

SERVES: 32 | SERVING SIZE: 1 TABLESPOON | PREP TIME: 5 MINUTES | COOKING TIME: NONE

Made with two kinds of olives, capers, garlic, herbs, and olive oil, this tapenade can transform almost any meal or snack from bland to extraordinary. If you don't have any Everyday Herb Oil (page 60) on hand, chop up 2 tablespoons of fresh herbs (like parsley, thyme, oregano, and basil) and add them instead.

1/2 cup pitted Niçoise or kalamata olives

1 1/2 cups pitted green olives (like Castelvatrano olives)

1 tablespoon capers

1 clove garlic, peeled

1 tablespoon Everyday Herb Oil (page 60)

1 tablespoon extra-virgin olive oil

1. Combine all ingredients in a food processor and purée until smooth.

2. Transfer tapenade to an airtight container and keep it in the refrigerator for up to 1 week.

EXCHANGES/CHOICES	1/2 Fat
CALORIES	25
CALORIES FROM FAT	20
TOTAL FAT	2.5 g
SATURATED FAT	0.3 g
TRANS FAT	0.0 g
CHOLESTEROL	0 mg
SODIUM	135 mg
POTASSIUM	0 mg
TOTAL CARBOHYDRATE	0 g
DIETARY FIBER	0 g
SUGARS	0 g
PROTEIN	0 g
PHOSPHORUS	0 mg

Roasted Eggplant Hummus

SERVES: 20 | SERVING SIZE: 2 TABLESPOONS | PREP TIME: 5 MINUTES | COOKING TIME: 35 MINUTES

Hummus is much more than just a party dip. It also makes for a great sandwich spread, pizza sauce, or pasta sauce (when thinned with a little chicken stock). In this recipe, roasted eggplant adds some extra flavor and gives the finished product a smooth, velvety texture. Though I chose cumin for seasoning, you can play with anything in your spice cabinet that goes well with eggplant and chickpeas, such as paprika, coriander, or turmeric.

- 1 small eggplant
- 1/4 cup extra-virgin olive oil, divided
- 2 tablespoons DIY Tahini (page 75)
- 2 cloves garlic, peeled (can use roasted)
- 1 teaspoon freshly grated lemon zest
- Juice of 1 lemon
- 1 (15-ounce) can chickpeas, drained and rinsed
- 1/4 teaspoon ground cumin
- 1/4 teaspoon fine sea salt
- 1/4 teaspoon freshly ground black pepper

1. Preheat the oven to 450°F.

2. Rub the eggplant with 1 tablespoon olive oil, then place it on a rimmed baking sheet and roast for 20–25 minutes, turning once halfway through, until it is easily pierced with the tip of a knife. Remove eggplant from the oven and let cool for about 10 minutes.

3. When it is cool enough to handle, cut eggplant in half lengthwise and scoop the flesh into the bowl of a food processor or blender. Discard eggplant skin.

4. Add the remaining 3 tablespoons olive oil, tahini, garlic, lemon zest, lemon juice, chickpeas, cumin, salt, and pepper to the food processor or blender and purée until smooth.

5. Transfer hummus to an airtight container and store it in the refrigerator for up to 1 week.

EXCHANGES/CHOICES	1/2 Carbohydrate
	1/2 Fat
CALORIES	60
CALORIES FROM FAT	25
TOTAL FAT	3.0 g
SATURATED FAT	0.4 g
TRANS FAT	0.0 g
CHOLESTEROL	0 mg
SODIUM	55 mg
POTASSIUM	65 mg
TOTAL CARBOHYDRATE	5 g
DIETARY FIBER	2 g
SUGARS	1 g
PROTEIN	2 g
PHOSPHORUS	35 mg

Smoked Butternut Squash–White Bean Dip

SERVES: 48 | SERVING SIZE: 2 TABLESPOONS | PREP TIME: 10 MINUTES | COOKING TIME: ABOUT 30 MINUTES

Rich and creamy, slightly sweet, earthy, and savory, this dip meets all the hors d'oeuvre requirements. Serve it up with whole-wheat pita chips, sliced carrots, bell peppers, cucumbers, or celery, or the socca on page 101.

3 cups cubed butternut squash

1/4 cup extra-virgin olive oil, divided

2 teaspoons smoked paprika

1 tablespoon Everyday Herb Oil (page 60)

1 tablespoon pure maple syrup (preferably grade B)

1/4 teaspoon fine sea salt

1/4 teaspoon freshly ground black pepper

1 (15-ounce) can cannellini beans, rinsed and drained OR 2 cups cooked white beans

2 tablespoons DIY Tahini (page 75)

1 teaspoon freshly grated orange zest

2 tablespoons freshly squeezed lemon juice

2 cloves garlic, peeled

1. Preheat the oven to 400°F.

2. In a medium bowl, toss butternut squash with 2 tablespoons olive oil, paprika, herb oil, maple syrup, salt, and pepper.

3. Arrange squash on a baking sheet in a single layer and roast for 20–25 minutes or until tender. Remove baking sheet from oven and let the squash cool for about 5 minutes.

4. In a food processor or blender, combine roasted squash, beans, tahini, orange zest, lemon juice, and garlic and purée until smooth.

5. Transfer dip to an airtight container and store it in the refrigerator for up to 1 week.

tip: If you don't have Everyday Herb Oil on hand, substitute 1 teaspoon of ground oregano or 2 teaspoons of chopped fresh oregano. If you're short on time, use defrosted, frozen butternut squash instead of fresh. You can just add it to the blender as is—no need to roast it first!

EXCHANGES/CHOICES	1/2 Fat
CALORIES	30
CALORIES FROM FAT	20
TOTAL FAT	2.0 g
SATURATED FAT	0.2 g
TRANS FAT	0.0 g
CHOLESTEROL	0 mg
SODIUM	20 mg
POTASSIUM	60 mg
TOTAL CARBOHYDRATE	3 g
DIETARY FIBER	1 g
SUGARS	0 g
PROTEIN	1 g
PHOSPHORUS	15 mg

Apples with Tahini, Honey, and Sunflower Seeds

SERVES: 4 | SERVING SIZE: 4 APPLE SLICES, 1 1/2 TEASPOONS TAHINI, 1/2 TEASPOON HONEY, 1 TEASPOON SUNFLOWER SEEDS
PREP TIME: 5 MINUTES | COOKING TIME: NONE

Sinking your teeth into a perfectly ripe apple can be seriously delicious, but I also appreciate the simple pairings that can make this familiar fruit taste extraordinary. I top the apples with tahini (sesame seed paste) and sunflower seeds in this recipe to add some healthy fats, protein, and additional fiber to really satisfy you. Bonus: they taste great!

2 medium gala or pink lady apples,
   cored and sliced into 8 pieces each

2 tablespoons tahini

2 teaspoons honey

4 teaspoons sunflower seeds

1. Arrange 4 apple slices on each of 4 serving plates. Drizzle each serving with 1 1/2 teaspoons of tahini and 1/2 teaspoon honey, and sprinkle each serving with 1 teaspoon sunflower seeds.

EXCHANGES/CHOICES	1 Fruit
	1 Fat
CALORIES	110
CALORIES FROM FAT	45
TOTAL FAT	5.0 g
SATURATED FAT	0.7 g
TRANS FAT	0.0 g
CHOLESTEROL	0 mg
SODIUM	10 mg
POTASSIUM	130 mg
TOTAL CARBOHYDRATE	15 g
DIETARY FIBER	3 g
SUGARS	10 g
PROTEIN	2 g
PHOSPHORUS	95 mg

"Everything" Deviled Eggs

SERVES: 8 | SERVING SIZE: 1 EGG (2 HALVES) | PREP TIME: 15 MINUTES | COOKING TIME: 10 MINUTES

I love deviled eggs! They are a great snack and the yolks have a naturally luxurious texture. Top them with the blend of salty and savory goodness that this recipe calls for, and you'll be hooked.

8 large eggs

4 tablespoons fat-free, plain strained yogurt (Greek or skyr)

2 teaspoons Dijon mustard

1 teaspoon whole-grain mustard

1/4 teaspoon fine sea salt

1/4 teaspoon freshly ground black pepper

4 teaspoons "Everything" Spice Blend (page 74)

1. Place eggs in a medium saucepan and cover them with cold water by 1 inch. Bring water to a boil over high heat, then cover the pan, turn off heat, and allow eggs to cook for 10 minutes.

2. While eggs cook, in a medium bowl stir together the yogurt, Dijon and whole-grain mustards, salt, and pepper, until well combined. Set aside.

3. When eggs are done cooking, peel them under cold running water and discard the shells.

4. Slice eggs in half lengthwise. Add 6 of the yolks to the yogurt mixture, reserving the remaining yolks for another use. Using a fork, mash the yolks into the yogurt mixture until very smooth. Divide yolk mixture evenly among egg white halves (about 1 tablespoon in each half). Garnish each egg half with 1/4 teaspoon of "Everything" Spice Blend.

EXCHANGES/CHOICES	1 Medium-Fat Protein
CALORIES	70
CALORIES FROM FAT	35
TOTAL FAT	4.0 g
SATURATED FAT	1.2 g
TRANS FAT	0.0 g
CHOLESTEROL	140 mg
SODIUM	240 mg
POTASSIUM	90 mg
TOTAL CARBOHYDRATE	2 g
DIETARY FIBER	0 g
SUGARS	1 g
PROTEIN	7 g
PHOSPHORUS	95 mg

Cucumber and Shishito Pickles

SERVES: 4 | SERVING SIZE: 1/2 CUP | PREP TIME: 5 MINUTES | REFRIGERATION TIME: 72 HOURS

Crunchy, slightly spicy, and oh, so zippy—I love pickles. Did you know you can pretty much pickle any fruit or vegetable? I mixed it up with this recipe by adding shishito peppers to a traditional cucumber pickle recipe.

1/2 pound whole shishito peppers

1 1/2 cups sliced English cucumber (1/2-inch-thick pieces)

1 cup distilled white vinegar

3 cloves garlic, peeled

2 tablespoons whole black peppercorns

2 tablespoons fine sea salt

1 tablespoon honey

1 tablespoon coriander seeds

1 1/2 cups hot water

1. Pack peppers and cucumbers into a clean 1-quart jar.

2. Add vinegar, garlic, peppercorns, salt, honey, and coriander to the jar. Pour hot water over vegetable mixture and seal the jar. Let pickles cool to room temperature, then refrigerate them for at least 72 hours. They will keep in the refrigerator for up to 1 month.

EXCHANGES/CHOICES	1 Nonstarchy Vegetable
CALORIES	25
CALORIES FROM FAT	0
TOTAL FAT	0.0 g
SATURATED FAT	0.0 g
TRANS FAT	0.0 g
CHOLESTEROL	0 mg
SODIUM	190 mg
POTASSIUM	230 mg
TOTAL CARBOHYDRATE	5 g
DIETARY FIBER	2 g
SUGARS	3 g
PROTEIN	1 g
PHOSPHORUS	30 mg

Moroccan Spiced Roasted Nuts

SERVES: 10.5 | SERVING SIZE: 3 TABLESPOONS | PREP TIME: 5 MINUTES | COOKING TIME: 20 MINUTES

I am determined to get you hooked on Moroccan spice blends! The earthy, sweet flavors really shine when they are roasted with nuts. This is the kind of robust flavor that turns an ordinary snack into an extraordinary one!

1/2 teaspoon freshly ground black pepper

2 tablespoons Moroccan Spice Blend (page 73)

2 cups raw, unsalted nuts (almonds, walnuts, hazelnuts, cashews, etc.)

1 tablespoon extra-virgin olive oil

1 teaspoon honey

1. Preheat the oven to 350°F. Line a rimmed baking sheet with parchment paper.

2. In a medium bowl, stir together pepper and spice blend.

3. To another medium bowl, toss nuts with olive oil and honey to combine. Add the spice blend and toss to evenly coat nuts. Add nuts to baking sheet.

4. Bake, stirring once, until fragrant and toasted, about 15–20 minutes. Let cool completely and then serve.

> **tip:** Use any leftover spice blend on meats, chicken, and/or root vegetables or in Moroccan Carrot and Red Lentil Soup (page 177).

EXCHANGES/CHOICES	1/2 Carbohydrate
	3 Fat
CALORIES	170
CALORIES FROM FAT	140
TOTAL FAT	15.0 g
SATURATED FAT	1.7 g
TRANS FAT	0.0 g
CHOLESTEROL	0 mg
SODIUM	20 mg
POTASSIUM	185 mg
TOTAL CARBOHYDRATE	7 g
DIETARY FIBER	2 g
SUGARS	2 g
PROTEIN	5 g
PHOSPHORUS	115 mg

Curry Roasted Chickpeas

SERVES: 4 | SERVING SIZE: 1/2 CUP | PREP TIME: 5 MINUTES | COOKING TIME: 35 MINUTES

Roasted chickpeas are one of my favorite healthy, munchy, crunchy snacks. There is nothing refined about these beauties as you roast up the whole bean. I enjoy trying a variety of spice blends to add flavor and dimension to this recipe.

1 (15-ounce) can chickpeas, rinsed,
   drained, and patted dry

2 teaspoons curry powder

2 tablespoons extra-virgin olive oil

1/4 teaspoon fine sea salt

1. Preheat the oven to 400°F.

2. In a small bowl, combine the chickpeas, curry powder, olive oil, and sea salt. Toss to evenly coat chickpeas.

3. Arrange chickpeas in a single layer on a rimmed baking sheet.

4. Transfer baking sheet to the oven and roast for 25–35 minutes, shaking the pan every 10–15 minutes, until the chickpeas are browned and crispy. Remove from the oven and serve chickpeas warm or at room temperature.

tip: You can cool the chickpeas and store them at room temperature in an airtight container. Change up this recipe by using the Moroccan Spice Blend (page 73) or the "Everything" Spice Blend (page 74) instead of the curry powder.

EXCHANGES/CHOICES	1 Starch
	1 Lean Protein
	1 Fat
CALORIES	170
CALORIES FROM FAT	70
TOTAL FAT	8.0 g
SATURATED FAT	1.1 g
TRANS FAT	0.0 g
CHOLESTEROL	0 mg
SODIUM	250 mg
POTASSIUM	195 mg
TOTAL CARBOHYDRATE	18 g
DIETARY FIBER	5 g
SUGARS	3 g
PROTEIN	6 g
PHOSPHORUS	110 mg

Savory Yogurt with Tapenade, Roasted Tomatoes, and Fresh Basil

SERVES: 4 | SERVING SIZE: 1/2 CUP YOGURT, 1 TABLESPOON TAPENADE, 2 TABLESPOONS TOMATO, 2 TABLESPOONS CUCUMBER, AND 1 TABLESPOON BASIL | PREP TIME: 5 MINUTES | COOKING TIME: NONE

Yes, it is true—yogurt can be enjoyed in savory dishes too! This is my take on a Mediterranean salad, but I use yogurt as the vehicle for the other ingredients. This recipe tastes best with in-season tomatoes; the quality of the ingredients really carries this dish.

2 cups fat-free, plain strained yogurt (Greek or skyr)

1/4 cup Olive Tapenade (page 113), or store-bought tapenade

1/2 cup Everyday Roasted Tomatoes (page 65), or store-bought whole-roasted tomatoes

1/2 cup diced English cucumber (1/2-inch-thick pieces)

1/4 cup sliced fresh basil

1 teaspoon freshly grated lemon zest (for garnish)

1. Spoon 1/2 cup of yogurt into each of 4 bowls. Top each serving with 1 tablespoon tapenade, 2 tablespoons roasted tomatoes, 2 tablespoons sliced cucumber, and 1 tablespoon fresh basil. Garnish with lemon zest.

tip: No time to make roasted tomatoes? You can use fresh tomatoes or roasted bell peppers instead.

EXCHANGES/CHOICES	1/2 Carbohydrate
	1 Lean Protein
	1/2 Fat
CALORIES	110
CALORIES FROM FAT	40
TOTAL FAT	4.5 g
SATURATED FAT	0.6 g
TRANS FAT	0.0 g
CHOLESTEROL	5 mg
SODIUM	250 mg
POTASSIUM	295 mg
TOTAL CARBOHYDRATE	7 g
DIETARY FIBER	1 g
SUGARS	4 g
PROTEIN	12 g
PHOSPHORUS	170 mg

Raw Multicolored Asparagus Salad with Grapes and Pistachios

SERVES: 4 | SERVING SIZE: 1 CUP ASPARAGUS, 1/2 CUP GRAPES, 1 TABLESPOON PISTACHIOS
PREP TIME: 10 MINUTES | COOKING TIME: NONE

White, purple, and green—have you enjoyed the many shades of deliciousness that asparagus has to offer? Thinly peeled, raw asparagus has a mild, spring-like flavor that makes the simplicity of this salad shine.

1 pound green asparagus, 1 inch of tough bottom stems removed

1 pound white and/or purple asparagus, 1 inch of tough bottom stems removed

1/2 teaspoon Dijon mustard

2 tablespoons extra-virgin olive oil

3 tablespoons champagne vinegar

1 tablespoon chopped fresh tarragon

1/4 teaspoon fine sea salt

1/4 teaspoon freshly ground black pepper

1 cup halved green grapes

1/4 cup chopped raw, unsalted pistachios

1. Shave green and white/purple asparagus into "ribbons' with a vegetable peeler, and place in a medium bowl.

2. In a small bowl, whisk together the mustard, olive oil, vinegar, tarragon, salt, and pepper.

3. Pour dressing over the asparagus and toss well to combine. Serve each portion topped with 1/4 cup grapes and 1 tablespoon chopped pistachios.

tip: If you cannot find white or purple asparagus, this recipe is just as delicious using only the green variety.

EXCHANGES/CHOICES	1/2 Fruit
	1 Nonstarchy Vegetable
	2 Fat
CALORIES	170
CALORIES FROM FAT	100
TOTAL FAT	11.0 g
SATURATED FAT	1.4 g
TRANS FAT	0.0 g
CHOLESTEROL	0 mg
SODIUM	160 mg
POTASSIUM	415 mg
TOTAL CARBOHYDRATE	16 g
DIETARY FIBER	4 g
SUGARS	9 g
PROTEIN	5 g
PHOSPHORUS	110 mg

Gingery Carrot, Apple, and Beet Slaw

SERVES: 8 | SERVING SIZE: 1/2 CUP | PREP TIME: 15 MINUTES | REFRIGERATION TIME: 30 MINUTES

Roasting beets can take a while, so why not enjoy them raw? This slaw is easy to whip up. Just grate your fruits and veggies, add the dressing, and you are good to go! The natural sweetness of the produce gets some zip from the ginger. This recipe is fun, colorful, and flavorful—sometimes even more flavorful the next day.

1/4 cup freshly squeezed orange juice

1 tablespoon apple cider vinegar

2 teaspoons grated fresh ginger

1 teaspoon freshly grated lemon zest

1 teaspoon freshly grated orange zest

1 tablespoon extra-virgin olive oil

1/4 teaspoon fine sea salt

1/4 teaspoon freshly ground black pepper

2 large carrots, peeled

1 large Granny Smith apple, peeled and cored

2 large red beets, peeled

1. In a large bowl, whisk together orange juice, cider vinegar, ginger, lemon zest, orange zest, olive oil, salt, and pepper.

2. Shred the carrots, apple, and beets using the large holes of a box grater. (Or, pulse each vegetable individually in a food processor.) Note: consider wearing gloves while shredding the beets as they may stain your hands.

3. Transfer the shredded vegetables and apple to the bowl with the dressing; toss to combine. Refrigerate salad for 30 minutes before serving.

EXCHANGES/CHOICES	1/2 Fruit
	1 Nonstarchy Vegetable
CALORIES	60
CALORIES FROM FAT	20
TOTAL FAT	2.0 g
SATURATED FAT	0.3 g
TRANS FAT	0.0 g
CHOLESTEROL	0 mg
SODIUM	105 mg
POTASSIUM	205 mg
TOTAL CARBOHYDRATE	10 g
DIETARY FIBER	2 g
SUGARS	7 g
PROTEIN	1 g
PHOSPHORUS	25 mg

Beet Salad with Citrus-Scented Ricotta, Orange Segments, and Chia

SERVES: 4 | SERVING SIZE: 4 BEET WEDGES, 2 TABLESPOONS RICOTTA MIXTURE, 2 ORANGE SEGMENTS, 1/2 TEASPOON CHIA SEEDS, AND 1 TABLESPOON SCALLIONS | PREP TIME: 10 MINUTES | COOKING TIME: 1 HOUR

Yes, roasting beets can take some time but it's fairly stress free. But if you are totally opposed to roasting them yourself, you are in luck because you can often buy precooked, un-dressed beets in the refrigerated section at your grocery store. Citrus and beets are a classic pairing that is made complete in this recipe with the addition of savory ricotta and the slight crunch of chia seeds.

1 pound red beets, trimmed

1 tablespoon extra-virgin olive oil

1/2 cup part-skim ricotta cheese

1/8 teaspoon ground cumin

1 teaspoon freshly squeezed lemon juice

1 teaspoon freshly grated lemon zest, divided

1 teaspoon freshly grated orange zest, divided

1/8 teaspoon fine sea salt

1/4 teaspoon freshly ground black pepper

1 medium navel orange, peeled and separated into 8 segments

2 teaspoons chia seeds

1/4 cup sliced scallions (green parts only)

1. Preheat the oven to 400°F.

2. Place beets in a large piece of foil and drizzle with the olive oil, then fold up the sides of the foil to form a sealed packet. Bake on a baking sheet for 40 minutes, or until beets are tender when pierced with a fork. Remove beets from the oven and transfer to a wire rack to cool.

3. When they are cool enough to handle, peel the beets, cut them in half, and cut each half into 4 equal-sized wedges. Toss with half the lemon and orange zests, and the salt and pepper.

4. In a small bowl, stir together ricotta, cumin, lemon juice, remaining lemon zest, and remaining orange zest.

5. Divide the ricotta mixture evenly among 4 bowls (2 tablespoons per bowl). Top each serving with 4 beet wedges, 2 orange segments, 1/2 teaspoon chia seeds, and 1 tablespoon scallion slices to garnish.

EXCHANGES/CHOICES	1/2 Fruit
	2 Nonstarchy Vegetable
	1 Fat
CALORIES	140
CALORIES FROM FAT	60
TOTAL FAT	7.0 g
SATURATED FAT	2.1 g
TRANS FAT	0.0 g
CHOLESTEROL	10 mg
SODIUM	160 mg
POTASSIUM	375 mg
TOTAL CARBOHYDRATE	14 g
DIETARY FIBER	4 g
SUGARS	9 g
PROTEIN	6 g
PHOSPHORUS	115 mg

Berry and Melon Salad with Basil, Lime, and Walnuts

SERVES: 4 | SERVING SIZE: 1 CUP ARUGULA AND 3/4 CUP FRUIT SALAD | PREP TIME: 10 MINUTES | COOKING TIME: NONE

This is a great example of how you can make fruit totally fabulous with the addition of a few ingredients. The mild spice of the basil and brightness of the lime take this fruity salad to the next level.

- 4 packed cups baby arugula
- 1 tablespoon extra-virgin olive oil
- 1 tablespoon freshly squeezed lemon juice
- 1 cup cubed watermelon (1-inch cubes)
- 1 cup cubed cantaloupe (1-inch cubes)
- 1 cup fresh berries (raspberries, blackberries, or blueberries)
- 1 tablespoon freshly squeezed lime juice
- 1 teaspoon freshly grated lime zest
- 2 tablespoons sliced fresh basil
- 1 tablespoon seltzer water
- 1/4 teaspoon fine sea salt
- 1/4 cup chopped raw, unsalted walnuts

1. In a medium bowl, toss arugula with olive oil and lemon juice. Divide dressed arugula evenly among 4 plates (1 cup per plate).

2. In the same bowl, combine watermelon, cantaloupe, berries, lime juice, zest, basil, seltzer, and salt. Toss to combine.

3. Top each plate of arugula with 3/4 cup fruit salad. Garnish each serving with 1 tablespoon chopped walnuts.

EXCHANGES/CHOICES	1/2 Fruit
	1 Nonstarchy Vegetable
	2 Fat
CALORIES	130
CALORIES FROM FAT	80
TOTAL FAT	9.0 g
SATURATED FAT	1.0 g
TRANS FAT	0.0 g
CHOLESTEROL	0 mg
SODIUM	160 mg
POTASSIUM	345 mg
TOTAL CARBOHYDRATE	12 g
DIETARY FIBER	4 g
SUGARS	8 g
PROTEIN	3 g
PHOSPHORUS	60 mg

Super Green Greek-Style Salad

SERVES: 4 | SERVING SIZE: 2 CUPS GREENS AND 1 1/4 CUPS VEGETABLE MIXTURE | PREP TIME: 10 MINUTES | COOKING TIME: NONE

While other people typically cook their dark leafy greens, I enjoy them in their raw form as well. This is my play on a traditional Greek salad; the standard Greek salad ingredients and all of their nutritional goodness take a ride on the bitterness of beautiful baby greens in this recipe.

2 packed cups baby spinach

2 packed cups baby kale

2 packed cups baby arugula

2 packed cups baby Swiss chard

1 cup halved grape tomatoes

1 cup halved and sliced English cucumber (1-inch-thick slices)

1 cup diced bell pepper (1-inch dice)

2 cups cooked or BPA-free canned chickpeas (if canned, rinsed and drained)

6 tablespoons Greek Dressing (page 87)

1. In a large bowl, toss together the spinach, kale, arugula, and chard. Set aside.

2. In a small bowl, mix together the tomato, cucumber, bell pepper, and chickpeas. Set aside.

3. Toss the greens with 3 tablespoons dressing and toss the vegetables with another 3 tablespoons dressing. Reserve remaining dressing for another meal.

4. Divide the greens among 4 plates (2 cups each) and top each plate with 1 1/4 cups of the vegetable mixture.

building a mason jar salad

You can turn any salad recipe into a mason-jar masterpiece. It's all about the layering. Start by adding the salad dressing to the bottom of the jar. Then add the ingredients that are the most dense (think hummus, beans, beets, chicken, etc.). Layer the ingredients with the heaviest on the bottom and the lightest on top. When you are ready to eat, simply give your ingredients a good shake or stir.

EXCHANGES/CHOICES	1 1/2 Starch
	1 Nonstarchy Vegetable
	1 Lean Protein
	1 1/2 Fat
CALORIES	250
CALORIES FROM FAT	110
TOTAL FAT	12.0 g
SATURATED FAT	1.7 g
TRANS FAT	0.0 g
CHOLESTEROL	0 mg
SODIUM	230 mg
POTASSIUM	700 mg
TOTAL CARBOHYDRATE	29 g
DIETARY FIBER	9 g
SUGARS	8 g
PROTEIN	10 g
PHOSPHORUS	200 mg

Southwest Kale Salad with Corn and Creamy Avocado Dressing

SERVES: 4 | SERVING SIZE: 2 CUPS KALE, 3/4 CUP VEGETABLE MIXTURE, 1 TABLESPOON PUMPKIN SEEDS
PREP TIME: 10 MINUTES | COOKING TIME: NONE

Creamy, rich avocado plays with corn, tomatoes, crunchy radishes, black beans, and kale in this flavorful and colorful entrée salad. This recipe will turn anyone into a raw kale advocate.

8 packed cups chopped lacinato or dinosaur kale

2 tablespoons minced shallot

1/2 cup diced bell pepper

1 cup halved grape tomatoes

1/2 cup quartered and sliced radishes

1/2 cup fresh or frozen (thawed) corn kernels

1/2 cup cooked or BPA-free canned black beans (if canned, rinsed and drained)

1/4 cup unsalted pumpkin seeds

6 tablespoons Creamy Avocado Dressing (page 88)

1. Place kale in a large bowl. In a smaller bowl, toss together shallot, pepper, tomatoes, radishes, corn, and black beans.

2. Toss kale with 1/4 cup Creamy Avocado Dressing, and toss vegetable mixture with another 2 tablespoons dressing. Reserve remaining dressing for another meal.

3. Arrange 2 cups kale on each of 4 plates. Top each serving with 3/4 cup vegetable mixture and 1 tablespoon sunflower seeds.

EXCHANGES/CHOICES	1 1/2 Starch
	2 Nonstarchy Vegetable
	1 Lean Protein
	1 1/2 Fat
CALORIES	180
CALORIES FROM FAT	90
TOTAL FAT	10.0 g
SATURATED FAT	1.5 g
TRANS FAT	0.0 g
CHOLESTEROL	0 mg
SODIUM	130 mg
POTASSIUM	610 mg
TOTAL CARBOHYDRATE	18 g
DIETARY FIBER	6 g
SUGARS	4 g
PROTEIN	7 g
PHOSPHORUS	195 mg

Sunshine Salad

SERVES: 6 | SERVING SIZE: 1 CUP | PREP TIME: 10 MINUTES | COOKING TIME: 5 MINUTES

As the title suggests, this salad is like sunshine in a bowl. A bunch of beautiful, yellow-hued veggies are tossed with an herbaceous dressing in this recipe. So dish some happiness and flavor onto your plate!

1 cup fresh corn kernels

1 1/2 cups halved yellow grape tomatoes

1 cup seeded and sliced yellow bell pepper

1 1/2 cups thinly sliced yellow squash

1 cup trimmed and halved yellow wax beans, blanched (see recipe note)

1/4 cup chopped fresh flat-leaf parsley

1 tablespoon chopped fresh chives

1 tablespoon chopped fresh dill

1 tablespoon champagne vinegar

2 tablespoons extra-virgin olive oil

1 teaspoon freshly grated lemon zest

1/4 teaspoon fine sea salt

1/2 teaspoon freshly ground black pepper

1. In a medium bowl, mix together the corn, tomatoes, bell pepper, squash, and beans. Add the herbs, vinegar, oil, zest, salt, and pepper. Toss to combine.

tip: To blanch the beans, cook them in simmering water for 3–5 minutes, then shock them in ice water to cool them and stop the cooking process.

EXCHANGES/CHOICES	1/2 Starch
	1 Nonstarchy Vegetable
	1/2 Fat
CALORIES	90
CALORIES FROM FAT	45
TOTAL FAT	5.0 g
SATURATED FAT	0.7 g
TRANS FAT	0.0 g
CHOLESTEROL	0 mg
SODIUM	95 mg
POTASSIUM	300 mg
TOTAL CARBOHYDRATE	10 g
DIETARY FIBER	2 g
SUGARS	3 g
PROTEIN	2 g
PHOSPHORUS	45 mg

Heirloom Tomato Salad with Fresh Oregano

SERVES: 6 | SERVING SIZE: ABOUT 2/3 CUP | PREP TIME: 10 MINUTES | COOKING TIME: NONE

This recipe speaks to my motto: quality ingredients are the key to good food. A ripe, in-season tomato needs nothing more than some olive oil, sea salt, citrus, and fresh oregano to make your taste buds feel alive.

4 cups assorted cored and halved vine-ripened heirloom tomatoes (cut halves into thick wedges if using large tomatoes)

1 teaspoon freshly grated lemon zest

2 tablespoons extra-virgin olive oil

2 tablespoons torn fresh oregano leaves

2 tablespoons torn fresh basil

2 tablespoons white balsamic vinegar

1/4 teaspoon fine sea salt

1/4 teaspoon freshly ground black pepper

1. In a large bowl, gently toss all of the ingredients together. Serve at room temperature.

tip: If tomatoes are out of season, opt for grape or cherry tomatoes instead as they tend to be flavorful all year round!

EXCHANGES/CHOICES	1 Nonstarchy Vegetable
	1 Fat
CALORIES	70
CALORIES FROM FAT	45
TOTAL FAT	5.0 g
SATURATED FAT	0.7 g
TRANS FAT	0.0 g
CHOLESTEROL	0 mg
SODIUM	100 mg
POTASSIUM	300 mg
TOTAL CARBOHYDRATE	6 g
DIETARY FIBER	2 g
SUGARS	4 g
PROTEIN	1 g
PHOSPHORUS	30 mg

Kale and Brussels Sprout Salad
with Cashews, Pears, and Pomegranate

SERVES: 4 | SERVING SIZE: ABOUT 2 CUPS | PREP TIME: 10 MINUTES | COOKING TIME: NONE

Put Brussels sprouts into the food processor and give them a whirl! The shredded sprouts add both crunch and a bit of spice to this recipe. With kale, crunchy cashews, and the sweetness of in-season pears and pomegranate seeds, this salad is perfect as a side dish, but is special enough for a holiday feast.

5 cups packed chopped curly kale

1 cup shredded Brussels sprouts

1/4 cup Everyday Vinaigrette
  (page 62)

1 cup diced pear

1/4 cup chopped raw, unsalted
  cashews

1/2 cup fresh pomegranate seeds

1. In a large bowl, toss the kale and Brussels sprouts with the vinaigrette. Divide mixture evenly among 4 plates (1 1/2 cups each).

2. Garnish each plate with 1/4 cup diced pear, 1 tablespoon cashews, and 2 tablespoons pomegranate seeds.

tip: I change this recipe with the seasons! If apples and pears are in season, I use them. When berries are in season, they are delicious as well!

EXCHANGES/CHOICES	1/2 Fruit 1 Nonstarchy Vegetable 2 Fat
CALORIES	170
CALORIES FROM FAT	100
TOTAL FAT	11.0 g
SATURATED FAT	1.8 g
TRANS FAT	0.0 g
CHOLESTEROL	0 mg
SODIUM	200 mg
POTASSIUM	340 mg
TOTAL CARBOHYDRATE	16 g
DIETARY FIBER	4 g
SUGARS	8 g
PROTEIN	4 g
PHOSPHORUS	90 mg

Spaghetti Squash with Walnut Arugula Pesto p. 148

vegetable sides and mains

A colorful plate is a healthy plate! This isn't just a ploy moms use to coax more veggies onto their kids' plates. In fact, each different vegetable pigment provides different health benefits, so by eating the rainbow, you can likely fulfill many of your daily nutritional needs—especially your need for micronutrients. Many vegetables may reduce inflammation, improve heart health, aid in circulation and healthy blood pressure, and could potentially reduce the risk of certain cancers. And of course it helps that vegetables include such a wide range of flavors and textures and can be prepared using just about any method imaginable. Let's be honest, we can all stand to eat more vegetables, and the recipes in this chapter will help!

Don't bother looking for ho-hum boiled Brussels sprouts or steamed cauliflower on the pages that follow. Instead, you'll find vegetarian sides and main dishes that explode with flavor and nutrients, like Sautéed Brussels Sprouts with Apples, Shallot, and Whole-Grain Mustard (page 140), Harissa-Roasted Root Vegetables with Cilantro Yogurt Sauce (page 141), and Sautéed Greens with Dried Cherries and Almonds (page 138).

Roasted Baby Artichokes
with Roasted Red Pepper Sauce

SERVES: 4 | SERVING SIZE: 6 ARTICHOKE HALVES AND 2 TABLESPOONS SAUCE | PREP TIME: 15 MINUTES | COOKING TIME: 15 MINUTES

One of my all-time favorite childhood meals was braised, stuffed artichokes. My mom used to stuff whole artichokes with a cheese and breadcrumb mixture and braise them in tomato sauce. It was pure and simple comfort food. This recipe is a quick, easy spin on that traditional dish. The red pepper sauce and cumin are a sophisticated twist on tomato sauce, and crispy, earthy baby artichokes cook up in a snap.

4 cups water

1/4 cup freshly squeezed lemon juice

12 baby artichokes

2 tablespoons extra-virgin olive oil

1 tablespoon freshly grated lemon zest

1/4 teaspoon fine sea salt

1/4 teaspoon freshly ground black pepper

1/2 cup Roasted Red Pepper Sauce (page 82)

1/4 teaspoon ground cumin

1. Preheat the oven to 425°F.

2. Combine the water and lemon juice in a large bowl. Cut 1/2 inch off the top of each artichoke. Cut off the stem of each artichoke to within 1 inch of the base; peel the stem and set it aside. Remove bottom leaves and tough outer leaves from each artichoke, leaving only the tender heart and bottom. Cut each artichoke in half lengthwise. Place the artichokes in the lemon water mixture.

3. Drain artichokes after 15 minutes and pat dry with paper towels. In a large bowl, whisk together the olive oil and lemon zest. Add artichokes, salt, and pepper and toss well to coat.

4. Arrange artichokes in a single layer on a rimmed baking sheet. Roast for 10 minutes, flip, and then roast for another 5 minutes, or until tender.

5. In a small bowl, whisk together the red pepper sauce and cumin. Serve sauce with the roasted artichokes for dipping.

EXCHANGES/CHOICES	3 Nonstarchy Vegetable
	1 1/2 Fat
CALORIES	150
CALORIES FROM FAT	80
TOTAL FAT	9.0 g
SATURATED FAT	1.5 g
TRANS FAT	0.0 g
CHOLESTEROL	0 mg
SODIUM	250 mg
POTASSIUM	335 mg
TOTAL CARBOHYDRATE	14 g
DIETARY FIBER	8 g
SUGARS	3 g
PROTEIN	5 g
PHOSPHORUS	100 mg

7 ways to save money at your local farmers' market

When you shop at your local farmers' market, not only do you get the freshest, most flavorful ingredients, but you also help support local agriculture and the environment. Sounds great, right? It's fantastic! But the farmers' market can also be overwhelming and, sometimes, expensive—especially during peak harvest times, when the farm stand tables overflow with bright produce and other exciting food items. Here are seven simple tips to help you navigate the local farmers' market like a pro and head home with plenty of goods in your basket . . . and money in your wallet.

1. **Take your time.** A little exploration goes a long way! It can be tempting to buy from the first farm stand you see, but by walking the entire market and visiting stands in different neighborhoods or on different days, you can compare prices, availability, and more. Don't be shy about chatting up the farmers; building a meaningful relationship with the people who grow your food can go a long way when it comes to saving some money.

2. **Be flexible.** Instead of showing up with a definitive shopping list, let the offerings of the day guide your choices. Prices on produce will vary depending on availability. Plentiful items will often cost less. Allowing the specials of the day to be your shopping guide may help you find kitchen inspiration. It can be fun to challenge yourself to create meals using your less expensive finds.

3. **Buy in bulk.** Berries, apples, tomatoes, and other staple goods are usually available in bulk, which can equate to monetary savings. Ask the farmer if they will cut you a deal if you order bulk goods ahead of time. Bulk buying options may not be advertised at the stand so make sure you inquire. Don't be overwhelmed by the task of utilizing a whole case of cucumbers, tomatoes, etc. Pickling, jarring, and freezing are all great ways to preserve your bulk summer bounty for enjoyment later in the year.

4. **Score on "seconds."** Don't overlook the ugly duckling. Less-than-perfect pieces of produce often taste just as good as their beautiful relatives. Misshapen fruits and veggies are harder to sell, so they often cost a lot less. Try to score a few freebies—buy some produce from a stand and ask it you can have the bruised peach for free. Scuffed-up tomatoes will taste wonderful in a sauce even if you don't want to use them in your salad.

5. **Consider the conventional.** There is a hefty price tag associated with the certified organic label that translates into the cost of the produce. Smaller, local farmers may not be able to afford to be certified organic, but they often use organic growing methods anyway. The result is "conventional" produce that is grown organically but costs much less. Again, get to know your local farmers as they can fill you in on their farm's growing practices.

6. **Keep it simple.** Sure, those heirloom tomatoes and beans are tempting, but they can be expensive. If you're trying to keep your costs low, stick with the basics—a local red tomato or green bean will cost much less than heirloom varieties. Also, avoid "trendy" foods like certain types of peppers or purslane, for example, as their price tags may mirror their popularity.

7. **Show up late.** The last thing a farmer wants is to pack up and head home with unsold goods. If you shop towards closing time, farmers are more willing to offer discounts and throw in freebies. This is also a good time to shop for seconds as the "perfect" produce will have already been picked through. As the market winds down and the crowd subsides there is more time to chat with farmers, which, as you hopefully have learned, is your most valuable tool.

Grilled Asparagus with Orange Zest and Chive

SERVES: 6 | SERVING SIZE: 3–4 ASPARAGUS SPEARS | PREP TIME: 5 MINUTES | COOKING TIME: 10 MINUTES

Asparagus has always held a special place in my heart. In season for only a few weeks each year, this spring vegetable takes 4 years of nurturing to reap one harvest. The asparagus shines in this recipe because the flavors of citrus and chive simply accent its natural goodness.

1 pound asparagus

2 tablespoons extra-virgin olive oil

1 tablespoon freshly grated orange zest

1/4 teaspoon fine sea salt

1/4 teaspoon freshly ground black pepper

1 tablespoon chopped fresh chives

2 tablespoons roasted walnut pieces

1. Preheat an outdoor grill or grill pan to medium-high heat.

2. Trim the asparagus by snapping off the tough, lower 1/3 of the stalk.

3. In a small bowl whisk together the olive oil and orange zest. Add salt and pepper. Toss asparagus with 1 tablespoon of the olive oil mixture.

4. Grill asparagus for 1–2 minutes per side or until crisp-tender. Remove from heat and toss with the remaining 1 tablespoon olive oil mixture and chives. Garnish with walnut pieces.

EXCHANGES/CHOICES	1 1/2 Fat
CALORIES	70
CALORIES FROM FAT	50
TOTAL FAT	6.0 g
SATURATED FAT	0.8 g
TRANS FAT	0.0 g
CHOLESTEROL	0 mg
SODIUM	95 mg
POTASSIUM	100 mg
TOTAL CARBOHYDRATE	2 g
DIETARY FIBER	1 g
SUGARS	1 g
PROTEIN	1 g
PHOSPHORUS	30 mg

Roasted Green Beans with Smoked Paprika

SERVES: 4 | SERVING SIZE: 1 CUP GREEN BEANS | PREP TIME: 5 MINUTES | COOKING TIME: 11–13 MINUTES

If steaming is the only method you know for cooking green beans, then I'm pretty sure this recipe will change your life forever. Coated with orange zest, paprika, and cumin, and then roasted until caramelized and tender, these green beans are an easy, delicious side for just about any meal.

1 pound green beans, trimmed

1 tablespoon extra-virgin olive oil

1 teaspoon freshly grated orange zest

1 tablespoon white wine vinegar

1/2 teaspoon smoked paprika

1/2 teaspoon ground cumin

1/4 teaspoon fine sea salt

1/4 teaspoon freshly ground black pepper

1 tablespoon freshly squeezed orange juice

1. Preheat the oven to 450°F.

2. In a medium bowl, toss the green beans with olive oil, orange zest, vinegar, paprika, cumin, salt, and pepper.

3. Arrange beans in a single layer on a rimmed baking sheet. Roast for 8 minutes, stir, and continue roasting for another 3–5 minutes until browned and tender. Remove beans from the oven, toss with fresh orange juice, and serve hot.

EXCHANGES/CHOICES	2 Nonstarchy Vegetable 1/2 Fat
CALORIES	70
CALORIES FROM FAT	30
TOTAL FAT	3.5 g
SATURATED FAT	0.5 g
TRANS FAT	0.0 g
CHOLESTEROL	0 mg
SODIUM	140 mg
POTASSIUM	160 mg
TOTAL CARBOHYDRATE	8 g
DIETARY FIBER	3 g
SUGARS	2 g
PROTEIN	2 g
PHOSPHORUS	30 mg

Sautéed Greens with Dried Cherries and Almonds

SERVES: 4 | SERVING SIZE: 3/4 CUP | PREP TIME: 5 MINUTES | COOKING TIME: 5 MINUTES

Use this recipe as an excuse to experiment with the different greens you find at the farmers' market. Try mixing chard with mustard greens, or kale with collards, noting the distinct flavors and textures that each one adds to the dish. The sweetness of the dried cherries helps to balance out the bitterness of the greens.

1 tablespoon extra-virgin olive oil

2 cloves garlic, chopped

2 pounds dark leafy greens (mustard greens, kale, Swiss chard), thick stems removed and greens cut crosswise into 1/2-inch-wide strips

2 tablespoons water

1 tablespoon white balsamic vinegar

1/2 cup unsweetened dried cherries

1/4 teaspoon fine sea salt

1/4 teaspoon freshly ground black pepper

1/4 cup sliced raw, unsalted almonds

1. Heat the oil in large nonstick skillet over medium heat. Add the garlic and sauté for 1 minute, then add the greens, water, and vinegar. Cook until greens are wilted and tender, 2–3 minutes. Add the cherries and stir to heat through.

2. Remove skillet from heat, season greens with salt and pepper, and serve garnished with sliced almonds.

EXCHANGES/CHOICES	1 Fruit
	1 Nonstarchy Vegetable
	1 1/2 Fat
CALORIES	160
CALORIES FROM FAT	60
TOTAL FAT	7.0 g
SATURATED FAT	0.8 g
TRANS FAT	0.0 g
CHOLESTEROL	0 mg
SODIUM	240 mg
POTASSIUM	630 mg
TOTAL CARBOHYDRATE	22 g
DIETARY FIBER	5 g
SUGARS	9 g
PROTEIN	6 g
PHOSPHORUS	100 mg

Roasted Broccoli with Walnut Arugula Pesto

SERVES: 4 | SERVING SIZE: 1 CUP | PREP TIME: 10 MINUTES | COOKING TIME: 10–15 MINUTES

This may be my all-time favorite broccoli recipe! When roasted, broccoli stems hold onto their crunch while the florets gently char and soften. Add to that fresh pesto that literally melts into every nook and cranny, and you will fall in love.

5 cups broccoli, large stems discarded, cut into 4-inch-long florets

1 tablespoon extra-virgin olive oil

1/4 teaspoon fine sea salt

1/4 teaspoon freshly ground black pepper

2 tablespoons Walnut Arugula Pesto (page 81)

Lemon wedges (for garnish)

1. Preheat the oven to 450°F.

2. On a rimmed baking sheet, toss the broccoli florets with olive oil, salt, and pepper. Spread broccoli out in a single layer and roast for 10–15 minutes, or until tender and slightly browned.

3. Transfer cooked broccoli to a large bowl, add pesto, and toss well to coat. Serve broccoli with lemon wedges (to be squeezed on top).

EXCHANGES/CHOICES	2 Nonstarchy Vegetable
	1 1/2 Fat
CALORIES	110
CALORIES FROM FAT	70
TOTAL FAT	8.0 g
SATURATED FAT	1.1 g
TRANS FAT	0.0 g
CHOLESTEROL	0 mg
SODIUM	200 mg
POTASSIUM	385 mg
TOTAL CARBOHYDRATE	8 g
DIETARY FIBER	3 g
SUGARS	2 g
PROTEIN	4 g
PHOSPHORUS	85 mg

Sautéed Brussels Sprouts
with Apples, Shallot, and Whole-Grain Mustard

SERVES: 6 | SERVING SIZE: 1 CUP | PREP TIME: 10 MINUTES | COOKING TIME: 15 MINUTES

What grows together goes together. That was my motto when I first developed this recipe. This dish combines two of my favorite fall ingredients: Brussels sprouts and apples. Both ingredients shine when paired with more savory ingredients like mustard.

1 pound fresh Brussels sprouts, trimmed and halved

1 shallot, thinly sliced

1 ounce reduced-fat, nitrate-free bacon, chopped

2 tablespoons extra-virgin olive oil

2 tablespoons whole-grain mustard

1 tablespoon Dijon mustard

2 tablespoons apple cider vinegar

1 red apple, cored and diced

1/8 teaspoon fine sea salt

1/2 teaspoon freshly ground black pepper

1. Preheat the oven to 450°F.

2. In baking dish, toss all ingredients together.

3. Bake the Brussels sprouts mixture, uncovered, for 10–15 minutes or until tender, stirring after 10 minutes to prevent burning.

4. Remove dish from the oven and serve hot.

EXCHANGES/CHOICES	1/2 Carbohydrate
	1 Nonstarchy Vegetable
	1 Fat
CALORIES	110
CALORIES FROM FAT	60
TOTAL FAT	7.0 g
SATURATED FAT	1.1 g
TRANS FAT	0.0 g
CHOLESTEROL	0 mg
SODIUM	230 mg
POTASSIUM	305 mg
TOTAL CARBOHYDRATE	11 g
DIETARY FIBER	3 g
SUGARS	5 g
PROTEIN	3 g
PHOSPHORUS	60 mg

Harissa-Roasted Root Vegetables with Cilantro Yogurt Sauce

SERVES: 10 | SERVING SIZE: 1/2 CUP VEGETABLES AND 2 TABLESPOONS SAUCE | PREP TIME: 15 MINUTES | COOKING TIME: 1 HOUR

In North Africa, harissa is the condiment of choice for livening up cooked meats and vegetables. Here, I use the spicy, garlicky chile paste to deepen the flavor of roasted root vegetables. Try serving this dish with chickpeas and whole-wheat couscous for a complete North African–style meal. Not up for making harissa yourself? You can purchase it in many stores and use it as a sandwich spread or marinade seasoning as well.

ROASTED VEGETABLES:

1 cup peeled and sliced carrots (cut into 1-inch-thick pieces)

1 cup peeled and sliced parsnips (cut into 1-inch-thick pieces)

1 cup diced sweet potato (1-inch dice)

1 cup peeled and diced turnip (1-inch dice)

1 cup peeled and diced rutabaga (1-inch dice)

3 tablespoons extra-virgin olive oil

1/4 teaspoon fine sea salt

2 tablespoons Harissa Paste (page 80)

1 tablespoon honey

CILANTRO YOGURT SAUCE:

1 1/4 cups fat-free, plain strained yogurt (Greek or skyr)

1/2 cup chopped fresh cilantro

1/4 teaspoon ground cumin

1/2 teaspoon freshly grated lime zest

1 tablespoon freshly squeezed lime juice

1. Preheat the oven to 425°F.

2. In a large bowl, toss all the root vegetables with olive oil, salt, harissa, and honey. Arrange vegetables in a single layer on 2 rimmed baking sheets and roast for 30–40 minutes, stirring after 15 minutes, until the vegetables are tender. Remove baking sheets from the oven.

3. In a blender or food processor, combine all the Cilantro Yogurt Sauce ingredients. Blend until smooth.

4. Serve roasted vegetables warm with 2 tablespoons of sauce per serving.

EXCHANGES/CHOICES	1/2 Starch
	1 Nonstarchy Vegetable
	1 Fat

CALORIES	100
CALORIES FROM FAT	40
TOTAL FAT	4.5 g
SATURATED FAT	0.6 g
TRANS FAT	0.0 g
CHOLESTEROL	0 mg
SODIUM	115 mg
POTASSIUM	280 mg
TOTAL CARBOHYDRATE	12 g
DIETARY FIBER	2 g
SUGARS	7 g
PROTEIN	4 g
PHOSPHORUS	75 mg

Curry-Roasted Cauliflower

SERVES: 4 | SERVING SIZE: 1 CUP | PREP TIME: 10 MINUTES | COOKING TIME: 20 MINUTES

If your reason for not eating more cauliflower has anything to do with its mild taste, then you're officially out of excuses. In this recipe, the naturally sweet flavor of this nutritious veggie is coaxed out through roasting and complemented with fragrant, warming spices.

1 clove garlic, chopped or grated

1 large shallot, halved and thinly sliced

1/2 cup no-sugar-added raisins

2 tablespoons extra-virgin olive oil

1 teaspoon freshly grated lime zest

1 tablespoon freshly squeezed lime juice

2 teaspoons curry powder

1 teaspoon grated fresh ginger

1/2 teaspoon mustard powder

1 teaspoon ground cumin

Pinch red pepper flakes (optional)

1/4 teaspoon fine sea salt

1/4 teaspoon freshly ground black pepper

1 large (30-ounce) head cauliflower, cut into florets

1/4 cup chopped fresh cilantro

Lime wedges (for garnish)

1. Preheat the oven to 450°F. Line a rimmed baking sheet with aluminum foil.

2. In a large bowl, combine the garlic, shallot, raisins, olive oil, lime zest, lime juice, curry powder, ginger, mustard powder, cumin, red pepper flakes (if using), salt, and pepper. Add cauliflower florets to the bowl; toss well to combine.

3. Spread cauliflower in a single layer on the prepared baking sheet. Roast for 20 minutes, stirring occasionally, until cauliflower is slightly browned and tender.

4. Garnish the cauliflower with the fresh cilantro and serve with lime wedges to squeeze on top.

EXCHANGES/CHOICES	1 Fruit
	2 Nonstarchy Vegetable
	1 1/2 Fat
CALORIES	160
CALORIES FROM FAT	70
TOTAL FAT	8.0 g
SATURATED FAT	1.1 g
TRANS FAT	0.0 g
CHOLESTEROL	0 mg
SODIUM	180 mg
POTASSIUM	600 mg
TOTAL CARBOHYDRATE	24 g
DIETARY FIBER	4 g
SUGARS	14 g
PROTEIN	4 g
PHOSPHORUS	90 mg

Smashed Potatoes with Everyday Herb Oil

SERVES: 8 | SERVING SIZE: 1/2 CUP | PREP TIME: 5 MINUTES | COOKING TIME: 30 MINUTES

Potatoes may be my favorite vegetable; they are always satisfying and comforting. This recipe marries my love for traditional roasted potatoes and delicious boiled potatoes. Crispy and bursting with herbaceous flavor, this may be the best potato you have ever tasted.

6 cups (1 1/2 pounds) fingerling potatoes

1 tablespoon extra-virgin olive oil

1 tablespoon Everyday Herb Oil (page 60)

1/4 teaspoon fine sea salt

1/4 teaspoon freshly ground black pepper

1. Place the potatoes in a medium saucepan over high heat and pour in enough cold water to cover them by 1 inch. Bring water to a boil, then reduce the heat to low, and simmer potatoes until they are barely fork tender, about 15 minutes. Drain potatoes.

2. Line a large baking sheet with parchment paper and arrange potatoes on the sheet in a single layer. Using a smaller baking dish, gently press down on the potatoes, smashing them to a 1/2-inch thickness. Set potatoes aside to cool completely.

3. Preheat your broiler on the high setting.

4. Season the cooled potatoes with the olive oil, herb oil, salt, and pepper, and toss well to combine. Spread potatoes out in a single layer and broil for 6–8 minutes, turning once halfway through cooking time, until they are brown on both sides.

EXCHANGES/CHOICES	1 Starch
	1/2 Fat
CALORIES	100
CALORIES FROM FAT	30
TOTAL FAT	3.5 g
SATURATED FAT	0.5 g
TRANS FAT	0.0 g
CHOLESTEROL	0 mg
SODIUM	70 mg
POTASSIUM	315 mg
TOTAL CARBOHYDRATE	16 g
DIETARY FIBER	2 g
SUGARS	1 g
PROTEIN	2 g
PHOSPHORUS	35 mg

Everyday Mashed Sweet Potatoes

SERVES: 4 | SERVING SIZE: 1/2 CUP | PREP TIME: 5 MINUTES | COOKING TIME: 30–40 MINUTES

Mashed sweet potatoes are an everyday (or every week) dish in my house. I try to maximize my oven space whenever I turn it on, so I usually cook a whole sweet potato or two while something else is cooking. I am always amazed at how sweet and flavorful the sweet potatoes become. They need nothing more than a good mash and some salt and pepper. Yum!

1 (10-ounce) sweet potato
1/8 teaspoon fine sea salt
1/8 teaspoon freshly ground black
    pepper

1. Preheat the oven to 450°F.
2. Poke holes in the sweet potato. Place on a baking sheet and roast in the oven for 30–40 minutes. Remove potato from oven. When cool enough to handle, peel and mash. Season with salt and pepper.

tip: Make extra of this recipe and freeze some. Use this mash in the Sweet Potato Oats recipe on page 96.

EXCHANGES/CHOICES	1 Starch
CALORIES	45
CALORIES FROM FAT	0
TOTAL FAT	0.0 g
SATURATED FAT	0.0 g
TRANS FAT	0.0 g
CHOLESTEROL	0 mg
SODIUM	90 mg
POTASSIUM	245 mg
TOTAL CARBOHYDRATE	11 g
DIETARY FIBER	2 g
SUGARS	3 g
PROTEIN	1 g
PHOSPHORUS	30 mg

Potato-Kale Cakes with Roasted Red Pepper Sauce

SERVES: 8 | SERVING SIZE: 1 CAKE AND 2 TABLESPOONS SAUCE | PREP TIME: 10 MINUTES | COOKING TIME: 45 MINUTES

If you love mashed potatoes as much as I do, then these potato cakes are everything you could want in a comfort food. They're crispy on the outside, creamy and rich on the inside, and paired with a yummy sauce to boot.

- 1 1/2 pounds unpeeled russet potatoes, scrubbed and cut into 1-inch cubes
- 2 tablespoons extra-virgin olive oil, divided
- 2 shallots, thinly sliced
- 2 tablespoons water
- 3 cups chopped kale
- 1/4 cup low-fat milk
- 2 tablespoons light sour cream
- 1 egg, lightly beaten
- 1/4 teaspoon fine sea salt
- 1/4 teaspoon freshly ground black pepper
- 2 tablespoons chopped fresh chives
- Nonstick cooking spray
- 1 cup Roasted Red Pepper Sauce (page 82)

1. Bring a large pot of salted water to a boil over high heat. Add the potatoes and boil for 25 minutes, or until they are fork tender. Remove pot from the heat and drain the potatoes, then return them to the same pot and set aside.

2. While potatoes are cooking, Heat 1 tablespoon olive oil in a medium sauté pan over medium heat. Add the shallots and sauté until soft, 3–4 minutes. Add the water and kale. Cook, stirring constantly, for 1–2 minutes, or until kale has wilted and water has evaporated. Remove pan from the heat and set aside.

3. In a medium bowl, whisk together the milk, sour cream, and egg. Add milk mixture to the potatoes and mash them until smooth with a potato masher. Season with the salt and pepper, and fold in the chives and kale mixture. Let potato-kale mixture cool to room temperature.

4. Preheat the broiler on the high setting. Coat a rimmed baking sheet lightly with nonstick cooking spray.

5. Shape 1/4-cup portions of the potato-kale mixture into cakes and place them on the prepared baking sheet. Spray the top of each cake with nonstick cooking spray and broil cakes for 6–8 minutes, or until browned.

6. Remove cakes from the oven and serve immediately, with the red pepper sauce on the side for dipping (2 tablespoons per serving).

EXCHANGES/CHOICES	1 Starch
	1 Nonstarchy Vegetable
	1 Fat
CALORIES	160
CALORIES FROM FAT	50
TOTAL FAT	6.0 g
SATURATED FAT	1.4 g
TRANS FAT	0.0 g
CHOLESTEROL	25 mg
SODIUM	150 mg
POTASSIUM	470 mg
TOTAL CARBOHYDRATE	21 g
DIETARY FIBER	2 g
SUGARS	3 g
PROTEIN	6 g
PHOSPHORUS	105 mg

Grilled Zucchini with Mint

SERVES: 4 | SERVING SIZE: 1/2 ZUCCHINI | PREP TIME: 5 MINUTES | COOKING TIME: 10 MINUTES

Summer would not be complete without grilling up some zucchini. Though this vegetable's fresh flavors can stand alone, a touch of mint really takes this recipe to the next level without making it complicated.

2 medium zucchini, trimmed and quartered

2 tablespoons extra-virgin olive oil, divided

1 teaspoon freshly grated lemon zest

1 tablespoon sliced fresh mint

1/4 teaspoon fine sea salt

1/4 teaspoon freshly ground black pepper

1. Preheat an outdoor grill or grill pan to medium-high.

2. In a large bowl, toss the zucchini with 1 tablespoon olive oil. Grill zucchini for 3–4 minutes per side, or until tender.

3. Return grilled zucchini to the large bowl and toss with the remaining 1 tablespoon olive oil, the lemon zest, mint, salt, and pepper. Serve immediately.

EXCHANGES/CHOICES	1 Nonstarchy Vegetable
	1 Fat
CALORIES	80
CALORIES FROM FAT	60
TOTAL FAT	7.0 g
SATURATED FAT	1.0 g
TRANS FAT	0.0 g
CHOLESTEROL	0 mg
SODIUM	150 mg
POTASSIUM	265 mg
TOTAL CARBOHYDRATE	4 g
DIETARY FIBER	1 g
SUGARS	2 g
PROTEIN	1 g
PHOSPHORUS	40 mg

Roasted Delicata Squash
with Maple-Chipotle Vinaigrette

SERVES: 4 | SERVING SIZE: 1/2 CUP | PREP TIME: 10 MINUTES | COOKING TIME: 20 MINUTES

My favorite of the winter squash varieties for its simplicity, the no-peel delicata squash is a breeze to cook up any night of the week. This mildly sweet squash is complemented by the sweet, smoky flavor of the vinaigrette in a way that encapsulates everything I love about fall.

1 tablespoon Everyday Herb Oil (page 60)

1 tablespoon pure maple syrup (preferably grade B)

2 teaspoons adobo sauce

1 tablespoon apple cider vinegar

1 (1–2 pound) delicata squash, halved, seeded, and sliced into 1/2-inch thick slices

1/4 teaspoon fine sea salt

1/4 teaspoon freshly ground black pepper

2 tablespoons raw, unsalted pumpkin seeds

1 tablespoon chopped fresh cilantro

1. Preheat the oven to 400°F.

2. In a large bowl, whisk together the herb oil, maple syrup, adobo sauce, and vinegar. Add squash to the bowl, along with salt and pepper; toss well to coat.

3. Arrange squash in a single layer on a rimmed baking sheet. Roast for 10 minutes, then flip squash, and roast for another 10 minutes, or until tender.

4. Remove squash from the oven, sprinkle with the pumpkin seeds and cilantro, and serve immediately.

tip: Can't find delicata squash? Try this recipe with butternut squash or sweet potatoes instead.

EXCHANGES/CHOICES	1 Starch
	1 1/2 Fat
CALORIES	140
CALORIES FROM FAT	60
TOTAL FAT	7.0 g
SATURATED FAT	1.1 g
TRANS FAT	0.0 g
CHOLESTEROL	0 mg
SODIUM	160 mg
POTASSIUM	425 mg
TOTAL CARBOHYDRATE	19 g
DIETARY FIBER	5 g
SUGARS	8 g
PROTEIN	3 g
PHOSPHORUS	80 mg

Spaghetti Squash with Walnut Arugula Pesto

SERVES: 6 | SERVING SIZE: 1 CUP | PREP TIME: 5 MINUTES | COOKING TIME: 30–40 MINUTES

No, it doesn't taste just like pasta, but spaghetti squash is fun and easily as delicious as pasta. With an earthy-sweet flavor, this squash can be made into whimsical, pasta-like strings when cooked, and you can flavor it just as you would pasta. In this recipe, I use pesto and tomatoes to round out the meal.

1 (3-pound) spaghetti squash, halved lengthwise and seeds removed

1/2 cup Walnut Arugula Pesto (page 81)

2 tablespoons water

1/4 teaspoon freshly ground black pepper

1 tablespoon freshly grated lemon zest

2 tablespoons freshly squeezed lemon juice

1/3 cup torn fresh basil

3 cups diced fresh tomato

1. Preheat the oven to 375°F. Line a rimmed baking sheet with parchment paper.

2. Place the squash cut-side down on the prepared baking sheet. Roast for 30–40 minutes, or until tender.

3. Remove squash from the oven, let it cool slightly, and then use a fork to scrape the spaghetti-like strands of squash flesh into a medium bowl.

4. Add the pesto, water, pepper, lemon zest, and lemon juice to the bowl and toss well to combine. Garnish with basil and tomatoes before serving.

EXCHANGES/CHOICES	3 Nonstarchy Vegetable
	2 Fat
CALORIES	160
CALORIES FROM FAT	110
TOTAL FAT	12.0 g
SATURATED FAT	1.8 g
TRANS FAT	0.0 g
CHOLESTEROL	0 mg
SODIUM	100 mg
POTASSIUM	465 mg
TOTAL CARBOHYDRATE	13 g
DIETARY FIBER	4 g
SUGARS	6 g
PROTEIN	3 g
PHOSPHORUS	70 mg

Rutabaga and Turnip Fries
with Peach and Mango Chipotle Ketchup

SERVES: 8 | SERVING SIZE: 1/2 CUP FRIES AND 2 TABLESPOONS OF KETCHUP | PREP TIME: 10 MINUTES | COOKING TIME: 45 MINUTES

Root vegetables, such as rutabaga and turnips, are often underappreciated, which is a shame. These inexpensive, versatile ingredients are both flavorful and nutrient dense. The natural sweetness of root vegetables is accentuated by roasting, which is why this recipe is so delicious. Once you've tried turnips and rutabagas crisped up and swimming in homemade ketchup—well, you won't miss french fries at all!

2 cups peeled and sliced rutabagas (cut into 2-inch french fry–like spears)

2 cups peeled and sliced turnips (cut into 2-inch spears)

1 tablespoon extra-virgin olive oil

1 teaspoon Everyday Herb Oil (page 60)

1/8 teaspoon fine sea salt

1/4 teaspoon freshly ground black pepper

1 cup Peach and Mango Chipotle Ketchup (page 79)

1. Preheat the oven to 450°F. Line a rimmed baking sheet with a baking rack.

2. In a large bowl, toss the rutabaga and turnip pieces with olive oil, herb oil, salt, and pepper until evenly coated.

3. Arrange fries in a single layer on the baking rack, leaving space between each piece so that they can crisp up in the oven. Roast the vegetables for 30–45 minutes, turning once during cooking time, or until they are browned and tender.

4. Remove fries from the oven and serve with the ketchup for dipping (2 tablespoons per serving).

EXCHANGES/CHOICES	1/2 Carbohydrate
	1 Nonstarchy Vegetable
	1/2 Fat
CALORIES	80
CALORIES FROM FAT	30
TOTAL FAT	3.5 g
SATURATED FAT	0.5 g
TRANS FAT	0.0 g
CHOLESTEROL	0 mg
SODIUM	240 mg
POTASSIUM	430 mg
TOTAL CARBOHYDRATE	12 g
DIETARY FIBER	3 g
SUGARS	8 g
PROTEIN	2 g
PHOSPHORUS	50 mg

Roasted Cabbage "Steaks" with Everyday Vinaigrette

SERVES: 4 | SERVING SIZE: 1 CABBAGE STEAK | PREP TIME: 5 MINUTES | COOKING TIME: 20 MINUTES

Move over, cauliflower! Cabbage "steaks" take center stage in this simple, nutritious, and super satisfying recipe. I love cabbage. It is inexpensive and I feel like I can make a few recipes out of just one head of this nutrient-dense cruciferous vegetable. It's the vegetable that keeps on giving. Here a tip: cut your "steaks" from the middle of the cabbage head and save the ends to make a slaw or salad.

1 medium head green cabbage, cut
   into 4 (1-inch-thick) round steaks

1/4 cup Everyday Vinaigrette
   (page 62)

1. Preheat the oven to 400°F.

2. Place cabbage steaks in a large baking dish. Gently toss them with the vinaigrette, evenly coating both sides of each steak. Roast for 20 minutes, or until cabbage is tender and the edges are golden.

EXCHANGES/CHOICES	2 Nonstarchy Vegetable
	1 1/2 Fat
CALORIES	100
CALORIES FROM FAT	60
TOTAL FAT	7.0 g
SATURATED FAT	1.0 g
TRANS FAT	0.0 g
CHOLESTEROL	0 mg
SODIUM	75 mg
POTASSIUM	290 mg
TOTAL CARBOHYDRATE	10 g
DIETARY FIBER	4 g
SUGARS	6 g
PROTEIN	2 g
PHOSPHORUS	45 mg

Balsamic Citrus Tempeh with Bitter Greens

SERVES: 4 | SERVING SIZE: 6 SLICES TEMPEH, 3/4 CUP GREENS | PREP TIME: 5 MINUTES | COOKING TIME: 15 MINUTES

Tempeh is a fermented soy product that originated in Indonesia. It has a firmer texture and a more distinctive flavor than tofu. Tempeh has a naturally nutty flavor that works well with bitter greens and the natural sweetness of citrus and balsamic vinegar.

1 teaspoon freshly grated orange zest

1/4 cup freshly squeezed orange juice

1/4 cup white balsamic vinegar

1 teaspoon grated fresh ginger

1 teaspoon tamari or soy sauce

2 (2-ounce) packages tempeh, each cut into 12 slices

1 tablespoon extra-virgin olive oil

2 cloves garlic, grated

6 cups roughly chopped Swiss chard or mustard greens, stems discarded

1/4 teaspoon fine sea salt

1/4 teaspoon freshly ground black pepper

1 tablespoon sesame seeds

1/4 cup sliced scallions (green parts only)

1. In a medium sauté pan, combine the orange zest, orange juice, vinegar, ginger, soy sauce, and tempeh slices. Bring mixture to a simmer over medium heat and cook the tempeh for 3–4 minutes per side, until sauce thickens and tempeh browns.

2. While the tempeh cooks, heat the olive oil in another medium sauté pan over medium heat. Add garlic and sauté for 1 minute. Add greens and sauté until they are tender and wilted, 3–4 minutes. Remove pan from the heat and season greens with salt and pepper.

3. Divide greens among 4 serving dishes and top each portion with 6 slices of tempeh. Garnish with sesame seeds and scallion.

EXCHANGES/CHOICES	1 Carbohydrate
	1 Medium-Fat Protein
CALORIES	140
CALORIES FROM FAT	70
TOTAL FAT	8.0 g
SATURATED FAT	1.3 g
TRANS FAT	0.0 g
CHOLESTEROL	0 mg
SODIUM	260 mg
POTASSIUM	410 mg
TOTAL CARBOHYDRATE	12 g
DIETARY FIBER	1 g
SUGARS	10 g
PROTEIN	7 g
PHOSPHORUS	125 mg

Herb-Roasted Tofu, Arugula, and Olive Tapenade

SERVES: 4 | SERVING SIZE: 2 SLICES TOFU, 1 1/2 CUPS ARUGULA, 1/4 CUP CUCUMBER, 2 TABLESPOONS TOMATOES, AND 1 TABLESPOON TAPENADE | PREP TIME: 1 HOUR | COOKING TIME: 20–25 MINUTES

If you associate tofu solely with Asian flavors, then you're missing out on a whole other world of applications for this versatile protein. This recipe takes tofu to the Greek isles with lemon vinaigrette and olive tapenade.

2 (14-ounce) packages firm tofu, drained and sliced into 8 pieces

1 teaspoon Everyday Herb Oil (page 60)

1 tablespoon white balsamic vinegar

1 teaspoon freshly grated lemon zest

1 teaspoon Dijon mustard

6 cups baby arugula

1/4 cup freshly squeezed lemon juice

2 tablespoons extra-virgin olive oil

1/4 teaspoon fine sea salt

1/4 teaspoon freshly ground black pepper

1 cup halved and sliced English cucumber

1/2 cup Everyday Roasted Tomatoes (page 65)

1/4 cup Olive Tapenade (page 113) or store-bought tapenade

1. Arrange the tofu slices in a single layer on a clean dish towel. Cover with another clean dish towel and a sheet pan or large plate to weigh it down. Let tofu drain for 20–30 minutes at room temperature to extract any excess liquid.

2. Pat the tofu dry and place in a medium bowl.

3. In a small bowl, whisk together the herb oil, vinegar, lemon zest, and mustard. Pour mixture over the tofu and let it marinate for 30 minutes at room temperature. While tofu marinates, preheat the oven to 450°F. Line a rimmed baking sheet with parchment paper.

4. Remove tofu from marinade and arrange it in a single layer on the baking sheet. Bake until tofu is firm and lightly browned, turning halfway through time, for 20–25 minutes.

5. Remove the tofu from the oven and set aside. In a medium bowl, toss the arugula with the lemon juice, olive oil, salt, and pepper.

6. Serve tofu hot over the arugula. Top with cucumbers, roasted tomatoes, and olive tapenade.

EXCHANGES/CHOICES	1/2 Carbohydrate 2 Medium-Fat Protein 2 Fat
CALORIES	280
CALORIES FROM FAT	190
TOTAL FAT	21.0 g
SATURATED FAT	3.4 g
TRANS FAT	0.0 g
CHOLESTEROL	0 mg
SODIUM	410 mg
POTASSIUM	570 mg
TOTAL CARBOHYDRATE	10 g
DIETARY FIBER	3 g
SUGARS	5 g
PROTEIN	18 g
PHOSPHORUS	275 mg

Curried Quinoa with Butternut Squash and Chickpeas p. 158
Citrus Farro Salad with Roasted Beets and Poppy Seeds p. 163

grains and beans

I don't know about you, but I often find myself in a dinnertime rut, alternating among starches such as potatoes, pasta, and rice to round out my weeknight meals. Now I keep a store of different options packed in airtight containers in my pantry, and I have one or two varieties of cooked grains in my fridge or freezer at all times. That way I'm always prepared to throw together a quick dish, I never get bored at mealtime, and I reap the nutritional benefits of whole grains and beans just about every day. Grains and beans couldn't be easier to prepare—just simmer them in water or broth—and they add a heck of lot more flavor to meals than bland white rice or potatoes.

As far as health benefits go, when it comes to carbohydrates, beans and whole grains are superheroes—providing the body with fiber, protein, vitamins, minerals, and more! They're filling, too, which makes them a great, delicious way to include carbohydrates on your plate!

Southwest Quinoa Salad

SERVES: 8 | SERVING SIZE: 1/2 CUP | PREP TIME: 10 MINUTES | COOKING TIME: 30 MINUTES

Bring this dish to your next potluck or barbecue and watch it disappear! With the familiar flavors of lime, onion, corn, bell peppers, tomatoes, and cilantro—and a healthy dose of protein from the quinoa—this dish makes a great light lunch or side dish, especially when served with grilled chicken or fish.

1 cup uncooked quinoa, rinsed and drained

2 cups water

1/2 cup finely diced red onion

1 cup fresh or frozen corn kernels

1 cup chopped bell peppers (red, orange, or yellow)

1 cup halved cherry tomatoes

1 cup BPA-free canned black beans, rinsed and drained

2 tablespoons freshly squeezed lime juice

1 teaspoon freshly grated lime zest

1 tablespoon red wine vinegar

2 tablespoons extra-virgin olive oil

1 teaspoon ground cumin

1/4 cup chopped fresh cilantro

1/4 teaspoon fine sea salt

1/4 teaspoon freshly ground black pepper

1. Add quinoa and water to a medium saucepan over high heat. Bring to a boil, then reduce heat to a simmer and cover. Cook for 12–15 minutes or until water is almost absorbed (do not stir while covered). Remove from heat and allow to cool.

2. Once cool, add the remaining ingredients and toss to combine. Serve immediately.

EXCHANGES/CHOICES	1 1/2 Starch 1 Nonstarchy Vegetable 1/2 Fat
CALORIES	170
CALORIES FROM FAT	45
TOTAL FAT	5.0 g
SATURATED FAT	0.7 g
TRANS FAT	0.0 g
CHOLESTEROL	0 mg
SODIUM	100 mg
POTASSIUM	355 mg
TOTAL CARBOHYDRATE	27 g
DIETARY FIBER	5 g
SUGARS	4 g
PROTEIN	6 g
PHOSPHORUS	155 mg

basic cooking instructions for grains

Cooking whole grains is very similar to cooking rice. You put the dry grains in a pot with water or broth, bring it to a boil, and then simmer until the liquid is absorbed.

Here are the general liquid amounts and cooking times for 1 cup dry portions of some of my favorite grains:

- **Amaranth:** Add 4–6 cups of water or broth, bring to a boil, cover, and simmer for 15–20 minutes. Adding more water will result in a more porridge-like consistency. (Makes 2 1/2 cups.)

- **Buckwheat:** Add 2 cups of water or broth, bring to a boil, cover, and simmer for 20 minutes. (Makes 4 cups.)

- **Bulgur:** Add 2 cups of water or broth, bring to a boil, turn off the heat, and cover for 10–12 minutes. (Makes 3 cups.)

- **Couscous:** Bring 1 1/2 cups of water or broth to a boil. Add the couscous, cover, and remove the pot from the heat. After 6 minutes, remove the lid and fluff the couscous with a fork. (Makes 3 cups.)

- **Farro, pearled:** Add 3–4 cups of water or broth, bring to a boil, cover, and simmer for 10–15 minutes. Drain, if necessary, after cooking. Whole-grain farro may take 30–45 minutes to cook. (Makes 2 cups.)

- **Millet, hulled:** Add 1–3 cups of water or broth, bring to a boil, cover, and simmer for 25–30 minutes. Less water will result in a fluffy grain, while more water will result in a more porridge-like consistency. (Makes 4 cups.)

- **Quinoa:** Add 2 cups of water or broth, bring to a boil, cover, and simmer for 15 minutes.

- **Rice (Brown):** Add 1 3/4–2 cups of water or broth, bring to a boil, cover, and simmer for 25–45 minutes. (Makes 3–4 cups.)

- **Whole-Grain Sorghum:** Add 3 cups water or broth, bring to a boil, and cover. Reduce heat to low and simmer until tender, about 45 minutes. (Makes 3 cups.)

- **Whole-grain Spelt/Wheat Berries:** Soak overnight then drain. Add 4 cups of water or broth, bring to a boil, and simmer, covered for 45–60 minutes. (Makes 3 cups.)

What is a pearled grain? Pearled grains have been polished, or "pearled," to remove some or all of the outer bran along with the hull. While this process removes some of the nutrient density of the grain, it can also decrease the cooking time of the grain significantly. Grains that tend to be pearled include barley and wheat grains like spelt, farro, and sorghum as they generally have longer cooking times.

Curried Quinoa
with Butternut Squash and Chickpeas

SERVES: 10 | SERVING SIZE: 1/2 CUP | PREP TIME: 15 MINUTES | COOKING TIME: 30 MINUTES

Curry powder, chickpeas, and squash are a classic combination in Indian cuisine. In this recipe, to liven up the curry flavor and add some welcome texture to the mix, I've also added fresh ginger, red wine vinegar, lime zest, and cilantro, along with nutty quinoa and crunchy pumpkin seeds. This dish is best made in the fall when mounds of butternut squash are available at the farmers' market but if you crave this spicy salad during the warmer months, feel free to use frozen (and thawed) squash instead.

1 small butternut squash, peeled, seeded, and cubed (2–3 cups)

2 tablespoons extra-virgin olive oil, divided

1/2 teaspoon fine sea salt, divided

1/4 teaspoon freshly ground black pepper, divided

1 cup uncooked quinoa

2 1/4 cups water

1 1/2 teaspoons curry powder

1 1/2 teaspoons ground cumin

2 teaspoons grated fresh ginger

1 teaspoon mustard powder

1 (14-ounce) can chickpeas, rinsed and drained

2 tablespoons red wine vinegar

1 teaspoon freshly grated lime zest

1/4 cup pumpkin seeds

1/4 cup chopped fresh cilantro

1. Preheat the oven to 400°F. Line a rimmed baking sheet with parchment paper.

2. In a medium bowl, mix the squash with 1 tablespoon olive oil, 1/4 teaspoon salt, and 1/8 teaspoon pepper. Toss to evenly coat. Spread squash onto the prepared baking sheet. Bake for about 15 minutes, stir, then bake for an additional 15 minutes, or until tender. Remove baking sheet from the oven and set aside.

3. While squash is in the oven, combine the quinoa, water, curry powder, cumin, ginger, and mustard powder in a medium saucepan over medium-high heat. Bring the mixture to a boil, then reduce the heat to low, cover, and simmer until the liquid is absorbed, about 12–15 minutes. Do not stir once covered.

4. In a large bowl, combine cooked quinoa, roasted squash, the remaining 1 tablespoon olive oil, chickpeas, red wine vinegar, lime zest, pumpkin seeds, and cilantro. Season with the remaining salt and pepper. Serve warm or at room temperature.

EXCHANGES/CHOICES	1 1/2 Starch
	1 Fat
CALORIES	160
CALORIES FROM FAT	50
TOTAL FAT	6.0 g
SATURATED FAT	0.8 g
TRANS FAT	0.0 g
CHOLESTEROL	0 mg
SODIUM	160 mg
POTASSIUM	285 mg
TOTAL CARBOHYDRATE	22 g
DIETARY FIBER	4 g
SUGARS	3 g
PROTEIN	6 g
PHOSPHORUS	165 mg

Carrot, Raisin, and Bulgur Salad

SERVES: 8 | SERVING SIZE: 1/2 CUP | PREP TIME: 5 MINUTES | COOKING TIME: 15 MINUTES

Moroccan couscous salad is a popular dish all over the country (and the world), but because couscous offers very little fiber, protein, and nutrients, I like to swap in bulgur instead. Not only does this nutty whole grain contain ten times the amount of protein and fiber that couscous does, it's also packed with vitamins and minerals that couscous lacks, such as vitamins B6, E, and K, thiamin, riboflavin, niacin, and folate. The natural sweetness of carrots and raisins make this savory salad an almost sweet treat and it reminds me of the carrot and raisin salad I used to eat as a kid.

1 cup uncooked bulgur wheat

2 cups boiling water

1 1/2 cups shredded carrot

1/2 cup raisins

1/4 cup sunflower seeds

1 teaspoon grated fresh ginger

1/4 cup chopped fresh flat-leaf parsley

1/4 teaspoon ground cinnamon

2 tablespoons freshly squeezed lemon juice

1 teaspoon freshly grated orange zest

2 tablespoons freshly squeezed orange juice

2 tablespoons extra-virgin olive oil

1/4 teaspoon fine sea salt

1/4 teaspoon freshly ground black pepper

1. In a heatproof bowl, combine the bulgur and boiling water. Cover the bowl with plastic wrap or foil and steam for 10 minutes or until the water is absorbed and bulgur is tender.

2. Allow bulgur to cool to room temperature, then mix in the carrot, raisins, sunflower seeds, ginger, parsley, cinnamon, lemon juice, orange zest, orange juice, olive oil, salt, and pepper. Mix well before serving.

EXCHANGES/CHOICES	1 Starch
	1/2 Fruit
	1 Fat
CALORIES	160
CALORIES FROM FAT	50
TOTAL FAT	6.0 g
SATURATED FAT	0.7 g
TRANS FAT	0.0 g
CHOLESTEROL	0 mg
SODIUM	85 mg
POTASSIUM	265 mg
TOTAL CARBOHYDRATE	26 g
DIETARY FIBER	5 g
SUGARS	7 g
PROTEIN	4 g
PHOSPHORUS	125 mg

Kaniwa Salad with Orange and Pistachios

SERVES: 8 | SERVING SIZE: 1/2 CUP | PREP TIME: 10 MINUTES | COOKING TIME: 30 MINUTES

Kaniwa is a small, grain-like seed that hails from the Peruvian Andes. Think of it as tiny quinoa. It's available at most grocery stores and online! Its flavor is sweet and nutty and, much like quinoa, it is considered a complete protein; it contains all nine essential amino acids and 7 grams of protein in each 1/2-cup serving (cooked). In this bright salad, kaniwa serves as a crunchy-soft base for citrus flavors, dried apricots, pistachios, and scallions.

1 cup uncooked kaniwa

2 cups water

1/2 cup chopped fresh flat-leaf parsley

1 1/2 teaspoons grated orange zest

1/3 cup freshly squeezed orange juice

Zest and juice of 1 lemon

2 tablespoons red wine vinegar

2 tablespoons extra-virgin olive oil, divided

1/4 teaspoon fine sea salt

1/4 teaspoon freshly ground black pepper

1/2 cup diced dried apricots (1/3-inch dice)

1/2 cup raw, unsalted pistachios, chopped

1/4 cup chopped scallions (white and light green parts)

1. In a medium saucepan, bring kaniwa and water to a boil over high heat. Cover, and simmer over medium heat until the liquid is absorbed, about 12–15 minutes.

2. When kaniwa is cooked, spread it out on a baking sheet to cool to room temperature.

3. In a large bowl, whisk together the parsley, orange zest, orange juice, lemon zest and juice, vinegar, and olive oil. Season with salt and pepper.

4. Add cooled kaniwa to the dressing mixture, along with the apricots, pistachios, and scallions; toss well to combine. Serve cold.

EXCHANGES/CHOICES	1 Starch
	1/2 Fruit
	1 1/2 Fat
CALORIES	180
CALORIES FROM FAT	70
TOTAL FAT	8.0 g
SATURATED FAT	1.0 g
TRANS FAT	0.0 g
CHOLESTEROL	0 mg
SODIUM	95 mg
POTASSIUM	365 mg
TOTAL CARBOHYDRATE	23 g
DIETARY FIBER	3 g
SUGARS	7 g
PROTEIN	5 g
PHOSPHORUS	140 mg

Cacio e Pepe Amaranth Polenta

SERVES: 6 | SERVING SIZE: 1/2 CUP | PREP TIME: 5 MINUTES | COOKING TIME: 1 HOUR

In Italian, *cacio e pepe* means "cheese and pepper" and refers to a classic Roman dish made simply of—you guessed it—cheese, black pepper, and spaghetti. For a fun twist, I use amaranth, which cooks down into a thick, polenta-like consistency. Because there are so few flavors in this recipe, the quality of the ingredients you use will really shine through. Spring for a block of aged Parmesan and use your best-quality extra-virgin olive oil, and you'll taste why this dish has been a part of Italian cuisine for centuries.

3 cups water

1 cup uncooked amaranth

1/2 cup freshly grated Parmesan
   cheese

2 tablespoons extra-virgin olive oil

1/4 teaspoon fine sea salt

1–2 teaspoons freshly ground black
   pepper

1. In a large pot, bring the water to a boil over high heat. Reduce the heat to low and pour the amaranth into the water in a steady stream, whisking constantly to prevent lumping. Simmer, stirring occasionally, until the mixture is soft and pudding-like, about 25–30 minutes, adding more water by the 1/4 cup if the mixture starts getting too thick.

2. Remove pot from the heat and stir in cheese, olive oil, salt, and pepper. Serve hot.

EXCHANGES/CHOICES	1 1/2 Starch
	1 1/2 Fat
CALORIES	190
CALORIES FROM FAT	70
TOTAL FAT	8.0 g
SATURATED FAT	2.1 g
TRANS FAT	0.0 g
CHOLESTEROL	5 mg
SODIUM	190 mg
POTASSIUM	170 mg
TOTAL CARBOHYDRATE	21 g
DIETARY FIBER	2 g
SUGARS	1 g
PROTEIN	7 g
PHOSPHORUS	220 mg

Herby Millet Tabbouleh

SERVES: 10 | SERVING SIZE: 1/2 CUP | PREP TIME: 10 MINUTES | COOKING TIME: 30 MINUTES

What's not to love about traditional Middle Eastern tabbouleh? With mounds of fresh herbs, hearty beans and grains, and the zip of lemon zest and juice, it's pure summertime in a bowl. This dish is purposefully herbaceous, so it should feel like an herb salad with a grain garnish.

1/2 cup uncooked millet

1 cup water

2 teaspoons freshly grated lemon zest

1/3 cup freshly squeezed lemon juice

2 tablespoons extra-virgin olive oil

1 (1-pound) seedless cucumber, diced

2 cups chopped fresh flat-leaf parsley

1 cup chopped fresh dill

1/2 cup chopped fresh mint

1 (14-ounce) can chickpeas, rinsed and drained

1/4 teaspoon fine sea salt

1/4 teaspoon freshly ground black pepper

1. Combine millet and water in a medium saucepan over medium-high heat. Bring the water to a boil, then reduce heat to low, cover, and simmer for 15–20 minutes, or until millet is tender and has absorbed the liquid. Remove pan from the heat and set it aside for 10 minutes, then fluff the millet with a fork.

2. In a large bowl, combine the lemon zest, lemon juice, olive oil, cucumber, parsley, dill, mint, chickpeas, salt, and pepper. Add the cooked millet and toss well to combine. Serve cooled.

EXCHANGES/CHOICES	1 Starch
	1/2 Fat
CALORIES	110
CALORIES FROM FAT	35
TOTAL FAT	4.0 g
SATURATED FAT	0.5 g
TRANS FAT	0.0 g
CHOLESTEROL	0 mg
SODIUM	105 mg
POTASSIUM	210 mg
TOTAL CARBOHYDRATE	17 g
DIETARY FIBER	3 g
SUGARS	2 g
PROTEIN	4 g
PHOSPHORUS	85 mg

Citrus Farro Salad
with Roasted Beets and Poppy Seeds

SERVES: 8 | SERVING SIZE: 1/2 CUP | PREP TIME: 5 MINUTES | COOKING TIME: 1 HOUR 30 MINUTES

Jewel-toned beets and citrus fruits make a beautiful pairing, for both the eyes and the taste buds. Add to that some incredibly nutritious farro, a hint of Dijon mustard, poppy seeds, and fresh parsley, and you've got an instant pick-me-up. For best results, make this salad in the winter, when beets and citrus are at their peak sweetness. You can swap poppy seeds for chia seeds, but there is something fun about sticking to poppy seeds; I think they are an underappreciated seed with spectacular flavor and nutrient density.

- 4 (4-ounce) medium beets, scrubbed, tops trimmed to 1 inch
- 3 tablespoons extra-virgin olive oil, divided
- 1 cup uncooked pearled farro
- 2 1/2 cups water
- 1 teaspoon freshly grated orange zest
- 3 teaspoons red wine vinegar, divided
- 1/4 cup freshly squeezed orange juice
- 1 teaspoon Dijon mustard
- 2 teaspoons poppy seeds
- 2 tablespoons chopped shallot
- 1/3 cup chopped fresh flat-leaf parsley
- 1/4 teaspoon fine sea salt
- 1/4 teaspoon freshly ground black pepper
- 1 navel orange, peeled and divided into segments

1. Preheat the oven to 400°F.

2. Rub the beets with 1 tablespoon olive oil, then wrap each beet in a piece of aluminum foil. Place the foil-wrapped beets on a rimmed baking sheet and roast for about 1 hour, or until tender. Remove beets from the oven and let them cool for 5–10 minutes, then unwrap them and peel off their skins. (This step can be done one day ahead and the peeled beets can be stored in the refrigerator.) Cut each roasted beet into 6–8 wedges.

3. In a medium saucepan over high heat, combine the farro and water. Bring water to a boil, then cover the pan, reduce heat to low, and simmer for 15–20 minutes, or until farro is tender. Remove pan from the heat.

4. Drain the cooked farro and transfer it to a large bowl, add 1 tablespoon olive oil and the orange zest. Stir to combine, and set aside to cool to room temperature.

5. In a small bowl, whisk the remaining 1 tablespoon olive oil with the vinegar, orange juice, mustard, poppy seeds, and shallot. Add this dressing and parsley to the farro, stir to combine, then season with the salt and pepper. Fold in the beets and orange segments and serve at room temperature.

EXCHANGES/CHOICES	1 1/2 Starch
	1 Nonstarchy Vegetable
	1 Fat
CALORIES	180
CALORIES FROM FAT	50
TOTAL FAT	6.0 g
SATURATED FAT	0.9 g
TRANS FAT	0.0 g
CHOLESTEROL	0 mg
SODIUM	120 mg
POTASSIUM	300 mg
TOTAL CARBOHYDRATE	26 g
DIETARY FIBER	5 g
SUGARS	5 g
PROTEIN	5 g
PHOSPHORUS	135 mg

Trail Mix Wild Rice Salad

SERVES: 6 | SERVING SIZE: 1/2 CUP | PREP TIME: 5 MINUTES | COOKING TIME: 40 MINUTES

While we often eat rice warm, it adds a delicious texture to cold recipes as well. This salad reminds me of a hearty trail mix—hence the name—as it is packed with nourishing nuts and seeds and naturally sweetened dried fruits, which are really satisfying.

1 cup freshly brewed mint tea

1 cup water

1 cup uncooked brown and wild rice blend

2 tablespoons raw, unsalted sunflower seeds

2 tablespoons chopped walnuts

2 tablespoons extra-virgin olive oil

2 tablespoons apple cider vinegar

2 tablespoons unsweetened dried cherries

2 tablespoons chopped unsweetened dried apricots

1 teaspoon freshly grated orange zest

1/4 cup sliced scallions (white and light green parts)

1 tablespoon chopped fresh mint

1/4 teaspoon fine sea salt

1/4 teaspoon freshly ground black pepper

1. In a medium saucepan over medium-high heat, combine the tea, water, and rice. Bring mixture to a boil, reduce heat to low, and cover the pan. Simmer for 30–40 minutes, without stirring, or until the rice is tender and all the liquid has been absorbed. Remove pan from the heat and let rice cool to room temperature.

2. In a small skillet over medium-high heat, toast sunflower seeds and walnuts for 2–3 minutes, or until they are lightly browned and aromatic, tossing frequently to prevent burning. Remove pan from the heat, transfer nuts to a plate, and let them cool to room temperature.

3. In a large bowl, combine the cooled rice with the olive oil, vinegar, dried cherries and apricots, orange zest, scallions, mint, toasted sunflower seeds and walnuts, salt, and pepper. Serve at room temperature.

tip: The unsweetened dried cherries called for in this recipe are a great substitute for dried cranberries, which almost always contain added sugars.

EXCHANGES/CHOICES	1 1/2 Starch
	1/2 Fruit
	1 1/2 Fat
CALORIES	200
CALORIES FROM FAT	80
TOTAL FAT	9.0 g
SATURATED FAT	1.0 g
TRANS FAT	0.0 g
CHOLESTEROL	0 mg
SODIUM	95 mg
POTASSIUM	215 mg
TOTAL CARBOHYDRATE	29 g
DIETARY FIBER	2 g
SUGARS	5 g
PROTEIN	4 g
PHOSPHORUS	160 mg

Freekeh Salad with Tarragon and Hazelnuts

SERVES: 8 | SERVING SIZE: 1/2 CUP | PREP TIME: 10 MINUTES | COOKING TIME: 20 MINUTES

Freekeh—a young, green wheat that has been roasted and cracked—is a rich source of protein. It tastes lovely in breakfast cereals, as a savory side dish, and, of course, in a salad like this one. The natural nuttiness of the grain complements the hazelnuts, and the lemon and tarragon brighten these flavors, creating a hearty yet refreshing dish.

1 cup uncooked freekeh

2 1/2 cups water

1 large shallot, minced (about 1/4 cup)

1 teaspoon Dijon mustard

3 tablespoons white wine vinegar

1 teaspoon freshly grated lemon zest

2 tablespoons extra-virgin olive oil

1 tablespoon hazelnut oil

1/4 teaspoon fine sea salt

1/4 teaspoon freshly ground black pepper

1/2 cup chopped fresh flat-leaf parsley

1/4 cup chopped fresh tarragon

1/2 cup chopped raw, unsalted hazelnuts

1. In a small saucepan over high heat, combine freekeh and water. Bring the water to a boil, then cover the pan, reduce heat to low, and simmer for 15 minutes, or until water is absorbed. Transfer freekeh to a large bowl and let it cool to room temperature.

2. Meanwhile, in a small bowl, whisk together the shallot, mustard, vinegar, lemon zest, olive oil, and hazelnut oil. Season with salt and pepper.

3. Pour dressing over the freekeh and add the parsley, tarragon, and hazelnuts. Toss well to combine. Serve at room temperature.

tip: If you can't find hazelnut oil or it is too expensive, try walnut oil or simply skip this ingredient.

EXCHANGES/CHOICES	1 Starch
	2 Fat
CALORIES	180
CALORIES FROM FAT	90
TOTAL FAT	10.0 g
SATURATED FAT	1.1 g
TRANS FAT	0.0 g
CHOLESTEROL	0 mg
SODIUM	85 mg
POTASSIUM	190 mg
TOTAL CARBOHYDRATE	19 g
DIETARY FIBER	5 g
SUGARS	1 g
PROTEIN	5 g
PHOSPHORUS	145 mg

Sorghum with Lemon Tahini Dressing

SERVES: 8 | SERVING SIZE: 3/4 CUP | PREP TIME: 5 MINUTES | COOKING TIME: 45 MINUTES

Relatively new to the gluten-free grain aisle in the grocery store, sorghum has a wonderful, toothsome texture and a mild nutty flavor that work perfectly with the peppery arugula and earthy tahini in this recipe. Rich in healthy fats, protein, and fiber, this recipe is delicious and satisfying!

1 cup uncooked sorghum

3 cups water

1 (14-ounce) can chickpeas, drained and rinsed

3 cups baby arugula

1/4 cup chopped fresh flat-leaf parsley

2 tablespoons extra-virgin olive oil

1 teaspoon freshly grated lemon zest

1/3 cup freshly squeezed lemon juice

1/4 teaspoon red pepper flakes (optional)

1 tablespoon tahini

1 small shallot, minced

1/4 teaspoon fine sea salt

1/4 teaspoon freshly ground black pepper

1. In a small saucepan over high heat, combine sorghum and water. Bring water to a boil, then cover the pan, reduce heat to low, and simmer for 45 minutes, or until sorghum is tender and the water has been absorbed. Remove pan from the heat and spread sorghum on a baking sheet to cool it to room temperature.

2. In a large bowl, combine cooled sorghum with the chickpeas, arugula, and parsley.

3. In a small bowl, whisk together the olive oil, lemon zest, lemon juice, red pepper flakes (if using), tahini, shallot, salt, and pepper. Pour dressing over the salad mixture and toss to combine. Serve cooled.

EXCHANGES/CHOICES	2 Starch
	1/2 Fat
CALORIES	190
CALORIES FROM FAT	50
TOTAL FAT	6.0 g
SATURATED FAT	0.8 g
TRANS FAT	0.0 g
CHOLESTEROL	0 mg
SODIUM	130 mg
POTASSIUM	235 mg
TOTAL CARBOHYDRATE	29 g
DIETARY FIBER	7 g
SUGARS	2 g
PROTEIN	6 g
PHOSPHORUS	145 mg

Lemony Barley Pilaf

SERVES: 8 | SERVING SIZE: 1/2 CUP | PREP TIME: 10 MINUTES | COOKING TIME: 35 MINUTES

A refreshing burst of lemon makes this barley pilaf the perfect side dish for summery fish and chicken recipes. This recipe speaks to the notion that simple is often best!

- 1 tablespoon extra-virgin olive oil
- 1 leek, trimmed and sliced (white part only)
- 1 cup finely diced red bell pepper
- 1 cup finely diced carrots
- 1 cup finely diced celery
- 1/4 teaspoon fine sea salt
- 1/4 teaspoon freshly ground black pepper
- 3/4 cup uncooked pearl barley
- 2 cups water
- 1/2 cup freshly squeezed lemon juice
- 1 tablespoon freshly grated lemon zest
- 1/4 cup chopped fresh flat-leaf parsley

1. Heat the oil in a medium saucepan over medium-high heat. Add the leek, pepper, carrots, celery, salt, and pepper, and sauté until vegetables begin to soften, about 5 minutes.

2. Add the barley and water to the saucepan and bring water to a boil. Then reduce the heat to low, give the barley mixture one last stir, and cover. Cook until barley is tender, 25–30 minutes.

3. Once barley is cooked, stir in the lemon juice and zest, cover the pan again, and remove from the heat. Let the pilaf rest for 10 minutes, then stir in the parsley and serve warm.

EXCHANGES/CHOICES	1 Starch
	1 Nonstarchy Vegetable
CALORIES	110
CALORIES FROM FAT	20
TOTAL FAT	2.0 g
SATURATED FAT	0.3 g
TRANS FAT	0.0 g
CHOLESTEROL	0 mg
SODIUM	95 mg
POTASSIUM	210 mg
TOTAL CARBOHYDRATE	20 g
DIETARY FIBER	4 g
SUGARS	3 g
PROTEIN	2 g
PHOSPHORUS	60 mg

Wheat Berries with Pesto, Kale, and White Beans

SERVES: 10 | SERVING SIZE: 1/2 CUP | PREP TIME: 5 MINUTES | COOKING TIME: 1 HOUR

I have been known to put pesto on just about anything, and this recipe is proof of that! Think of this dish as a spin-off of pasta with pesto; I just swapped the pasta for wheat berries—a hearty, filling whole grain—and the rest is history.

2 cups uncooked wheat berries (or farro)

7 cups water

1/2 cup Walnut Arugula Pesto (page 81)

1 teaspoon freshly grated lemon zest

1 tablespoon freshly squeezed lemon juice

2 cups chopped lacinato kale

1 cup halved grape tomatoes

1 cup BPA-free canned navy beans, drained and rinsed

1. Combine wheat berries and water in a medium saucepan over medium-high heat. Bring water to a boil, then cover the pan, reduce heat to low, and simmer for 1 hour, or until wheat berries are tender. Drain and set aside.

2. Meanwhile, in a large bowl, combine the pesto, lemon zest, lemon juice, kale, tomatoes, and navy beans. Add the cooked wheat berries and toss well to combine. Serve warm or cold.

beans, beans, they're good for your heart

In my mind, beans are the number one "superfood" on the market—they are extremely good for you *and* very inexpensive! Beans are an excellent source of complex carbohydrate, protein, and fiber, as well as vitamins and minerals (calcium, potassium, vitamin B6, and folate to name a few). I am a huge fan of beans, and we eat them regularly in my house. Though it is healthiest to cook beans from their dry state, this can take quite a long time. To save some time, cook beans in bulk and use them in various recipes throughout the week. I always have some BPA-free canned beans on hand as well for those last-minute recipes, but I make sure to rinse canned beans before using them to help decrease the residual sodium.

Beans can cause gas—yes, it is true! To reduce their gassy effect, try adding a piece of kombu (seaweed) to the cooking water. The kombu helps make the beans more digestible!

EXCHANGES/CHOICES	2 Starch
	1 Fat
CALORIES	210
CALORIES FROM FAT	60
TOTAL FAT	7.0 g
SATURATED FAT	1.1 g
TRANS FAT	0.0 g
CHOLESTEROL	0 mg
SODIUM	90 mg
POTASSIUM	325 mg
TOTAL CARBOHYDRATE	30 g
DIETARY FIBER	7 g
SUGARS	1 g
PROTEIN	7 g
PHOSPHORUS	165 mg

Tuscan White Beans

SERVES: 8 | SERVING SIZE: 1/2 CUP | PREP TIME: 5 MINUTES | COOKING TIME: 1 HOUR

This recipe reminds me of my childhood and the traditional Italian bean recipes my great aunt Anita used to make. Rustic and flavorful, this dish of white beans with savory herbs and a touch of salty pancetta truly speaks to my Italian roots and a lifetime of memories.

2 tablespoons Everyday Herb Oil (page 60) or extra-virgin olive oil, divided

1 ounce pancetta, diced

2 cups dried white beans (cannellini or Great Northern beans), sorted and rinsed

10 cups water

2 fresh sage sprigs

5 cloves garlic, smashed

1/2 teaspoon fine sea salt

1/2 teaspoon freshly ground black pepper

1. Heat 1 tablespoon oil in a large Dutch oven over medium heat. Add the pancetta and cook for 3–4 minutes, then add the beans, water, sage, and garlic. Cover the pot, reduce heat to medium-low, and simmer for 1 hour, or until beans are tender.

2. Remove pot from the heat, drain the beans, and return them to the pot. Season with salt, pepper, and remaining 1 tablespoon oil. Serve hot.

basic cooking instructions for dried beans

1. Rinse the beans and sort out any that are broken, blistered looking, wrinkled, or shriveled.

2. Place the beans in a large pot with 3 cups of water for every cup of beans. Let the beans soak for 6–8 hours or overnight. (If you don't have time for an overnight soak, bring the beans and water to a boil and let boil for 2 minutes. Remove from the heat, cover, and let the pot sit at room temperature for 1 hour.) Then drain and rinse the beans.

3. To cook the beans, return them to the pot they soaked in and add 3 cups of water for every cup of beans. Bring to a boil; then reduce heat and simmer, partially covered, until the beans are tender, about 1–1 1/2 hours. The beans are done when they can be easily mashed with a fork or between two fingers. Cooked beans should be refrigerated or frozen. One cup of dry beans yields 2–3 cups of cooked beans, depending on the variety of bean.

EXCHANGES/CHOICES	2 Starch
	1 Lean Protein
CALORIES	190
CALORIES FROM FAT	45
TOTAL FAT	5.0 g
SATURATED FAT	1.0 g
TRANS FAT	0.0 g
CHOLESTEROL	5 mg
SODIUM	200 mg
POTASSIUM	500 mg
TOTAL CARBOHYDRATE	26 g
DIETARY FIBER	8 g
SUGARS	3 g
PROTEIN	11 g
PHOSPHORUS	220 mg

Green Lentil Salad with Tomatoes and Dill

SERVES: 12 | SERVING SIZE: 1/2 CUP | PREP TIME: 15 MINUTES | COOKING TIME: 20 MINUTES

I like to think of lentils as the no-soak bean; they cook up quickly with very little fuss. If lentils are new to you, this is the perfect beginner recipe as it includes familiar ingredients like tomatoes and cucumber as well as popular herbs such as parsley, basil, and dill. It's a bowl of summer flavors that I know you will love!

- 4 cups water
- 1 cup dried lentils (preferably green or French)
- 1 shallot, finely diced
- 2 cups chopped tomatoes (or halved grape tomatoes)
- 1 cup diced seedless cucumber

- 1/4 cup chopped fresh dill
- 1/4 cup chopped fresh flat-leaf parsley
- 1/4 cup chopped fresh basil
- 2 tablespoons red wine vinegar
- 1 teaspoon freshly grated lemon zest

- 2 tablespoons freshly squeezed lemon juice
- 2 tablespoons extra-virgin olive oil
- 1/4 teaspoon fine sea salt
- 1/4 teaspoon freshly ground black pepper

1. In a medium, heavy-bottomed saucepan over medium-high heat, combine the water and lentils. Bring water to a boil, then cover the pan, reduce heat to low, and simmer for 15–25 minutes, or until lentils are tender but not mushy. Remove pan from the heat and drain the lentils in a large sieve; transfer them to a large bowl and let them cool to room temperature.

2. When lentils have cooled, add the shallot, tomatoes, cucumber, dill, parsley, and basil. Set aside.

3. In a small bowl, whisk together the vinegar, lemon zest, lemon juice, olive oil, salt, and pepper. Pour dressing over the lentil mixture and toss well to combine. Serve at room temperature.

tip: This recipe works best with green or brown lentils because these varieties are not hulled and hold their shape when cooked. Hulled lentils, like yellow and red varieties, tend to disintegrate when cooked, so they work best in soups and stews like the Moroccan Carrot and Red Lentil Soup on page 177.

EXCHANGES/CHOICES	1 Starch
CALORIES	80
CALORIES FROM FAT	20
TOTAL FAT	2.5 g
SATURATED FAT	0.4 g
TRANS FAT	0.0 g
CHOLESTEROL	0 mg
SODIUM	50 mg
POTASSIUM	255 mg
TOTAL CARBOHYDRATE	11 g
DIETARY FIBER	4 g
SUGARS	2 g
PROTEIN	4 g
PHOSPHORUS	85 mg

Red Lentil Dal

SERVES: 8 | SERVING SIZE: 1/2 CUP | PREP TIME: 10 MINUTES | COOKING TIME: 40–45 MINUTES

This Indian-inspired dish will fill your home with the aroma of warm, exotic spices. But that's not all the spices are good for. For instance, turmeric may have anti-inflammatory effects and cumin provides iron. And that's just a couple of the spices I've included in this recipe.

1 tablespoon extra-virgin olive oil

1 cup diced onion

3 cloves garlic, minced

3/4 teaspoon ground turmeric

3/4 teaspoon ground cumin

1/2 teaspoon mustard powder

1/4 teaspoon ground cinnamon

1/2 teaspoon ground coriander

1/2 teaspoon ground cardamom

1 teaspoon grated fresh ginger

3 cups water

1 cup crushed tomatoes with juice

1 cup dried red lentils

1/4 teaspoon fine sea salt

1/2 teaspoon freshly ground black pepper

1. Heat the olive oil in a medium saucepan over medium heat. Add the onion and garlic and sauté until tender, about 5 minutes. Stir in the turmeric, cumin, mustard powder, cinnamon, coriander, cardamom, and ginger, and cook until aromatic, about 1 minute.

2. Add the water, tomatoes, and lentils to the pan, and bring mixture to a boil. Reduce heat to low, cover the pan, and simmer for 15 minutes, or until lentils are tender but not mushy.

3. Remove pan from the heat, season with salt and pepper, and serve hot.

EXCHANGES/CHOICES	1 Starch
	1 Nonstarchy Vegetable
CALORIES	120
CALORIES FROM FAT	20
TOTAL FAT	2.0 g
SATURATED FAT	0.3 g
TRANS FAT	0.0 g
CHOLESTEROL	0 mg
SODIUM	110 mg
POTASSIUM	365 mg
TOTAL CARBOHYDRATE	18 g
DIETARY FIBER	6 g
SUGARS	3 g
PROTEIN	7 g
PHOSPHORUS	130 mg

Smoky Seafood Stew p. 181

soups and stews

I am obsessed with one-pot meals—particularly soups and stews! They are like a warm, cozy hug in a bowl. Whether they are minimalist and brothy, stick-to-your-ribs hearty, or luxuriously creamy, boy, are the good. While it's nice to imagine a cauldron of stew bubbling for hours on the stove, many of the one-pot wonders in this chapter come together in less than 30 minutes on a busy weeknight; and if we're being realistic, that is more in line with what we can actually accomplish on a weekday.

Of course, like many other comfort foods, some soup and stew recipes include excess sodium, sugars, and fats that cancel out the natural health benefits of the whole foods they contain. But in this chapter, you'll find a few of my favorite soups and stews that celebrate all that is good for you—fresh vegetables, lean meats, whole grains, legumes, and other ingredients that will satisfy your appetite and fortify your body. There's the 10-Minute Miso Soup Mugs (page 174), made in individual mugs for ultimate convenience, and the Gingery Chicken and Vegetable Soup (page 182), which takes 30 minutes to cook from start to finish. If you like it smooth, there are blended soups like Roasted Eggplant and Tomato Soup (page 180), Poblano-Ginger Butternut Squash Soup (page 179), and Roasted Beet and Apple Soup (page 175), all of which forgo the typical heavy cream but don't sacrifice a drop of flavor. And then, for those extra-chilly winter nights, there's Chipotle-Chocolate Chicken and Root Vegetable Chili (page 183), Beef, Barley, and Mushroom Stew (page 185), and Smoky Seafood Stew (page 181) to keep you warm.

10-Minute Miso Soup Mugs

SERVES: 4 | SERVING SIZE: 1 CUP | PREP TIME: 2 MINUTES | COOKING TIME: 8 MINUTES

Trust me, once you try this ridiculously simple soup, it's sure to become a staple in your home. I like to think of this soup as a more satisfying version of a cup of tea. Miso is rich in probiotics, healthy bacteria that support digestion and overall health. Plus, the slightly salty and savory flavor profile is really cozy and delicious.

4 1/2 cups water

1 (1-inch) piece kombu (seaweed)

4 teaspoons white miso paste

1/4 cup sliced scallions (white and
    light green parts)

1. In a medium stock pot, bring the water and kombu to a boil over high heat. Then immediately remove pot from the heat, remove and discard kombu, and divide the broth evenly among 4 mugs.

2. Whisk 1 teaspoon miso paste into each mug. Garnish with scallions and serve hot.

the health benefits of fermented foods

Fermentation is the process of exposing foods to bacteria, causing them to break down, which makes the food easier to digest. It is therefore easier for our bodies to absorb nutrients from fermented foods. The speed of fermentation may vary depending on the culture used, the fuel (the fermenting food), and the temperature at which fermentation takes place.

Fermentation changes the flavor, texture, and nutritive value of the food. One major change is the increase in its probiotic (healthy bacteria) content. Eating foods that contain these healthy bacteria may support both digestive and immune health.

EXCHANGES/CHOICES	Free food
CALORIES	10
CALORIES FROM FAT	0
TOTAL FAT	0.0 g
SATURATED FAT	0.0 g
TRANS FAT	0.0 g
CHOLESTEROL	0 mg
SODIUM	115 mg
POTASSIUM	25 mg
TOTAL CARBOHYDRATE	3 g
DIETARY FIBER	0 g
SUGARS	1 g
PROTEIN	0 g
PHOSPHORUS	10 mg

Roasted Beet and Apple Soup

SERVES: 6 | SERVING SIZE: 1 CUP | PREP TIME: 10 MINUTES | COOKING TIME: 1 HOUR 30 MINUTES

Earthy and slightly sweet, I love to make this scarlet-hued soup in mid- to late fall when apples and beets are at their peak ripeness. It's the perfect starter for an autumn-themed meal, and its contrasting sweet and tart flavors complement all sorts of seasonal dishes, from pork and chicken to roasted cauliflower and Brussels sprouts.

1/2 pound red beets, trimmed and scrubbed (about 3 medium beets)

2 tablespoons extra-virgin olive oil

1 leek, sliced (white and pale green parts)

2 cloves garlic, chopped

2 Granny Smith apples, peeled, cored, and diced

1/8 teaspoon ground ginger

1/4 cup freshly squeezed orange juice

1 teaspoon freshly grated orange zest

4 cups low-sodium vegetable broth

2 tablespoons freshly squeezed lemon juice

1/4 teaspoon fine sea salt

1/4 teaspoon freshly ground black pepper

1. Preheat the oven to 350°F.

2. Wrap each beet in a piece of foil and roast until they are tender when pierced with fork, about 1 hour. Remove beets from the oven, unwrap them, and let them cool for 5 minutes. Then peel off the skins and cut the beets into 1/2-inch dice.

3. Heat the oil in a medium, heavy-bottomed saucepan over medium-high heat. Add the leek and garlic, and cook for 5–8 minutes, or until tender. Stir in the apples, diced beets, and ginger. Cook for 1–2 minutes, stirring constantly, then add the orange juice, orange zest, and broth.

4. Bring the liquid to a boil, then reduce heat to low, cover the pan, and simmer until the vegetables are very tender, about 25 minutes.

5. Remove pan from the heat, stir in the lemon juice, and let soup cool slightly. Carefully transfer soup to a blender or food processor, in batches if necessary, and purée until smooth. Season with salt and pepper and serve immediately.

EXCHANGES/CHOICES	1/2 Fruit
	1 Nonstarchy Vegetable
	1 Fat
CALORIES	110
CALORIES FROM FAT	40
TOTAL FAT	4.5 g
SATURATED FAT	0.7 g
TRANS FAT	0.0 g
CHOLESTEROL	0 mg
SODIUM	220 mg
POTASSIUM	325 mg
TOTAL CARBOHYDRATE	15 g
DIETARY FIBER	3 g
SUGARS	10 g
PROTEIN	1 g
PHOSPHORUS	85 mg

Chipotle-Honey Sweet Potato Soup

SERVES: 8 | SERVING SIZE: 1 CUP | PREP TIME: 10 MINUTES | COOKING TIME: 45 MINUTES

This is not your grandma's cream of potato soup. In this recipe, smoky and spicy Southwest flavors blend with sweet potato to create a smooth, decadent texture without any added fat. If you like it extra spicy, add 1/2 teaspoon of adobo sauce to the broth.

2 tablespoons extra-virgin olive oil

1 medium onion, chopped

4 cloves garlic, chopped

1 teaspoon ground coriander

2 teaspoons ground cumin

2 large sweet potatoes, diced (about 6 cups)

4 cups low-sodium vegetable broth

2 cups water

1/2–1 chipotle pepper in adobo, chopped

1 teaspoon honey

1/4 teaspoon fine sea salt

1/4 teaspoon freshly ground black pepper

1/4 cup chopped fresh cilantro

1. Heat the olive oil in a large pot over medium-high heat. Add the onion and cook for 5 minutes, or until it begins to soften. Add the garlic, coriander, and cumin, and cook for 1 minute. Stir in the sweet potatoes, broth, and water.

2. Bring the liquid to a boil, then reduce heat to low, cover the pot, and simmer for 25–30 minutes, or until the sweet potatoes are tender. Add the chipotle pepper and honey and season with salt and pepper.

3. Remove pot from the heat and allow the soup to cool slightly. Carefully transfer soup to a blender or food processor, in batches if necessary, and purée until smooth. Garnish with fresh cilantro and serve immediately.

EXCHANGES/CHOICES	1 1/2 Starch
	1 Nonstarchy Vegetable
CALORIES	140
CALORIES FROM FAT	30
TOTAL FAT	3.5 g
SATURATED FAT	0.5 g
TRANS FAT	0.0 g
CHOLESTEROL	0 mg
SODIUM	200 mg
POTASSIUM	460 mg
TOTAL CARBOHYDRATE	25 g
DIETARY FIBER	4 g
SUGARS	7 g
PROTEIN	2 g
PHOSPHORUS	95 mg

Moroccan Carrot and Red Lentil Soup

SERVES: 8 | SERVING SIZE: 1 CUP SOUP AND 1 TABLESPOON YOGURT | PREP TIME: 10 MINUTES | COOKING TIME: 45 MINUTES

This vegetarian soup is one tasty powerhouse of a meal. Both lentils and carrots contain enough dietary fiber to really fill you up. Trust me, if you are not yet familiar with Moroccan flavor profiles, you want to be. A combination of earthy, savory, and sweet flavors, the spice blend in this soup complements the carrots and lentils in a magical way.

1 tablespoon extra-virgin olive oil

1 Spanish onion, chopped

5 cloves Everyday Roasted Garlic (page 64)

1 1/2 pounds large carrots, peeled and cut into 1/2-inch dice (about 4 cups)

3 tablespoons Moroccan Spice Blend (page 73)

4 cups low-sodium vegetable broth

2 cups water

1 cup dried red lentils

1 teaspoon raw honey

1/4 teaspoon fine sea salt

1/4 teaspoon freshly ground black pepper

8 tablespoons fat-free, plain strained yogurt (Greek or skyr), stirred

1. Heat the olive oil in a large saucepan over medium-high heat. Add the onion and garlic and sauté for 2 minutes, then add the carrots and spice blend and cook for 1 minute.

2. Add the broth, water, and lentils. Bring liquid to a boil, then reduce heat to low, cover the pan, and simmer until carrots and lentils are tender, about 30–35 minutes.

3. Remove pot from the heat. Carefully transfer soup to a blender or food processor, in batches if necessary, and purée until smooth. Return blended soup to the pot and stir in the honey, salt, and pepper.

4. Divide soup among 8 bowls and drizzle each serving with 1 tablespoon yogurt. Serve hot.

EXCHANGES/CHOICES	1 Starch
	2 Nonstarchy Vegetable
	1 Fat
CALORIES	170
CALORIES FROM FAT	35
TOTAL FAT	4.0 g
SATURATED FAT	0.6 g
TRANS FAT	0.0 g
CHOLESTEROL	0 mg
SODIUM	240 mg
POTASSIUM	640 mg
TOTAL CARBOHYDRATE	27 g
DIETARY FIBER	9 g
SUGARS	8 g
PROTEIN	8 g
PHOSPHORUS	210 mg

African Peanut Stew

SERVES: 10 | SERVING SIZE: 1 CUP | PREP TIME: 15 MINUTES | COOKING TIME: 1 HOUR

If you're new to peanut stew, the combination of greens, vegetables, and peanut butter might seem strange. But all it takes is one spoonful, and you'll be hooked for life! This traditional West African meal is packed with nutrients from fresh vegetables, rich, warming spices, and bitter greens. The peanut butter brings it all together into one mind-blowing flavorful bite.

1 tablespoon extra-virgin olive oil

1 1/2 cups chopped onion

1 cup chopped carrot

1 cup chopped celery

2 tablespoons minced garlic

2 tablespoons grated fresh ginger

1 tablespoon curry powder

1 tablespoon ground cumin

1 (14-ounce) can low-sodium diced tomatoes with juice

4 cups low-sodium vegetable broth

1 large sweet potato, peeled and cubed

1 (15-ounce) can chickpeas, drained and rinsed

1/4 cup unsweetened crunchy natural peanut butter (or almond butter or other nut butter; preferably organic)

1/4 cup chopped fresh cilantro

1 bunch kale, tough stems discarded, leaves chopped (about 5 cups)

1/4 teaspoon red pepper flakes or freshly ground black pepper

1. Heat the olive oil in a Dutch oven over medium heat. Add the onions, carrots, and celery; sauté until soft and translucent, about 5 minutes. Add the garlic, ginger, curry powder, and cumin, and sauté until fragrant, about 1 minute. Add the tomatoes and cook for 10 minutes to reduce the liquid a bit.

2. Add the broth and sweet potatoes and bring mixture to a boil. Reduce heat to low, and simmer for about 30 minutes, or until the sweet potatoes are tender and the broth starts to thicken.

3. Add the chickpeas and peanut butter, stir to combine, and then stir in the cilantro and kale. Cook for another 2 minutes or until all ingredients are heated through and kale has wilted. Top with pepper flakes. Serve hot.

EXCHANGES/CHOICES	1 Starch
	1 Nonstarchy Vegetable
	1 Fat
CALORIES	150
CALORIES FROM FAT	50
TOTAL FAT	6.0 g
SATURATED FAT	0.9 g
TRANS FAT	0.0 g
CHOLESTEROL	0 mg
SODIUM	140 mg
POTASSIUM	455 mg
TOTAL CARBOHYDRATE	20 g
DIETARY FIBER	5 g
SUGARS	6 g
PROTEIN	5 g
PHOSPHORUS	140 mg

Poblano-Ginger Butternut Squash Soup

SERVES: 10 | SERVING SIZE: 1 CUP | PREP TIME: 10 MINUTES | COOKING TIME: 50 MINUTES

There will always be a place in my heart for the pure flavor of plain butternut squash soup, but this version—with the added flavor boost from ginger and poblano peppers—is just what I crave as the first gusts of fall weather blow in. Poblano peppers are on the mild side, so they add more of a smoky flavor than an in-your-face heat.

- 1–2 medium poblano peppers (depending on desired heat)
- 2 tablespoons extra-virgin olive oil
- 1 onion, diced
- 4 cloves Everyday Roasted Garlic (page 64)
- 1 tablespoon grated fresh ginger
- 1 medium or large butternut squash, peeled, seeded, and cubed (about 6 cups)
- 2 small apples, peeled, cored, and cubed
- 4 cups low-sodium vegetable broth
- 2 cups water
- 1 tablespoon raw honey
- 1/4 teaspoon fine sea salt
- 1/4 teaspoon freshly ground black pepper

1. If you have a gas stove, turn on one burner and char the poblano(s) on all sides over the open flame, about 5 minutes. Or preheat the broiler on high with a rack set as close to the heat source as possible. Place the poblano(s) directly on the rack in the oven and broil for 5–10 minutes, turning occasionally, until all sides are charred. Place charred pepper(s) in a metal bowl and cover bowl with plastic wrap. Let the pepper(s) steam in the bowl for 10 minutes, and then uncover the bowl. Carefully remove the skin, stem(s), and seeds and set roasted peppers aside.

2. Heat the olive oil in a large pot over high heat. Add the onion, roasted garlic, roasted poblano(s), and ginger. Sauté vegetables for 2–3 minutes, or until onion is tender. Add the squash, apples, broth, and water to the pot. Bring mixture to a boil, reduce heat to low, and simmer, stirring occasionally, until squash is tender, about 20 minutes. Add the honey and stir.

3. Remove pot from the heat. Carefully transfer soup to a blender or food processor, in batches if necessary, and purée until smooth. Season with salt and pepper before serving.

EXCHANGES/CHOICES	1/2 Starch
	1 Nonstarchy Vegetable
	1 Fat

CALORIES	100
CALORIES FROM FAT	35
TOTAL FAT	4.0 g
SATURATED FAT	0.6 g
TRANS FAT	0.0 g
CHOLESTEROL	0 mg
SODIUM	120 mg
POTASSIUM	420 mg
TOTAL CARBOHYDRATE	18 g
DIETARY FIBER	3 g
SUGARS	7 g
PROTEIN	1 g
PHOSPHORUS	70 mg

Roasted Eggplant and Tomato Soup

SERVES: 10 | SERVING SIZE: 1 CUP | PREP TIME: 10 MINUTES | COOKING TIME: 1 HOUR

The eggplant in this soup serves many functions. It provides a host of vitamins, minerals, and other nutrients, it balances the acidity of the tomatoes and adds earthy-sweet flavor, and, when blended, it creates a texture so luscious and smooth that you'll swear someone added heavy cream to the soup when you weren't looking.

2 tablespoons extra-virgin olive oil, divided

1 large eggplant, halved lengthwise

2 cups diced onion

4 cloves garlic, chopped

1 (28-ounce) can low-sodium crushed tomatoes with juice

3 cups water

1/4 cup chopped fresh basil

2 tablespoons chopped fresh oregano

1/4 teaspoon fine sea salt

1/4 teaspoon freshly ground black pepper

1. Preheat the oven to 425°F. Lightly grease a rimmed baking sheet with 1 tablespoon olive oil.

2. Place the eggplant on the prepared baking sheet, cut-side down, and roast until tender, about 30–45 minutes. Remove eggplant from the oven, allow to cool slightly, then peel off the skin and chop the flesh. Place the chopped eggplant in a medium bowl and set aside.

3. Meanwhile, heat the remaining 1 tablespoon olive oil in a large Dutch oven or heavy saucepan over medium-high heat. Add the onion and sauté for 5–8 minutes until it is soft and translucent. Add the garlic and sauté for 1 more minute. Stir in the tomatoes, water, and eggplant flesh with any accumulated juices. Simmer, partially covered, for 15 minutes. Stir in the basil, oregano, salt, and pepper, and simmer for an additional 2–3 minutes.

4. Remove pot from the heat and let it cool slightly. Carefully transfer soup to a blender or food processor, in batches if necessary, and purée until smooth.

5. Pour the blended soup back into the pot and reheat on the stove if necessary. Serve hot.

EXCHANGES/CHOICES	3 Nonstarchy Vegetable 1/2 Fat
CALORIES	90
CALORIES FROM FAT	25
TOTAL FAT	3.0 g
SATURATED FAT	0.4 g
TRANS FAT	0.0 g
CHOLESTEROL	0 mg
SODIUM	60 mg
POTASSIUM	360 mg
TOTAL CARBOHYDRATE	13 g
DIETARY FIBER	4 g
SUGARS	6 g
PROTEIN	2 g
PHOSPHORUS	45 mg

Smoky Seafood Stew

SERVES: 6 | SERVING SIZE: 1 1/2 CUPS | PREP TIME: 1 HOUR 15 MINUTES | COOKING TIME: 45 MINUTES

This stew is great year-round, but it's best in late summer when bell peppers are extra plump and abundant at the farmers' market. When buying fresh clams, make sure they are still alive with their shells tightly closed. This recipe is my rendition of the clambakes and lobster boils I loved as a kid.

2 tablespoons Everyday Herb Oil (page 60) or extra-virgin olive oil

1 cup chopped onion

1/2 cup chopped celery

1 cup chopped red bell pepper

1/4 teaspoon fine sea salt

1/2 teaspoon freshly ground black pepper, divided

3 cloves garlic, minced

1/2 teaspoon red pepper flakes

1 teaspoon smoked paprika

1 tablespoon no-salt-added tomato paste

4 cups low-sodium vegetable broth or low-sodium seafood stock

1 (15-ounce) can no-salt-added crushed tomatoes

2 cups quartered white potatoes

1/2 teaspoon freshly grated lemon zest

1 tablespoon freshly squeezed lemon juice

1 pound littleneck clams, soaked in water for 1 hour

1/2 pound medium shrimp, peeled and deveined, tails left on

1/2 pound white fish fillets (such as hake or cod), cut into 1-inch pieces

3 tablespoons chopped fresh flat-leaf parsley

2 tablespoons chopped fresh oregano

1. Heat the oil in a large pot over medium heat. Add the onion, celery, bell pepper, salt, and black pepper, and cook, stirring occasionally, until vegetables have softened, 6–8 minutes. Add the garlic, red pepper flakes, paprika, and tomato paste. Continue to cook, stirring, for 1–2 minutes.

2. Pour in the broth and tomatoes with their juices. Bring mixture to a boil, then add the potatoes. Reduce heat to low and cover the pot. Simmer for 15–20 minutes, or until the potatoes are tender.

3. When potatoes are tender, increase heat to medium and add the lemon zest, lemon juice, and clams. Cover the pot and cook for 3 minutes. Stir in the shrimp and fish, cover again, and simmer for about 5 more minutes, until the clams open and the fish and shrimp are firm and opaque. Stir in the parsley and oregano, and serve immediately.

EXCHANGES/CHOICES	1/2 Starch
	2 Nonstarchy Vegetable
	2 Lean Protein
	1/2 Fat
CALORIES	210
CALORIES FROM FAT	50
TOTAL FAT	6.0 g
SATURATED FAT	0.8 g
TRANS FAT	0.0 g
CHOLESTEROL	70 mg
SODIUM	430 mg
POTASSIUM	915 mg
TOTAL CARBOHYDRATE	21 g
DIETARY FIBER	4 g
SUGARS	8 g
PROTEIN	18 g
PHOSPHORUS	265 mg

Gingery Chicken and Vegetable Soup

SERVES: 6 | SERVING SIZE: 1 CUP | PREP TIME: 10 MINUTES | COOKING TIME: 20 MINUTES

Over the years, I've tinkered with many different variations on chicken and vegetable soup, and eventually, this recipe emerged as the undisputed favorite. The Asian flavors of kombu, ginger, shiitake, and miso always soothe my soul after a long day, and the added boost of antioxidants, vitamins, and minerals from these ingredients may help stave off sickness when temperatures begin to drop outside.

2 teaspoons extra-virgin olive oil

1 teaspoon sesame oil

1/2 medium onion, cut into 3/4-inch dice

2 cloves garlic, thinly sliced

1 tablespoon grated fresh ginger

5 cups water

1 (1-inch) piece kombu (seaweed)

1 celery stalk, thinly sliced

1/2 medium carrot, halved lengthwise and thinly sliced into half moons

10 fresh shiitake mushrooms, stems discarded, caps thinly sliced

8 ounces poached chicken, shredded

1 cup very thinly sliced bok choy or Napa cabbage

1 teaspoon tamari or low-sodium soy sauce

2–3 tablespoons white miso paste

1 scallion, thinly sliced (white and light green parts)

1. Heat the olive oil and sesame oil in a heavy, 3–4-quart saucepan over medium-high heat. Add the onion and cook, stirring constantly, until it begins to brown, about 5 minutes. Add the garlic and ginger, and cook just until they become aromatic, about 30 seconds.

2. Add the water, kombu, celery, carrot, mushrooms, and chicken, reduce heat to low, and simmer, covered, until carrot is just tender, about 5–8 minutes. Remove pan from the heat, remove and discard the kombu, and stir in the bok choy and tamari.

3. Put the miso paste in a small bowl and add 1/4 cup hot broth from the soup, whisking until the miso is fully incorporated. Stir the miso mixture into the hot soup.

4. Garnish soup with scallions and serve immediately.

EXCHANGES/CHOICES	1 Nonstarchy Vegetable
	1 Lean Protein
	1 Fat
CALORIES	130
CALORIES FROM FAT	45
TOTAL FAT	5.0 g
SATURATED FAT	1.0 g
TRANS FAT	0.0 g
CHOLESTEROL	30 mg
SODIUM	190 mg
POTASSIUM	350 mg
TOTAL CARBOHYDRATE	7 g
DIETARY FIBER	2 g
SUGARS	3 g
PROTEIN	12 g
PHOSPHORUS	120 mg

Chipotle-Chocolate Chicken and Root Vegetable Chili

SERVES: 10 | SERVING SIZE: 1 CUP | PREP TIME: 15 MINUTES | COOKING TIME: 45 MINUTES

Dessert for dinner? Yes, please! You read the title right; chocolate is the secret ingredient in this chicken chili recipe. Not only does it infuse the other ingredients with traditional mole flavor, but it also adds an extra kick of antioxidants to an already nutrient-packed meal. Cinnamon is another noteworthy ingredient in this chili; its natural sweetness pairs perfectly with root vegetables.

2 tablespoons vegetable oil

1 large yellow onion, diced

2 cloves garlic, minced

1 red bell pepper, seeded and diced

1 pound ground chicken

1/2 large sweet potato, peeled and cut into 1/2-inch pieces

1 cup chopped butternut squash (1/2-inch pieces)

2 tablespoons chili powder

2 tablespoons ground cumin

1 tablespoon dried oregano

1 tablespoon unsweetened cocoa powder

1 1/2 teaspoons ground cinnamon

1 (28-ounce) can diced tomatoes with juice

2 chipotle peppers in adobo, diced, plus 1 tablespoon adobo sauce

4 cups low-sodium chicken stock

1 (15-ounce) can mixed beans, rinsed and drained (or your bean of choice)

1. Heat the oil in a medium Dutch oven or stock pot over medium-high heat. Add the onion, garlic, and bell pepper and cook, stirring, until vegetables begin to soften, about 3 minutes. Add the chicken and sauté for 6–8 minutes, until chicken is browned and crumbled.

2. Add the sweet potato and squash and cook, stirring occasionally, for about 5 minutes. Stir in the chili powder, cumin, oregano, cocoa powder, and cinnamon, and cook for 1 minute to toast the spices.

3. Add the tomatoes, chipotle peppers, adobo sauce, and stock. Partially cover the pot, reduce heat to low, and simmer the chili until the vegetables are tender, about 30 minutes. Stir in the beans and cook, uncovered, for 10 more minutes, or until chili is heated through.

EXCHANGES/CHOICES	1/2 Starch
	2 Nonstarchy Vegetable
	1 Lean Protein
	1 Fat
CALORIES	180
CALORIES FROM FAT	60
TOTAL FAT	7.0 g
SATURATED FAT	1.5 g
TRANS FAT	0.0 g
CHOLESTEROL	40 mg
SODIUM	250 mg
POTASSIUM	765 mg
TOTAL CARBOHYDRATE	18 g
DIETARY FIBER	5 g
SUGARS	5 g
PROTEIN	13 g
PHOSPHORUS	175 mg

Chicken, Sausage, and Lentil Soup

SERVES: 6 | SERVING SIZE: 1 CUP | PREP TIME: 10 MINUTES | COOKING TIME: 50 MINUTES

It seems that every big Italian family has their own version of this old-school favorite, and this is mine. High-quality, sweet Italian chicken sausage (I like to buy it raw and take it out of the casing before cooking) has all the flavor of pork sausage but with only a fraction of the fat content. This hearty soup is bursting with flavor in each satisfying bite.

1 tablespoon extra-virgin olive oil

3/4 pound sweet Italian chicken sausage, casings removed

2 cups chopped onion

2 large cloves garlic, chopped or sliced

1 tablespoon chopped fresh thyme

1 teaspoon fennel seeds

1/8 teaspoon fine sea salt

1/2 teaspoon freshly ground black pepper

2 tablespoons no-salt-added tomato paste

1 1/2 cups dried French lentils

4 cups low-sodium chicken stock

2 cups water

3 cups chopped Swiss chard

1. Heat the olive oil in a stock pot or large Dutch oven over medium-high heat. Add the sausage and cook for 6–8 minutes, breaking it up with a wooden spoon, until it is lightly browned. Add the onions, garlic, thyme, fennel seed, salt, and pepper, and cook for 8–10 minutes, or until the vegetables have softened.

2. Stir in the tomato paste for 30 seconds, then add the lentils, stock, and water. Bring mixture to a boil, reduce heat to low, and simmer until lentils are tender, about 30 minutes. Add the chard and stir to wilt. Serve immediately.

EXCHANGES/CHOICES	2 Starch
	1 Nonstarchy Vegetable
	2 Lean Protein
	1/2 Fat
CALORIES	300
CALORIES FROM FAT	70
TOTAL FAT	8.0 g
SATURATED FAT	1.9 g
TRANS FAT	0.0 g
CHOLESTEROL	45 mg
SODIUM	450 mg
POTASSIUM	945 mg
TOTAL CARBOHYDRATE	35 g
DIETARY FIBER	12 g
SUGARS	6 g
PROTEIN	25 g
PHOSPHORUS	380 mg

Beef, Barley, and Mushroom Stew

SERVES: 8 | SERVING SIZE: 1 CUP | PREP TIME: 10 MINUTES | COOKING TIME: 2 HOURS

Is there anything cozier than the smell of beef stew bubbling on the stove? Unlike other beef stew recipes that use an unhealthy amount of meat, this one calls for just 1 pound of beef and rounds out the meaty, robust flavor with the umami flavor and great texture of the mushrooms—not to mention the barley and vegetables!

2 tablespoons extra-virgin olive oil, divided

4 cups quartered cremini mushrooms

2 tablespoons Everyday Herb Oil (page 60) or extra-virgin olive oil

2 cups diced onion

1/2 cup diced carrot

1/2 cup diced celery

2 cloves garlic, minced

1 pound lean beef round, cubed

1/4 teaspoon fine sea salt

1/2 teaspoon freshly ground black pepper

4 cups low-sodium beef stock, divided

2 cups water

1 (15-ounce) can crushed tomatoes with juice

1 cup uncooked barley

1/4 cup fresh marjoram

1/2 cup chopped fresh flat-leaf parsley

1. Heat 1 tablespoon olive oil in a 5-quart Dutch oven over medium-high heat. Add the mushrooms and sauté for 5–8 minutes or until lightly browned. Remove mushrooms from the pot and set aside in a large bowl. Add the herb oil, onion, carrot, celery, and garlic to the pot; sauté for 4 minutes, or until vegetables begin to soften. Transfer vegetable mixture to the large bowl with the mushrooms.

2. In the same pot, heat the remaining 1 tablespoon olive oil over medium-high heat. Add the beef; season with salt and pepper and cook for 3 minutes, browning meat on all sides. Add 1 cup stock to the pot, scraping the bottom to loosen any browned bits. Then add the remaining 3 cups stock, the water, and crushed tomatoes. Bring mixture to a boil; cover the pot, reduce heat to medium-low, and simmer for 1 hour, or until the beef is just tender.

3. Stir in the barley and cooked vegetable mixture; cover and cook for 30 minutes, or until the barley is tender. Remove lid, add the marjoram, and cook for an additional 15 minutes. Serve garnished with fresh parsley.

EXCHANGES/CHOICES	1 Starch
	3 Nonstarchy Vegetable
	2 Lean Protein
	1 Fat

CALORIES	270
CALORIES FROM FAT	80
TOTAL FAT	9.0 g
SATURATED FAT	1.7 g
TRANS FAT	0.1 g
CHOLESTEROL	35 mg
SODIUM	260 mg
POTASSIUM	830 mg
TOTAL CARBOHYDRATE	30 g
DIETARY FIBER	7 g
SUGARS	5 g
PROTEIN	21 g
PHOSPHORUS	295 mg

Salmon with Thyme-Roasted Grapes p. 198
Curry-Roasted Cauliflower p. 142

fish and seafood

If there is one thing I have learned from working with my clients it's that people can be intimidated by cooking fish. Fish is a nutrient-dense, lean protein that deserves to grace your plate, so my mission with the recipes in this chapter is to change people's minds about fish—to prove to you that cooking fish can be simple and quick! Did you know you can season and roast a piece of fish in less than 15 minutes? Take the Maple and Mustard Salmon (page 199), for example: you simply stir together a few household ingredients to create a glaze, coat the salmon, and into the oven it goes. You'll have dinner on your plate in no time! Don't like salmon? How about a flaky, mild white fish instead? I have you covered with a variety of flavorful sauces and toppings in these recipes that you might even dare to mix and match!

Seared Halibut with Herbed Tomato and Corn Salad

SERVES: 4 | SERVING SIZE: 1 (4-OUNCE) HALIBUT FILLET AND 1/2 CUP SALAD | PREP TIME: 10 MINUTES | COOKING TIME: 15 MINUTES

Crunchy, raw corn pairs with sweet, juicy tomatoes and a bouquet of herbs to create a vibrant salad fit for any fish. Is halibut too expensive? Opt for another mild, white-fleshed fish like cod or flounder instead.

- 4 (4-ounce) skin-on halibut fillets
- 1/2 teaspoon freshly cracked black pepper, divided
- 1/4 teaspoon fine sea salt, divided
- 1 cup fresh corn kernels (or defrosted frozen sweet corn kernels)
- 1 cup halved grape or cherry tomatoes
- 2 tablespoons thinly sliced scallions (white and light green parts)
- 1 tablespoon chopped fresh basil
- 1 tablespoon chopped fresh mint
- 1/2 teaspoon freshly grated lemon zest
- 2 tablespoons freshly squeezed lemon juice
- 1 tablespoon minced shallot
- 2 tablespoons extra-virgin olive oil, divided

1. Pat the halibut dry and season with 1/4 teaspoon pepper and 1/8 teaspoon salt.

2. In a small bowl, combine the corn, tomatoes, scallions, basil, mint, lemon zest, lemon juice, shallot, and 1 tablespoon olive oil. Season with the remaining 1/4 teaspoon pepper and 1/8 teaspoon salt. Set aside.

3. Heat the remaining 1 tablespoon olive oil in a medium sauté pan over medium-high heat. Add the fish to the pan, skin-side down. Cook for 4–5 minutes, flip the fillets, and cook for another 3–4 minutes, or until fish flakes easily with a fork.

4. Serve each halibut fillet topped with 1/2 cup of the tomato and corn salad.

EXCHANGES/CHOICES	1/2 Starch
	1 Nonstarchy Vegetable
	3 Lean Protein
	1/2 Fat
CALORIES	230
CALORIES FROM FAT	90
TOTAL FAT	10.0 g
SATURATED FAT	1.4 g
TRANS FAT	0.0 g
CHOLESTEROL	35 mg
SODIUM	210 mg
POTASSIUM	725 mg
TOTAL CARBOHYDRATE	10 g
DIETARY FIBER	2 g
SUGARS	2 g
PROTEIN	25 g
PHOSPHORUS	290 mg

Grilled Halibut with Saffron-Walnut Romesco Sauce

SERVES: 4 | SERVING SIZE: 1 (4-OUNCE) HALIBUT FILLET AND 2 TABLESPOONS SAUCE
PREP TIME: 5 MINUTES | COOKING TIME: 10 MINUTES

Cooking fish is really easy—especially if you have a go-to sauce on hand to complete the dish. This Saffron-Walnut Romesco Sauce (page 85) is nutty, sweet, and packed with immune-boosting vitamin C.

1 tablespoon freshly squeezed
    lemon juice

2 tablespoons extra-virgin olive oil

4 (4-ounce) halibut fillets

1/4 teaspoon fine sea salt

1/4 teaspoon freshly ground
    black pepper

1/2 cup Saffron-Walnut Romesco
    Sauce (page 85)

1. Preheat an outdoor grill to medium-high heat.

2. Combine the lemon juice and olive oil in a small baking dish. Add the halibut and turn to coat.

3. Remove fish from oil mixture and season with salt and pepper. Grill the halibut for 3–4 minutes per side. Serve with Saffron-Walnut Romesco Sauce.

EXCHANGES/CHOICES	3 Lean Protein
	2 1/2 Fat
CALORIES	260
CALORIES FROM FAT	140
TOTAL FAT	16.0 g
SATURATED FAT	2.0 g
TRANS FAT	0.0 g
CHOLESTEROL	35 mg
SODIUM	270 mg
POTASSIUM	625 mg
TOTAL CARBOHYDRATE	4 g
DIETARY FIBER	1 g
SUGARS	2 g
PROTEIN	25 g
PHOSPHORUS	280 mg

Roasted Halibut with Zucchini Salsa Verde

SERVES: 4 | SERVING SIZE: 1 (4-OUNCE) HALIBUT FILLET AND 2 TABLESPOONS SAUCE
PREP TIME: 5 MINUTES | COOKING TIME: 15 MINUTES

Zucchini Salsa Verde offers another unique way to fit extra vegetables into your meal. The raw zucchini adds flavor and oomph to this traditional, herbaceous Mediterranean sauce. This seemingly fancy recipe can be whipped up in about 15 minutes.

4 (4-ounce) halibut fillets

1 tablespoon extra-virgin olive oil

1/4 teaspoon fine sea salt

1/4 teaspoon freshly ground black pepper

1/2 cup Zucchini Salsa Verde (page 86)

1. Preheat the oven to 375°F.

2. Arrange the halibut fillets in a rimmed baking dish. Top with the olive oil, salt, and pepper.

3. Bake for 10–12 minutes, or until fish reaches your desired doneness. Serve topped with the Zucchini Salsa Verde.

EXCHANGES/CHOICES	3 Lean Protein
	3 Fat
CALORIES	290
CALORIES FROM FAT	180
TOTAL FAT	20.0 g
SATURATED FAT	2.7 g
TRANS FAT	0.0 g
CHOLESTEROL	35 mg
SODIUM	300 mg
POTASSIUM	620 mg
TOTAL CARBOHYDRATE	3 g
DIETARY FIBER	1 g
SUGARS	1 g
PROTEIN	24 g
PHOSPHORUS	270 mg

En Papillote Red Snapper with Cilantro Ginger Vinaigrette and Bok Choy

SERVES: 4 | SERVING SIZE: 1 (4-OUNCE) SNAPPER FILLET AND 2 TABLESPOONS VINAIGRETTE
PREP TIME: 10 MINUTES | COOKING TIME: 25–30 MINUTES

This recipe is proof that you do not need a buttery, rich sauce to make your fish taste delicious. Bright and acidic, this punchy vinaigrette plays perfectly with the sweetness of the snapper and the crunch of the bok choy. Plus, cooking in parchment packets, or *en papillote*, is a healthy, mess-free alternative to traditional roasting or steaming methods.

Parchment paper

4 heads baby bok choy, quartered lengthwise

4 (4-ounce) fillets skin-on red snapper

1/4 teaspoon fine sea salt

1/4 teaspoon freshly ground black pepper

1/2 cup Cilantro Ginger Vinaigrette (page 88)

1/4 cup chopped scallions (green parts only)

1. Preheat the oven to 400°F.

2. Fold 4 (18-inch-long) pieces of parchment paper in half, then open and lay them flat on your work surface. On 1/2 of each of the parchment pieces, place 4 pieces of bok choy. Top each serving of bok choy with 1 snapper fillet. Season each piece of fish with salt, pepper, and 2 tablespoons vinaigrette.

3. Fold the other half of each parchment paper sheet over the ingredients. Make small, overlapping folds to seal the edges, forming packets. Twist the ends to firmly close each packet.

4. Place packets on a rimmed baking sheet and bake for 25–30 minutes, or until fish is opaque, flaky, and cooked through. Transfer fillets to a plate; spoon cooking liquid and bok choy pieces on top. Garnish with scallions and serve.

EXCHANGES/CHOICES	3 Lean Protein
	2 Fat
CALORIES	240
CALORIES FROM FAT	140
TOTAL FAT	15.0 g
SATURATED FAT	2.2 g
TRANS FAT	0.0 g
CHOLESTEROL	40 mg
SODIUM	330 mg
POTASSIUM	490 mg
TOTAL CARBOHYDRATE	1 g
DIETARY FIBER	0 g
SUGARS	0 g
PROTEIN	23 g
PHOSPHORUS	180 mg

Cucumber Relish

SERVES: 8 | SERVING SIZE: 1/4 CUP
PREP TIME: 5 MINUTES
REFRIGERATION TIME: 1 HOUR

1 English cucumber, diced

1/4 teaspoon fine sea salt

1/4 teaspoon freshly ground pepper

1 tablespoon unseasoned
   rice wine vinegar

1 tablespoon freshly squeezed
   orange juice

1 teaspoon freshly grated orange zest

1 teaspoon black sesame seeds

1/4 cup thinly sliced scallions
   (green part only)

1. Thoroughly combine all
   ingredients in a bowl. Cover and
   refrigerate for 1 hour prior to use.
   Store in a sealed container in the
   refrigerator for 2–3 days.

EXCHANGES/CHOICES	Free food
CALORIES	15
CALORIES FROM FAT	0
TOTAL FAT	0.0 g
SATURATED FAT	0.0 g
TRANS FAT	0.0 g
CHOLESTEROL	0 mg
SODIUM	70 mg
POTASSIUM	95 mg
TOTAL CARBOHYDRATE	3 g
DIETARY FIBER	0 g
SUGARS	1 g
PROTEIN	0 g
PHOSPHORUS	15 mg

Sesame Orange Miso Cod with Cucumber Relish

SERVES: 4 | SERVING SIZE: 1 (4-OUNCE) COD FILLET AND 1/4 CUP RELISH
PREP TIME: 10 MINUTES | COOKING TIME: 15 MINUTES

Savory and salty miso comes alive with the sweetness of citrus and the crunch of cucumber relish. This dish, with its well-rounded flavors, is both refreshing and satisfying.

2 tablespoons freshly squeezed
   orange juice

1 teaspoon freshly grated orange zest

2 tablespoons rice wine vinegar

1 tablespoon white miso

1 teaspoon honey

4 (4-ounce) skinless cod fillets

1 tablespoon extra-virgin olive oil

1 teaspoon black sesame seeds

1 cup Cucumber Relish (at left)

1. Preheat the oven to broil on the high setting. Set a rack 12 inches from the heat source. Line a rimmed baking sheet with parchment paper.

2. In a small bowl, whisk together the orange juice, zest, vinegar, miso, and honey. Set aside.

3. Arrange the fish fillets on the baking sheet lined with olive oil–coated parchment paper. Brush fillets generously with the miso glaze, then sprinkle with the sesame seeds.

4. Broil fish until the fillets are browned on top and opaque throughout, 8–10 minutes. Remove from oven, garnish with the relish, and serve immediately.

EXCHANGES/CHOICES	1/2 Carbohydrate 3 Lean Protein
CALORIES	160
CALORIES FROM FAT	45
TOTAL FAT	5.0 g
SATURATED FAT	0.7 g
TRANS FAT	0.0 g
CHOLESTEROL	50 mg
SODIUM	220 mg
POTASSIUM	340 mg
TOTAL CARBOHYDRATE	7 g
DIETARY FIBER	1 g
SUGARS	5 g
PROTEIN	21 g
PHOSPHORUS	155 mg

Grilled Fish Tacos with Strawberry-Mango Salsa

SERVES: 4 | SERVING SIZE: 2 TACOS AND 1/4 CUP SALSA | PREP TIME: 30 MINUTES | COOKING TIME: 15 MINUTES

This fish taco recipe becomes extra lively when you top if off with juicy strawberry-mango salsa. The sweet berries and tropical mango are the perfect combo for this festive summer dish.

FISH TACOS

1 tablespoon extra-virgin olive oil

2 tablespoons freshly squeezed lime juice

1 teaspoon freshly grated lime zest

1/4 teaspoon chipotle chili powder

1/2 teaspoon ground cumin

1/4 teaspoon fine sea salt

1/4 teaspoon freshly ground black pepper

1 pound cod (or similar flaky white fish)

8 corn tortillas

SALSA

1/2 cup chopped strawberries

1/2 cup chopped mango

1 small shallot, minced

1/4 teaspoon freshly grated lime zest

2 tablespoons freshly squeezed lime juice

1/4 cup chopped fresh cilantro

1. In a medium bowl, whisk together the oil, lime juice, lime zest, chili powder, cumin, salt, and pepper. Add the cod and marinate in the refrigerator for 15–20 minutes.

2. While fish is marinating, stir together all the salsa ingredients in a medium bowl.

3. Preheat an outdoor grill or grill pan to medium-high heat.

4. Remove the cod from the marinade and grill for 3–4 minutes on one side. Then flip and grill 1–2 minutes on the other side, or until fish flakes easily with a fork.

5. Transfer the cod to a plate and let it rest for 5 minutes, then use a fork to flake it into bite-size pieces.

6. Working in batches if necessary, grill the tortillas for 20 seconds each. Divide the fish evenly among the tortillas, garnish with the salsa (about 2 tablespoons per taco), and serve.

EXCHANGES/CHOICES	1 1/2 Starch
	1/2 Fruit
	3 Lean Protein
CALORIES	260
CALORIES FROM FAT	40
TOTAL FAT	4.5 g
SATURATED FAT	0.6 g
TRANS FAT	0.0 g
CHOLESTEROL	50 mg
SODIUM	170 mg
POTASSIUM	415 mg
TOTAL CARBOHYDRATE	31 g
DIETARY FIBER	4 g
SUGARS	5 g
PROTEIN	24 g
PHOSPHORUS	300 mg

Lemon Sole with Roasted Tomato and Grapefruit Salsa

SERVES: 4 | SERVING SIZE: 1 (4-OUNCE) SOLE FILLET AND 1/2 CUP SALSA | PREP TIME: 10 MINUTES | COOKING TIME: 30 MINUTES

Oven-roasted tomatoes are like nature's candy. Their natural sweetness calms the tart overtones of the grapefruit in this recipe to create a simple yet exciting dish.

1 cup halved grape tomatoes

2 tablespoons extra-virgin olive oil, divided

1/4 teaspoon fine sea salt, divided

1/2 teaspoon freshly ground black pepper, divided

2 cloves garlic, halved

4 (4-ounce) lemon sole fillets

2 tablespoons freshly squeezed lemon juice, divided

1 teaspoon freshly grated lemon zest

2 tablespoons chopped fresh chives

1 red grapefruit, segmented and chopped (about 1 cup)

1. Preheat the oven to 425°F. Line two rimmed baking sheets with parchment paper.

2. In a medium bowl, toss the tomatoes with 1 tablespoon olive oil and season with 1/8 teaspoon salt and 1/4 teaspoon pepper. Add the garlic and toss to combine. Arrange the mixture in a single layer on one of the prepared baking sheets. Roast the tomatoes for 20–25 minutes, or until lightly browned.

3. While the tomatoes are roasting, place the sole on the other prepared baking sheet. Season the fish with the remaining 1/8 teaspoon salt and 1/4 teaspoon black pepper, the remaining 1 tablespoon olive oil, and 1 tablespoon lemon juice. Roast the fish for 8–10 minutes, or until it flakes easily with a fork.

4. Remove tomatoes from the oven and return them to their original bowl. Toss with the remaining 1 tablespoon lemon juice, the lemon zest, chives, and grapefruit segments. Set aside.

5. When fish is cooked, serve topped with the tomato-grapefruit salsa.

EXCHANGES/CHOICES	1/2 Carbohydrate
	3 Lean Protein
	1/2 Fat
CALORIES	200
CALORIES FROM FAT	70
TOTAL FAT	8.0 g
SATURATED FAT	1.3 g
TRANS FAT	0.0 g
CHOLESTEROL	60 mg
SODIUM	250 mg
POTASSIUM	515 mg
TOTAL CARBOHYDRATE	8 g
DIETARY FIBER	1 g
SUGARS	5 g
PROTEIN	22 g
PHOSPHORUS	275 mg

Turbot with Lemony Wild Mushroom and Leek Sauté

SERVES: 6 | SERVING SIZE: 1 (4-OUNCE) TURBOT FILLET AND 1/2 CUP MUSHROOMS
PREP TIME: 10 MINUTES | COOKING TIME: ABOUT 15 MINUTES

Buttery turbot becomes even more soulful when it is topped with earthy mushrooms and sweet leeks. This is the perfect fish recipe for a cool fall evening. The flavors feel decadent and cozy, yet the dish is healthy and nourishing.

FISH

6 (4-ounce) turbot fillets

1 tablespoon extra-virgin olive oil

2 tablespoons freshly squeezed lemon juice

1 teaspoon freshly grated lemon zest

1/4 teaspoon fine sea salt

1/4 teaspoon freshly ground black pepper

MUSHROOM AND LEEK SAUTÉ

1 tablespoon Everyday Herb Oil (page 60)

1 cup halved and sliced leek (white part only)

3 cups wild mushrooms, sliced

1 tablespoon freshly grated lemon zest

1/4 cup chopped fresh flat-leaf parsley

1/4 teaspoon fine sea salt

1/4 teaspoon freshly ground black pepper

1. Preheat the oven to 375°F.

2. Place turbot fillets on a parchment paper–lined baking sheet. Top with the remaining fish ingredients. Roast fillets for 10–12 minutes, or until they reach your desired doneness.

3. While the fish is cooking, heat the herb oil in a medium sauté pan over medium-high heat. Add the leeks and sauté for 2–3 minutes. Add the mushrooms and cook for 3–5 minutes, or until mushrooms are browned and tender. Add the lemon zest, parsley, salt, and pepper, and stir to combine.

4. Remove turbot fillets from the oven. Serve with mushroom/leek mixture.

EXCHANGES/CHOICES	1 Nonstarchy Vegetable
	3 Lean Protein
	1/2 Fat
CALORIES	170
CALORIES FROM FAT	70
TOTAL FAT	8.0 g
SATURATED FAT	1.3 g
TRANS FAT	0.0 g
CHOLESTEROL	55 mg
SODIUM	360 mg
POTASSIUM	435 mg
TOTAL CARBOHYDRATE	5 g
DIETARY FIBER	1 g
SUGARS	1 g
PROTEIN	19 g
PHOSPHORUS	190 mg

Grilled Spice-Rubbed Salmon

SERVES: 4 | SERVING SIZE: 1 (4-OUNCE) PIECE OF SALMON | PREP TIME: 20 MINUTES | COOKING TIME: 15 MINUTES

This salmon is a favorite in my house. I am always amazed at the vibrancy of flavor that the spices impart to the fish. Save yourself some time and mix up a large batch of the spice blend so you'll have some on hand for other dishes. It's great on vegetables and other animal proteins. This is my go-to grilled salmon recipe.

1 pound skin-on wild salmon, cut into 4 (4-ounce) pieces

1 teaspoon extra-virgin olive oil

1/4 teaspoon fine sea salt

1/4 teaspoon freshly ground black pepper

1/2 teaspoon fennel seeds

1/2 teaspoon freshly grated lime zest

1 tablespoon red wine vinegar

1 teaspoon honey

1 teaspoon ground cumin

1 teaspoon smoked paprika

1 tablespoon finely chopped fresh oregano

4 lime wedges

1. Preheat an outdoor grill or grill pan to medium-high.

2. Brush the salmon pieces with the olive oil and season all over with the salt and pepper. Set aside.

3. In a small bowl, combine the fennel seeds (rub them in the palms of your hands first to release their oils), lime zest, vinegar, honey, cumin, paprika, and oregano to create a paste. Brush the spice mixture generously over the flesh side of the salmon, then place the salmon flesh-side up in an airtight container and let it marinate in the refrigerator for 15 minutes.

4. Place the salmon skin-side up on an oiled grill or grill rack; cover and cook until the edges begin to turn pink, about 6 minutes. Flip salmon and cook for another 3–5 minutes, or until it reaches your desired doneness.

5. Remove salmon from the grill and serve with lime wedges (for squeezing over the fish).

EXCHANGES/CHOICES	3 Lean Protein
	1 Fat
CALORIES	190
CALORIES FROM FAT	80
TOTAL FAT	9.0 g
SATURATED FAT	1.9 g
TRANS FAT	0.0 g
CHOLESTEROL	65 mg
SODIUM	230 mg
POTASSIUM	445 mg
TOTAL CARBOHYDRATE	2 g
DIETARY FIBER	1 g
SUGARS	2 g
PROTEIN	23 g
PHOSPHORUS	315 mg

Steamed Cod with Basil and Caper Dressing

SERVES: 4 | SERVING SIZE: 1 (4-OUNCE) COD FILLET AND 2 TABLESPOONS DRESSING
PREP TIME: 10 MINUTES | COOKING TIME: 15 MINUTES

Simple steamed cod becomes extraordinary once it is drizzled with the robust dressing in this recipe. You can even use any leftover dressing for salads, vegetables, or as a marinade for tomorrow night's meal.

1 tablespoon chopped shallot

1 teaspoon chopped capers

1 teaspoon freshly grated lemon zest

1 tablespoon freshly squeezed lemon juice

2 tablespoons white wine vinegar

2 tablespoons extra-virgin olive oil

1/2 cup chopped fresh basil, divided

1/3 cup chopped fresh tomato

1/4 teaspoon fine sea salt

1/4 teaspoon freshly ground black pepper

4 (4-ounce) cod fillets

1. Preheat the oven to 400 F.

2. In a small bowl, combine the shallot, capers, lemon zest, lemon juice, vinegar, olive oil, 1/4 cup basil, tomato, salt, and pepper. Set aside.

3. Prepare 4 pieces of aluminum foil or parchment paper that are twice as long as each cod fillet. Place each piece of cod on a piece of foil. Top each fillet with about 2 tablespoons of the dressing.

4. Fold the foil or parchment paper into packets, making sure to seal the edges tightly. Bake for 15 minutes.

5. Remove fish from oven (use caution when opening the packets), top with remaining basil, and serve.

EXCHANGES/CHOICES	3 Lean Protein
	1/2 Fat
CALORIES	160
CALORIES FROM FAT	70
TOTAL FAT	8.0 g
SATURATED FAT	0.9 g
TRANS FAT	0.0 g
CHOLESTEROL	50 mg
SODIUM	220 mg
POTASSIUM	545 mg
TOTAL CARBOHYDRATE	2 g
DIETARY FIBER	1 g
SUGARS	1 g
PROTEIN	20 g
PHOSPHORUS	240 mg

Salmon with Thyme-Roasted Grapes

SERVES: 4 | SERVING SIZE: 1 (5-OUNCE) SALMON FILLET AND 1/4 CUP ROASTED GRAPES
PREP TIME: 5 MINUTES | COOKING TIME: 30 MINUTES

Grapes are not just for snacking! Sweet, juicy, and succulent, they are divine when roasted. I love pairing grapes with savory herbs like fresh oregano or, in this dish, thyme.

2 cups red grapes, stems removed

2 tablespoons extra-virgin olive oil, divided

2 cloves garlic, sliced

3 sprigs thyme, leaves removed from stem

1/4 teaspoon fine sea salt, divided

1/4 teaspoon freshly ground black pepper, divided

4 (5-ounce) salmon fillets

1. Preheat the oven to 450 F.

2. In a small bowl, toss grapes with 1 tablespoon olive oil, garlic, thyme, 1/8 teaspoon salt, and 1/8 teaspoon pepper. Arrange the grapes in a rimmed baking dish and roast for 20 minutes, or until slightly brown and bursting.

3. While the grapes are roasting, arrange the salmon fillets on a rimmed baking sheet. Drizzle with remaining olive oil and season with remaining salt and pepper.

4. Once the grapes are roasted, remove from the oven. Decrease oven temperature to 400°F and roast the salmon for 10–12 minutes, or until salmon reached your desired doneness.

5. Remove salmon from the oven, top with the roasted grapes, and serve.

tip: Did you know you can use grapes in place of tomatoes in many recipes? They have a similar flavor profile. Give it a try!

EXCHANGES/CHOICES	1 Fruit
	4 Lean Protein
	2 Fat
CALORIES	320
CALORIES FROM FAT	140
TOTAL FAT	16.0 g
SATURATED FAT	3.2 g
TRANS FAT	0.0 g
CHOLESTEROL	80 mg
SODIUM	230 mg
POTASSIUM	670 mg
TOTAL CARBOHYDRATE	14 g
DIETARY FIBER	1 g
SUGARS	12 g
PROTEIN	29 g
PHOSPHORUS	405 mg

Maple and Mustard Salmon

SERVES: 4 | SERVING SIZE: 1 (4-OUNCE) FILLET | PREP TIME: 5 MINUTES | COOKING TIME: 15 MINUTES

Say hello to your new weeknight meal staple! Ready in about 15 minutes, this crowd-pleasing salmon dish uses ingredients that you probably already have in your pantry. That means you can whip it up in a snap any night of the week.

1 tablespoon pure maple syrup
   (preferably grade B)
2 teaspoons Dijon mustard
2 teaspoons whole-grain mustard
1 teaspoon freshly grated orange zest
4 (4-ounce) salmon fillets

1. Preheat the oven to broil on the high setting. Line a rimmed baking sheet with parchment paper.

2. In a small bowl, whisk together the maple syrup, both mustards, and orange zest.

3. Place the salmon skin-side down on the prepared baking sheet. Spoon and spread 2 teaspoons of the maple-mustard mixture on the flesh side of each fillet.

4. Transfer baking sheet to the oven and broil on the middle rack for 8–10 minutes, or until the salmon reaches your desired doneness. Serve immediately.

EXCHANGES/CHOICES	3 Lean Protein
	1 Fat
CALORIES	190
CALORIES FROM FAT	70
TOTAL FAT	8.0 g
SATURATED FAT	1.8 g
TRANS FAT	0.0 g
CHOLESTEROL	65 mg
SODIUM	180 mg
POTASSIUM	430 mg
TOTAL CARBOHYDRATE	4 g
DIETARY FIBER	0 g
SUGARS	3 g
PROTEIN	23 g
PHOSPHORUS	315 mg

Shrimp Saganaki

SERVES: 4 | SERVING SIZE: 4–5 SHRIMP, 1/2 CUP SAUCE, AND 1/2 OUNCE CHEESE
PREP TIME: 15 MINUTES | COOKING TIME: 15 MINUTES

This quick and easy recipe was inspired by a trip I took to Greece. I love the fresh flavors and simplicity of the ingredients. This recipe uses lots of herbs to create flavor and brighten the heartier aspects of the dish. Trust me, it is delicious!

1 tablespoon extra-virgin olive oil

3/4 cup thinly sliced yellow onions

1 clove garlic, thinly sliced

1/2 teaspoon red pepper flakes

1 pound U16–20 shrimp, peeled and deveined (tails left on)

1 cup halved grape or cherry tomatoes

1/4 cup pitted kalamata olives, rinsed

1/2 cup low-sodium vegetable broth

1 tablespoon chopped fresh oregano

1 tablespoon chopped fresh dill

1 tablespoon chopped fresh flat-leaf parsley

2 ounces reduced-fat feta cheese, crumbled

1/8 teaspoon fine sea salt

1/4 teaspoon freshly ground black pepper

1. Heat the olive oil in a large skillet over medium-high heat. Add the onion, garlic, and red pepper flakes, and cook for about 5 minutes, or until onion is soft.

2. Add the shrimp, tomatoes, olives, stock, and oregano, and cook for 3–5 minutes, stirring occasionally, until shrimp are pink and almost completely opaque. Add the dill, parsley, and feta, and cook for 1–2 minutes to heat through.

3. Remove skillet from the heat. Season with the salt and pepper and serve hot.

EXCHANGES/CHOICES	1 Nonstarchy Vegetable
	2 Lean Protein
	1 Fat
CALORIES	170
CALORIES FROM FAT	70
TOTAL FAT	8.0 g
SATURATED FAT	1.8 g
TRANS FAT	0.0 g
CHOLESTEROL	125 mg
SODIUM	420 mg
POTASSIUM	350 mg
TOTAL CARBOHYDRATE	6 g
DIETARY FIBER	2 g
SUGARS	2 g
PROTEIN	19 g
PHOSPHORUS	230 mg

Oven-Roasted Shrimp with Chive and Lemon Pistou

SERVES: 4 | SERVING SIZE: 4–5 SHRIMP AND 2 TABLESPOONS SAUCE | PREP TIME: 10 MINUTES | COOKING TIME: 10 MINUTES

Have you ever tried roasted shrimp? If not, prepare yourself to be wowed—they are so simple, tender, and juicy. Roasting shrimp is fairly mess free and super quick; they cook in less than 10 minutes. I have been known to make a large batch of roasted shrimp to enjoy throughout the week.

- 1 pound U16–20 shrimp, peeled and deveined
- 1 tablespoon extra-virgin olive oil
- 1 teaspoon freshly grated lemon zest
- 1 cup Everyday Roasted Tomatoes (page 65)
- 1/4 teaspoon fine sea salt
- 1/4 teaspoon freshly ground black pepper
- 1/2 cup Chive and Lemon Pistou (page 83)

1. Preheat the oven to 400°F.

2. In a medium bowl, combine the shrimp, olive oil, lemon zest, tomatoes, salt, and pepper.

3. Arrange the shrimp mixture in a single layer on a parchment paper–lined baking sheet, and roast for 6–8 minutes, or until shrimp are pink, firm, and cooked through.

4. Set aside to cool slightly. Serve with the pistou.

EXCHANGES/CHOICES	1 Nonstarchy Vegetable
	2 Lean Protein
	1 1/2 Fat
CALORIES	180
CALORIES FROM FAT	100
TOTAL FAT	11.0 g
SATURATED FAT	1.5 g
TRANS FAT	0.0 g
CHOLESTEROL	120 mg
SODIUM	430 mg
POTASSIUM	415 mg
TOTAL CARBOHYDRATE	5 g
DIETARY FIBER	2 g
SUGARS	2 g
PROTEIN	17 g
PHOSPHORUS	180 mg

Curried Scallops with Mango and Apple Slaw

SERVES: 4 | SERVING SIZE: 3 SCALLOPS AND 1/2 CUP SLAW | PREP TIME: 15 MINUTES | COOKING TIME: 4 MINUTES

What is the key to a great scallop dish? Buy scallops fresh, pat them dry before cooking, and only flip them once while cooking. The scallops in this recipe are dusted with curry spices then paired with a sweet and tangy slaw of mango and apples. Yum!

SCALLOPS

12 large sea scallops

1/8 teaspoon fine sea salt

1/4 teaspoon freshly ground black pepper

1 tablespoon curry powder

1 tablespoon extra-virgin olive oil

SLAW

1/2 cup peeled and julienned large Granny Smith apple (matchsticks)

1/2 cup peeled and julienned mango (matchsticks)

1/2 teaspoon grated fresh ginger

1 tablespoon freshly squeezed lime juice

1/2 teaspoon freshly grated lime zest

1/4 cup chopped fresh cilantro

1/4 teaspoon fine sea salt

1/4 teaspoon freshly ground black pepper

1. Remove the muscle from the side of each scallop. Pat scallops dry using a kitchen towel or paper towel. Season with salt and pepper.

2. Spread the curry powder onto a plate, and coat the top and bottom of each scallop with the curry powder by gently pressing onto the plate.

3. Add the olive oil to a 12-inch nonstick skillet and heat over medium heat until hot. Cook the scallops, without crowding the pan, on one side for 2 minutes, or until golden brown. Then flip the scallops and cook an additional 1–2 minutes.

4. In a small bowl, combine all the slaw ingredients. Serve over the cooked scallops.

EXCHANGES/CHOICES	1 Carbohydrate
	2 Lean Protein
CALORIES	140
CALORIES FROM FAT	40
TOTAL FAT	4.5 g
SATURATED FAT	0.7 g
TRANS FAT	0.0 g
CHOLESTEROL	30 mg
SODIUM	400 mg
POTASSIUM	315 mg
TOTAL CARBOHYDRATE	11 g
DIETARY FIBER	1 g
SUGARS	5 g
PROTEIN	15 g
PHOSPHORUS	320 mg

Pasta with Cannellini Beans, Greens, Seared Scallops, and Pesto

SERVES: 4 | SERVING SIZE: 4 SCALLOPS AND 2 CUPS PASTA/VEGETABLE MIXTURE
PREP TIME: 10 MINUTES | COOKING TIME: 25–30 MINUTES

I love adding beans to pasta. It's a great way to increase the protein and fiber content of your meal. Cannellini beans are really creamy and rich so they add a lovely texture to this dish. Bitter greens like kale and arugula add a pop of green and a boost of nutrients that pair perfectly with the pesto and sweet seared scallops.

12 large sea scallops

1 cup whole-wheat fusilli

2 tablespoons extra-virgin olive oil, divided

1/4 teaspoon red pepper flakes

1 cup sliced yellow onion

1/2 cup freshly squeezed lemon juice

1 tablespoon freshly grated lemon zest

3/4 cup BPA-free canned cannellini beans, rinsed and drained

2 cups baby arugula

2 cups chopped kale

6 tablespoons Walnut Arugula Pesto (page 81)

1. Remove the muscle from the side of each scallop. Pat the scallops dry with a kitchen towel or a paper towel and refrigerate until ready to use.

2. Bring 4 cups of water to a boil in a medium saucepan. Cook the fusilli for 8–10 minutes, or until it reaches your desired doneness. Drain the pasta, reserving 1/2 cup of the pasta cooking water, and set pasta aside.

3. To a large sauté pan over medium heat, add 1 tablespoon olive oil, red pepper flakes, and onion. Sauté for 2–3 minutes to soften onion. Add the reserved pasta water, lemon juice, and lemon zest, and simmer for 2–3 minutes to reduce liquid. Add the cannellini beans, baby arugula, and kale, and sauté for another 2–3 minutes to wilt. Add the cooked pasta and pesto and reduce heat to low for 1–2 minutes, then turn off the heat and cover. Set aside while cooking the scallops.

4. Meanwhile, in a separate sauté pan, heat the remaining 1 tablespoon olive oil. Add scallops to the pan in a single layer. Cook about 2 minutes, or until golden brown on the bottom side, then flip with tongs and cook an additional 1–2 minutes.

5. Serve the scallops over the pasta mixture.

EXCHANGES/CHOICES	1 1/2 Starch
	1/2 Carbohydrate
	1 Nonstarchy Vegetable
	2 Lean Protein
	3 Fat

CALORIES	390
CALORIES FROM FAT	190
TOTAL FAT	21.0 g
SATURATED FAT	3.1 g
TRANS FAT	0.0 g
CHOLESTEROL	30 mg
SODIUM	330 mg
POTASSIUM	640 mg
TOTAL CARBOHYDRATE	32 g
DIETARY FIBER	6 g
SUGARS	3 g
PROTEIN	23 g
PHOSPHORUS	455 mg

Roasted Moroccan Turkey Breast with Root Vegetables p. 208
Grilled Asparagus with Orange Zest and Chive p. 136

lean meats and poultry

Look around—it's hard not to be inspired by your lush garden or your local farmers' market overflowing with colorful produce, but for most omnivores, the idea of planning a meal around carrots sounds, well, lackluster at best. Fortunately, a vegetable-centric plate can include lean meats and poultry, too. The key is mindfully rearranging your plate so that the veggies are the star and the animal proteins play a supporting role.

Why is it so important to eat mindfully? By purposefully changing the way we view our plate, we can continue to enjoy all of the foods we love, including meat and poultry, in conjunction with a plentitude of nourishing, plant-based foods. Slow down and savor your food, and a few ounces of animal protein will feel just as satisfying as a whole plateful.

In this chapter, you will find healthful recipes to appease even the staunchest meat lovers in your life—from comfort-food staples like meat loaf and Bolognese, to summery kabobs, wintry braises, and elegant date-night eats.

Turkey and Quinoa Meat Loaf

SERVES: 6 | SERVING SIZE: 4 OUNCES MEAT LOAF | PREP TIME: 10 MINUTES | COOKING TIME: 25–30 MINUTES

This play on a traditional meat loaf quickly became a favorite in our house. In this recipe, quinoa (a gluten-free grain) takes the place of bread crumbs to bind the ingredients together and lock in moisture. Fresh vegetables add natural flavor and a satisfying texture to each bite of this dish. For easy weekday meals, combine the ingredients ahead of time and store the meat loaf mixture in an airtight container in the freezer for up to 1 month. Then you can just defrost and cook on a busy night!

1 large egg

1/4 red bell pepper, seeded and chopped

1 small shallot, peeled

1 clove garlic, peeled

1 (2-inch) piece carrot, peeled and shredded

1 tablespoon Everyday Herb Oil (page 60)

1/2 cup cooked quinoa (see page 157 for cooking instructions)

1 1/2 pounds ground turkey breast

1/4 teaspoon fine sea salt

1/4 teaspoon freshly ground black pepper

1. Preheat the oven to 375°F. Line a rimmed baking sheet with parchment paper.

2. In a blender or food processor, combine the egg, bell pepper, shallot, garlic, carrot, and herb oil; purée until smooth.

3. Transfer the puréed vegetable mixture to a large bowl and add the cooked quinoa and ground turkey. Season with salt and pepper and mix well to combine.

4. On the prepared baking sheet, form the meat mixture into a loaf about 4 inches wide and 1–2 inches high. Bake the meat loaf, uncovered, for 25–30 minutes, or until cooked through. Serve hot.

EXCHANGES/CHOICES	1/2 Carbohydrate
	4 Lean Protein
CALORIES	200
CALORIES FROM FAT	50
TOTAL FAT	6.0 g
SATURATED FAT	1.3 g
TRANS FAT	0.0 g
CHOLESTEROL	95 mg
SODIUM	160 mg
POTASSIUM	405 mg
TOTAL CARBOHYDRATE	5 g
DIETARY FIBER	1 g
SUGARS	1 g
PROTEIN	31 g
PHOSPHORUS	310 mg

Turkey and Lentil Bolognese

SERVES: 6 | SERVING SIZE: 1 1/2 CUPS PASTA MIXTURE | PREP TIME: 10 MINUTES | COOKING TIME: 1 HOUR

Every Italian cook needs a go-to recipe for Bolognese, and this is mine. Ground turkey is much leaner than the traditional mix of beef, pork, and veal, and turkey's milder flavor is complemented by bright vegetables like bell pepper, carrot, and celery. I also add a generous helping of earthy lentils to my Bolognese to cut the fat content and add richness as well as an extra boost of protein.

2 tablespoons extra-virgin olive oil

3/4 pound ground turkey breast

1 cup chopped onion

1/2 cup finely chopped carrot

1/2 cup finely chopped celery

1/2 cup finely chopped red bell pepper

4 cloves garlic, minced

1/4 teaspoon fine sea salt

1/4 teaspoon freshly ground black pepper

1 tablespoon tomato paste

1 (28-ounce) can low-sodium crushed tomatoes with juice

1 cup water

1 tablespoon dried oregano

1/2 cup French lentils

1 cup dried whole-grain pasta (such as fusilli)

1/2 cup chopped fresh basil

1. Heat the oil in a large Dutch oven over medium-high heat. Add the ground turkey and sauté for 5–8 minutes, or until it is no longer pink. Using a slotted spoon or spatula, transfer the cooked turkey to a paper towel–lined plate and set aside.

2. To the same Dutch oven, add the onion, carrot, celery, bell pepper, garlic, salt, and pepper, and cook over medium-low heat until vegetables soften, about 15 minutes.

3. Increase heat to medium-high and add the tomato paste. Cook for 2–3 minutes, stirring constantly, then add the tomatoes with their juice, water, and oregano. Cover the pot and cook for 10 minutes. Stir in the lentils and cooked turkey, cover the pot again, and cook for 20–25 minutes, or until lentils are tender.

4. Meanwhile, bring a large pot of water to a boil over high heat and cook the pasta to al dente according to the package instructions.

5. Add the pasta to the sauce and stir to combine. Garnish with basil right before serving.

EXCHANGES/CHOICES	1 Starch
	3 Nonstarchy Vegetable
	2 Lean Protein
	1/2 Fat

CALORIES	280
CALORIES FROM FAT	60
TOTAL FAT	7.0 g
SATURATED FAT	1.1 g
TRANS FAT	0.0 g
CHOLESTEROL	30 mg
SODIUM	170 mg
POTASSIUM	900 mg
TOTAL CARBOHYDRATE	31 g
DIETARY FIBER	8 g
SUGARS	8 g
PROTEIN	23 g
PHOSPHORUS	305 mg

Roasted Moroccan Turkey Breast with Root Vegetables

SERVES: 12 | SERVING SIZE: 4 OUNCES TURKEY AND 1/2 CUP ROOT VEGETABLES
PREP TIME: 15 MINUTES | COOKING TIME: 1 HOUR PLUS 20 MINUTES RESTING TIME

Moroccan spices, such as cinnamon, cardamom, cumin, and coriander, are ideal seasonings for roasted vegetables and meats. During roasting, they coax the sweetness and deep flavors out of whatever they're coating, and their rich, warm flavors transport the taste buds to exotic locales. Make this dish in the winter when oranges are in season and cabin fever has begun to set in.

1 (4-pound) bone-in, skin-on turkey breast

3 tablespoons extra-virgin olive oil, divided

1 teaspoon fine sea salt, divided

1 teaspoon freshly ground black pepper, divided

2 tablespoons Moroccan Spice Blend (page 73)

5 cloves garlic, smashed

1 onion, halved, peeled, and then quartered

3 celery ribs, trimmed and cut into thirds

2 cups peeled, chopped carrots (cut into 2-inch pieces)

2 cups peeled, chopped rutabaga (cut into 2-inch pieces)

1 cup peeled, chopped turnip (cut into 2-inch pieces)

1 cup peeled, chopped sweet potato (cut into 2-inch pieces)

1 tablespoon chopped fresh oregano

1 tablespoon freshly grated orange zest

1 orange, halved and then quartered

1 teaspoon cumin

1/2 teaspoon mild or hot smoked paprika

1. Preheat the oven to 425°F.

2. Loosen the skin from the turkey breast by gently pushing your fingers between the skin and the meat. Season under the skin with 1 tablespoon olive oil, 1/2 teaspoon salt, and 1/2 teaspoon pepper. Rub the spice blend under and over the loosened skin and then set the turkey breast in a roasting pan.

3. In a small bowl, toss together the remaining oil, the remaining salt and pepper, the garlic, onion, celery, carrots, rutabaga, turnip, sweet potato, oregano, orange zest, orange, cumin, and smoked paprika. Arrange the vegetable mixture in a single layer around the turkey breast.

4. Transfer the pan to the oven and roast the turkey and vegetables, uncovered, for 15 minutes. Cover the pan loosely with foil. Reduce the oven temperature to 325°F and roast for an additional 30–45 minutes, or until an instant-read thermometer inserted into the meaty part of the turkey breast registers 165°F.

5. Remove pan from oven, transfer the turkey to a cutting board, and tent it loosely with foil. Let the turkey rest for 20 minutes, then discard the skin and slice the meat.

6. Remove and discard the oranges from the roasted vegetables, give vegetables a good stir, and serve them with the sliced turkey.

EXCHANGES/CHOICES	2 Nonstarchy Vegetable
	3 Lean Protein
CALORIES	200
CALORIES FROM FAT	40
TOTAL FAT	4.5 g
SATURATED FAT	0.7 g
TRANS FAT	0.0 g
CHOLESTEROL	75 mg
SODIUM	280 mg
POTASSIUM	540 mg
TOTAL CARBOHYDRATE	10 g
DIETARY FIBER	3 g
SUGARS	4 g
PROTEIN	28 g
PHOSPHORUS	235 mg

Chicken Sausage and Sweet Potato Cassoulet

SERVES: 6 | SERVING SIZE: 1 CUP | PREP TIME: 10 MINUTES | COOKING TIME: 1 HOUR 15 MINUTES

Cassoulet is a classic French casserole of white beans, meat, and herbs that is baked slowly in a covered dish to harmonize the different flavors. In my version of this dish, I use chicken sausage (instead of pork sausage), lots of nutrient-packed sweet potatoes, creamy cannellini beans, and fresh leeks, thyme, sage, oregano, and parsley.

2 tablespoons extra-virgin olive oil, divided

1 1/2 cups sliced leeks (white parts only)

3 cloves garlic, minced

12 ounces sweet Italian chicken sausage, casings removed

2 cups diced sweet potato

3/4 cup low-sodium vegetable stock

1 teaspoon chopped fresh thyme

1 tablespoon chopped fresh sage

1 tablespoon chopped fresh oregano

1 (15-ounce) can cannellini beans, drained and rinsed

1/2 cup whole-grain panko bread crumbs

1/4 cup freshly grated Parmesan cheese

1/4 cup chopped fresh flat-leaf parsley

1. Preheat the oven to 375°F.

2. Heat 1 tablespoon olive oil in a large Dutch oven or other large oven-safe pot over medium-high heat. Add the leeks and garlic, and sauté for 6–8 minutes, or until softened. Add the sausage and sauté for 5 minutes, breaking it up with a wooden spoon. Then stir in the sweet potatoes, stock, thyme, sage, oregano, and beans.

3. Cover the Dutch oven and transfer it to the oven. Bake for 30–40 minutes, stirring once, until the sweet potato is almost fork tender. Remove Dutch oven from the oven.

4. In a small bowl, stir together the bread crumbs and cheese; sprinkle the mixture evenly over the cassoulet.

5. Return cassoulet to the oven and bake, uncovered, for an additional 15 minutes, or until the topping is browned. Remove cassoulet from the oven and serve hot, garnished with parsley.

EXCHANGES/CHOICES	1 1/2 Starch
	1 Nonstarchy Vegetable
	2 Lean Protein
	1 Fat

CALORIES	270
CALORIES FROM FAT	100
TOTAL FAT	11.0 g
SATURATED FAT	2.6 g
TRANS FAT	0.0 g
CHOLESTEROL	45 mg
SODIUM	440 mg
POTASSIUM	470 mg
TOTAL CARBOHYDRATE	28 g
DIETARY FIBER	5 g
SUGARS	5 g
PROTEIN	16 g
PHOSPHORUS	185 mg

Parmesan Dijon Chicken

SERVES: 4 | SERVING SIZE: 1 CHICKEN CUTLET | PREP TIME: 5 MINUTES | COOKING TIME: 15 MINUTES

This is my take on Chicken Dijon: the ever-popular potluck staple of chicken in creamy Dijon mustard sauce. Instead of using the traditional calorie-laden sauce, I coat the chicken with mustard and Parmesan cheese before baking. The result is moist, flavorful chicken with just the right amount of cheesiness in each bite.

2 tablespoons country Dijon mustard

1 tablespoon fat-free, plain strained yogurt (Greek or skyr)

1/4 teaspoon freshly ground black pepper

1 pound boneless, skinless chicken breast, cut into 4 equal pieces

1/2 cup cooked quinoa

7 tablespoons shredded Parmesan cheese

2 tablespoons fresh flat-leaf parsley

1. Line a rimmed baking sheet with parchment paper.

2. In a small bowl, combine the mustard, yogurt, and pepper. Coat the chicken cutlets with the mustard mixture and set them aside.

3. In another bowl, combine the quinoa, cheese, and parsley. Coat the chicken, on all sides, with the quinoa mixture. Place the coated chicken on the prepared baking sheet.

4. Set an oven rack in the middle position and preheat the oven to broil on the high setting. Broil the chicken on the middle rack in the oven, without flipping, for 10–12 minutes, or until an instant-read thermometer inserted into the thickest part of each cutlet registers 165°F.

EXCHANGES/CHOICES	1/2 Carbohydrate
	4 Lean Protein
CALORIES	200
CALORIES FROM FAT	50
TOTAL FAT	6.0 g
SATURATED FAT	2.2 g
TRANS FAT	0.0 g
CHOLESTEROL	70 mg
SODIUM	370 mg
POTASSIUM	275 mg
TOTAL CARBOHYDRATE	6 g
DIETARY FIBER	1 g
SUGARS	1 g
PROTEIN	29 g
PHOSPHORUS	280 mg

Baked Chicken Thighs
with Pears, Maple, Mustard, and Herbs

SERVES: 8 | SERVING SIZE: 1 CHICKEN THIGH | PREP TIME: 10 MINUTES | COOKING TIME: 40 MINUTES

In the fall, when pears are in season and the air is crisp, do yourself a favor and bake up a batch of this warm, aromatic chicken for dinner. And trust me: keep the skins on the pears. Not only do they add extra flavor to the dish, but they also contain powerful phytonutrients that may help boost your immune system and reduce inflammation in the body.

8 skinless, bone-in chicken thighs

1 shallot, sliced

1/2 cup white balsamic vinegar

2 tablespoons pure maple syrup (preferably grade B)

2 tablespoons whole-grain mustard

1 tablespoon Dijon mustard

2 tablespoons Everyday Herb Oil (page 60)

2 medium pears, skins on, cored and sliced

1/4 teaspoon fine sea salt

1/4 teaspoon freshly ground black pepper

1. Preheat the oven to 400°F.

2. In a large bowl, toss together the chicken, shallot, vinegar, maple syrup, both mustards, herb oil, and pears. Season with salt and pepper, and toss again.

3. Transfer the chicken mixture to a rimmed baking dish. Cover the dish with foil and bake for 30 minutes; then uncover and bake for an additional 10–15 minutes, or until an instant-read thermometer inserted into the thickest part of a thigh registers 165°F.

4. Remove baking dish from the oven and serve the chicken and pears hot.

EXCHANGES/CHOICES	1/2 Fruit
	1/2 Carbohydrate
	2 Lean Protein
	1 Fat
CALORIES	190
CALORIES FROM FAT	80
TOTAL FAT	9.0 g
SATURATED FAT	1.8 g
TRANS FAT	0.0 g
CHOLESTEROL	75 mg
SODIUM	220 mg
POTASSIUM	255 mg
TOTAL CARBOHYDRATE	14 g
DIETARY FIBER	2 g
SUGARS	10 g
PROTEIN	14 g
PHOSPHORUS	140 mg

Chicken Tikka Kabob
with Pomegranate and Pistachios

SERVES: 8 | SERVING SIZE: 1 KABOB | PREP TIME: 10 MINUTES (PLUS 30 MINUTES FOR SOAKING SKEWERS)
COOKING TIME: 10 MINUTES

In Indian cuisine, chicken is often marinated in yogurt and spices to add flavor and ensure that the meat won't dry out when cooked at high temperatures (like when it's grilled). In this recipe, I brighten up the traditional kabob (and add an extra boost of antioxidants) with a sprinkling of pomegranate seeds, pistachios, and cilantro.

8 wooden or metal skewers

1/2 cup fat-free, plain strained yogurt (Greek or skyr)

2 tablespoons Dijon mustard

1 tablespoon freshly squeezed lime juice

1 teaspoon grated fresh ginger

1 teaspoon grated garlic

1 teaspoon ground cumin

1/2 teaspoon ground coriander

1/2 teaspoon ground turmeric

1/4 teaspoon red pepper flakes

2 pounds boneless, skinless chicken breasts, cut into 24 (2-inch) pieces

1/4 teaspoon fine sea salt

1/4 teaspoon freshly ground black pepper

1 tablespoon extra-virgin olive oil

1/2 cup fresh pomegranate seeds

1/4 cup raw, unsalted pistachios, chopped

1/4 cup chopped fresh cilantro

1. If you're using wooden skewers, place them in a shallow bowl and soak in water for 30 minutes.

2. In a medium bowl, combine the yogurt, mustard, lime juice, ginger, garlic, cumin, coriander, turmeric, and red pepper flakes. Allow the spices to hydrate and bloom for 5 minutes.

3. In another medium bowl, toss the chicken pieces with the salt and pepper. Add the chicken to the yogurt mixture and let marinate for at least 15 minutes in the refrigerator.

4. Preheat an outdoor grill or grill pan to medium-high and coat with olive oil.

5. Thread 3 pieces of chicken onto each skewer. Grill the kebabs until chicken is just cooked through, about 2 minutes per side, for a total of 8–10 minutes.

6. Remove kebobs from the grill and serve immediately garnished with the pomegranate seeds, pistachios, and cilantro.

EXCHANGES/CHOICES	1/2 Carbohydrate 3 Lean Protein 1/2 Fat
CALORIES	190
CALORIES FROM FAT	60
TOTAL FAT	7.0 g
SATURATED FAT	1.3 g
TRANS FAT	0.0 g
CHOLESTEROL	65 mg
SODIUM	230 mg
POTASSIUM	320 mg
TOTAL CARBOHYDRATE	5 g
DIETARY FIBER	1 g
SUGARS	3 g
PROTEIN	26 g
PHOSPHORUS	230 mg

Chorizo Chicken Sausage, Sweet Potato, and Mushroom Tostadas

SERVES: 6 | SERVING SIZE: 1 TOSTADA AND 2 TABLESPOONS SALSA | PREP TIME: 10 MINUTES | COOKING TIME: 40 MINUTES

Tostadas are the Mexican equivalent of open-faced sandwiches; they are crispy corn tortillas piled with any number of toppings. While they are usually topped with cheese or dollops of sour cream, these additions are more functional than anything, serving as the glue to adhere toppings to the tortilla base. In my version of this dish, tender cubes of sweet potato serve the same function as the cheese.

1 tablespoon extra-virgin olive oil

1 small onion, diced (about 1 cup)

3/4 pound chorizo chicken sausage, casings removed

3/4 cup chopped cremini mushrooms

1 small sweet potato, peeled and cut into small cubes

1/2–1 jalapeño pepper, minced

1/2 teaspoon ground cumin

1/4 cup water

2 cups chopped kale

6 corn tortillas

Nonstick cooking spray

1/4 cup finely chopped fresh cilantro

3/4 cup Tomatillo Salsa (page 89)

1. Preheat the oven to 350°F.

2. Heat the oil in a large sauté pan over medium-high heat. Add the onion, and cook for 3–4 minutes to soften, stirring constantly. Add the chorizo and cook for 4–5 minutes, breaking it up with a wooden spoon, until it is heated through. Add the mushrooms and sauté for 2–3 minutes to soften.

3. Add the sweet potato, jalapeño, cumin, and water. Reduce heat to medium-low, cover the pan, and simmer for 15 minutes, or until the sweet potato is tender. Once sweet potato is tender, add the kale and sauté for 1–2 minutes, or until bright green.

4. While the meat mixture is cooking, spray both sides of each tortilla lightly with nonstick cooking spray and spread them out in a single layer on two baking sheets. Transfer baking sheets to the oven and bake for 10–12 minutes, or until tortillas are slightly brown and crispy.

5. Divide the meat mixture evenly between the 6 tortillas. Top each tostada with cilantro and 2 tablespoons of tomatillo salsa.

EXCHANGES/CHOICES	1 Starch
	1 Nonstarchy Vegetable
	1 Lean Protein
	1 Fat

CALORIES	200
CALORIES FROM FAT	70
TOTAL FAT	8.0 g
SATURATED FAT	1.8 g
TRANS FAT	0.0 g
CHOLESTEROL	50 mg
SODIUM	410 mg
POTASSIUM	550 mg
TOTAL CARBOHYDRATE	23 g
DIETARY FIBER	3 g
SUGARS	4 g
PROTEIN	12 g
PHOSPHORUS	215 mg

Garlicky Grilled Pork Chops with Navy Beans

SERVES: 4 | SERVING SIZE: 1 PORK CHOP AND 1/2 CUP NAVY BEAN MIXTURE
PREP TIME: 10 MINUTES PLUS 1 HOUR MARINATING TIME | COOKING TIME: 10 MINUTES

After soaking in a delicious marinade of roasted garlic, citrus, and herb oil, these pork chops grill up perfectly in minutes!

4 cloves Everyday Roasted Garlic (page 64)

2 teaspoons freshly grated lemon zest, divided

1/3 cup freshly squeezed lemon juice, divided

1 teaspoon freshly grated orange zest

1 tablespoon Everyday Herb Oil (page 60)

1/8 teaspoon fine sea salt

1/4 teaspoon freshly ground black pepper

4 (4-ounce) boneless pork loin chops

2 cups BPA-free canned navy beans, rinsed and drained

1/4 cup Olive Tapenade (page 113)

1/4 cup chopped fresh flat-leaf parsley

1. In a large bowl, whisk together the roasted garlic, 1 teaspoon lemon zest, 1/4 cup lemon juice, the orange zest, herb oil, salt, and pepper. Add the pork chops to the bowl and turn to coat. Cover the bowl and marinate the pork chops for at least 1 hour in the refrigerator.

2. Preheat an outdoor grill or grill pan to medium-high. Grill the marinated pork chops for 4–5 minutes per side.

3. While the pork chops are cooking, combine the navy beans, tapenade, parsley, and remaining lemon juice and lemon zest in a small bowl.

4. Transfer cooked pork chops to a plate and let them rest for 5 minutes before serving. Serve each pork chop topped with 1/2 cup navy bean mixture.

tip: Save time by marinating your pork the night before so it is ready to cook come dinner time!

EXCHANGES/CHOICES	1 1/2 Starch
	4 Lean Protein
	1 1/2 Fat
CALORIES	370
CALORIES FROM FAT	140
TOTAL FAT	16.0 g
SATURATED FAT	3.8 g
TRANS FAT	0.0 g
CHOLESTEROL	60 mg
SODIUM	450 mg
POTASSIUM	705 mg
TOTAL CARBOHYDRATE	27 g
DIETARY FIBER	10 g
SUGARS	1 g
PROTEIN	29 g
PHOSPHORUS	315 mg

a cut above the rest

When it comes to choosing lean animal proteins, the cut of meat or poultry can make all the difference. Try some of these lean cuts in your next recipe!

- **Beef:** Opt for the loin cuts (sirloin, tenderloin, etc.) or round cuts, which tend to be lower in fat but do not lack in flavor. Grass-fed beef is lower in saturated fat than its grain-fed counterparts.

- **Bison:** This is a flavorful alternative to beef that is lower in saturated fat and rich in nutrients. Bison tends to be grass-fed, which adds to its earthy, rich flavor.

- **Poultry:** While white meat portions are lower in saturated fat than dark meat portions, don't fear a bone-in, skin-on cut. Cooking poultry with the bone in and skin on helps to lock in the flavor and moisture—and you can remove the skin prior to eating the meat.

Pork, Pepper, and Green Olive Stew

SERVES: 8 | SERVING SIZE: 1 1/2 CUPS | PREP TIME: 10 MINUTES | COOKING TIME: 2 HOURS

This Mediterranean-style stew is a true one-pot wonder! It's fragrant with garlic and studded with multicolored bell peppers, potatoes, and plump, green olives.

1 tablespoon extra-virgin olive oil

2 pounds boneless, lean pork sirloin roast, cut into 2-inch pieces

2 tablespoons Everyday Herb Oil (page 60)

2 cups diced yellow onion

2 cups diced bell pepper (red, orange, yellow, or a mix)

4 cloves garlic, smashed

1/2 teaspoon fine sea salt

1/2 teaspoon freshly ground black pepper

1 tablespoon tomato paste

1 cup low-sodium chicken stock

2 cups water

2 cups quartered small white potatoes

1 cup green olives (like Castelvetrano), pitted

1/2 cup chopped fresh flat-leaf parsley

1. In a 6-quart Dutch oven, heat the oil over medium or medium-high heat. Add half the pork and sear well on all sides for about 10 minutes total. Transfer seared pork to a large bowl or rimmed baking sheet and repeat with the remaining pork.

2. Once all the pork has been seared and removed, add the herb oil, onion, bell pepper, and garlic to the pot, season with salt and pepper, and cook for 3–5 minutes, or until the onions and pepper begin to soften. Add the tomato paste and cook for another 1–2 minutes. Add the chicken stock to deglaze the bottom of the pan, scraping up any browned bits.

3. Return the pork to the pot along with any accumulated juices. Add the water and lower the heat to maintain a simmer.

4. Cover the pot and simmer for 45 minutes, then add the potatoes and olives, cover the pot again, and cook for another 45–60 minutes, or until the pork and potatoes are tender.

5. Remove pot from the heat and serve hot, garnished with the parsley.

EXCHANGES/CHOICES	1/2 Starch
	1 Nonstarchy Vegetable
	3 Lean Protein
	1 1/2 Fat

CALORIES	260
CALORIES FROM FAT	90
TOTAL FAT	10.0 g
SATURATED FAT	2.3 g
TRANS FAT	0.0 g
CHOLESTEROL	65 mg
SODIUM	440 mg
POTASSIUM	640 mg
TOTAL CARBOHYDRATE	16 g
DIETARY FIBER	3 g
SUGARS	4 g
PROTEIN	25 g
PHOSPHORUS	280 mg

Grilled Lamb Chops and Lemony Barley Pilaf

SERVES: 4 | SERVING SIZE: 1 LAMB CHOP, 1 TABLESPOON SALSA, AND 1/2 CUP PILAF
PREP TIME: 15 MINUTES | COOKING TIME: 10 MINUTES

When you're looking for an impressive main course that's ready in a flash, you can't go wrong with these lamb chops slathered with Zucchini Salsa Verde.

1 tablespoon extra-virgin olive oil

1 tablespoon freshly grated lemon zest

1/4 teaspoon fine sea salt

1/4 teaspoon freshly ground black pepper

4 lamb chops

1/4 cup Zucchini Salsa Verde (page 86)

2 cups Lemony Barley Pilaf (page 167)

1 tablespoon thinly sliced fresh mint

1. Preheat an outdoor grill or grill pan to medium-high.

2. In a large bowl, whisk together the olive oil, lemon zest, salt, and pepper. Add the lamb chops and toss well to coat. Marinate in the refrigerator for 10 minutes.

3. Transfer the chops to the grill or grill pan and sear for 2–3 minutes per side or until they reach your desired doneness.

4. Remove chops from the grill and divide them among 4 plates. Top each serving with 1 tablespoon Zucchini Salsa Verde and 1/2 cup Lemony Barley Pilaf. Garnish with fresh mint and serve.

EXCHANGES/CHOICES	1 1/2 Starch
	2 Lean Protein
	3 Fat
CALORIES	330
CALORIES FROM FAT	160
TOTAL FAT	18.0 g
SATURATED FAT	3.8 g
TRANS FAT	0.0 g
CHOLESTEROL	55 mg
SODIUM	330 mg
POTASSIUM	500 mg
TOTAL CARBOHYDRATE	21 g
DIETARY FIBER	5 g
SUGARS	3 g
PROTEIN	21 g
PHOSPHORUS	205 mg

Cinnamon-Spiced Beef Meatballs and Tabbouleh

SERVES: 6 | SERVING SIZE: 2 MEATBALLS, 1/4 CUP TOMATO SAUCE, AND 1 CUP TABBOULEH
PREP TIME: 10 MINUTES PLUS 1 HOUR REFRIGERATION TIME | COOKING TIME: 20 MINUTES

Meatballs made with ground beef and lamb tend to be high in fat, but by reducing the amount of meat in the recipe and rounding it out instead with minced fresh mushrooms and cooked bulgur, you can have your meatballs and eat them, too. Serve these meatballs as appetizers for your next gathering, or make them the main course and enjoy with spaghetti squash and sautéed greens.

3/4 pound 95% lean ground beef

1/4 pound ground lamb

1 pound cremini mushrooms, finely chopped (or pulsed in your food processor)

1/2 cup cooked bulgur (see cooking instructions on page 157)

1 large egg, lightly beaten

2 cloves garlic, grated

2 tablespoons chopped fresh flat-leaf parsley

1 tablespoon finely chopped fresh oregano

1/2 teaspoon ground cumin

1/4 teaspoon ground allspice

1/2 teaspoon ground cinnamon

1/2 teaspoon red pepper flakes

1/8 teaspoon fine sea salt

1/4 teaspoon freshly ground black pepper

1 tablespoon extra-virgin olive oil

1 (8-ounce) can no-salt-added tomato sauce

1 (8-ounce) can regular tomato sauce

1 cinnamon stick

4 cups Herby Millet Tabbouleh (page 162)

1. In a large bowl, combine all the ingredients *except for* the cinnamon stick, tomato sauces, and tabbouleh. Mix well, cover, and refrigerate for 1 hour. Shape the meat mixture into 12 equally sized meatballs.

2. Preheat the oven to 375°F. Line a rimmed baking sheet with parchment paper.

3. Arrange the meatballs in a single layer on the prepared baking sheet and bake for 15–20 minutes, or until cooked through.

4. While meatballs are baking, simmer both kinds of tomato sauce with the cinnamon stick in a small saucepan over medium heat for 10 minutes.

5. Remove meatballs from oven and serve with the tomato sauce for dipping and the tabbouleh on the side.

EXCHANGES/CHOICES	1 Starch
	3 Nonstarchy Vegetable
	2 Lean Protein
	2 Fat
CALORIES	340
CALORIES FROM FAT	130
TOTAL FAT	14.0 g
SATURATED FAT	3.7 g
TRANS FAT	0.1 g
CHOLESTEROL	80 mg
SODIUM	430 mg
POTASSIUM	1100 mg
TOTAL CARBOHYDRATE	32 g
DIETARY FIBER	7 g
SUGARS	7 g
PROTEIN	24 g
PHOSPHORUS	375 mg

Seared Flank Steak with Horseradish Chimichurri

SERVES: 4 | SERVING SIZE: 4 OUNCES SLICED STEAK, 2 TABLESPOONS CHIMICHURRI, AND 1 CUP MASHED SWEET POTATOES
PREP TIME: 5 MINUTES PLUS 1 HOUR MARINATING TIME AND 15 MINUTES RESTING TIME | COOKING TIME: 6 MINUTES

You might be tempted to shorten the marinating time in this recipe, but trust me: the full time makes all the difference. Flank steak, a lean cut of beef, can be tough depending on the preparation. The marinade acts as a tenderizer to keep the meat moist and tender.

1 (1-pound) flank steak, trimmed of all visible fat

1 tablespoon extra-virgin olive oil

1 teaspoon ground cumin

1/4 teaspoon fine sea salt

1/4 teaspoon freshly ground black pepper

1/2 cup Horseradish Chimichurri (page 84)

4 cups Everyday Mashed Sweet Potatoes (page 144)

1. Place the flank steak in a medium bowl. Season steak with the olive oil, cumin, salt, and pepper. Cover and refrigerate for at least 1 hour.

2. Preheat an outdoor grill or grill pan to medium high.

3. Remove steak from the refrigerator and allow it to rest at room temperature for 15 minutes. Then grill steak for 2–3 minutes per side. Transfer the steak to a cutting board, let it rest for 5–10 minutes, then slice it thinly against the grain.

4. Serve the sliced steak topped with the Horseradish Chimichurri and with the Everyday Mashed Sweet Potatoes on the side.

EXCHANGES/CHOICES	1 1/2 Starch
	3 Lean Protein
	1 1/2 Fat
CALORIES	310
CALORIES FROM FAT	120
TOTAL FAT	13.0 g
SATURATED FAT	3.4 g
TRANS FAT	0.0 g
CHOLESTEROL	60 mg
SODIUM	440 mg
POTASSIUM	845 mg
TOTAL CARBOHYDRATE	23 g
DIETARY FIBER	4 g
SUGARS	7 g
PROTEIN	25 g
PHOSPHORUS	240 mg

Everyday Grilled Chicken Breasts

SERVES: 8 | SERVING SIZE: 4 OUNCES CHICKEN | PREP TIME: 30 MINUTES | COOKING TIME: 15 MINUTES

Simple yet wildly flavorful and unique, this chicken recipe will become a staple in your house. Rich herbs such as rosemary, oregano, and thyme marry with crisp citrus zest and smoky paprika in this vibrant dish. I seriously make some variation of this chicken recipe every single week!

2 tablespoons Everyday Herb Oil (page 60)

1 teaspoon smoked paprika

1 teaspoon freshly grated orange zest

1 teaspoon grated fresh garlic

1/4 teaspoon fine sea salt

1/2 teaspoon freshly ground black pepper

8 (5-ounce) boneless, skinless chicken breasts, butterflied lengthwise

1. In a medium bowl, combine the herb oil, paprika, orange zest, garlic, salt, and pepper. Add the chicken, cover, and refrigerate for at least 30 minutes.

2. Preheat a grill or grill pan over medium-high heat.

3. Remove chicken from refrigerator and sear on the grill, cooking for 3–4 minutes per side to create grill marks. Serve immediately.

tip: Make a few extra breasts of chicken each week so you have them on hand for lunches, salads, or an easy precooked dinner.

EXCHANGES/CHOICES	4 Lean Protein
CALORIES	190
CALORIES FROM FAT	60
TOTAL FAT	7.0 g
SATURATED FAT	1.4 g
TRANS FAT	0.0 g
CHOLESTEROL	80 mg
SODIUM	140 mg
POTASSIUM	255 mg
TOTAL CARBOHYDRATE	0 g
DIETARY FIBER	0 g
SUGARS	0 g
PROTEIN	30 g
PHOSPHORUS	220 mg

Beef, Mushroom, and Brown Rice Lettuce Cups

SERVES: 4 | SERVING SIZE: 3/4 CUP FILLING AND 3 LARGE LETTUCE CUPS | PREP TIME: 10 MINUTES | COOKING TIME: 9–12 MINUTES

Crunchy, cool lettuce wraps are the perfect complement to this slightly spicy beef and mushroom blend. Festive and fun, this recipe is a go-to in my house when I am craving Asian flavors!

- 1 tablespoon bottled chile-garlic sauce
- 2 teaspoons toasted sesame oil
- 1 tablespoon reduced-sodium soy sauce
- 1 tablespoon hoisin sauce
- 2 tablespoons rice vinegar
- 2 teaspoons avocado oil

- 1 tablespoon grated or finely chopped fresh garlic
- 2 tablespoons minced fresh ginger
- 3/4 cup diced yellow onion
- 1/2 pound 90% lean ground beef
- 3/4 pound cremini mushrooms, finely chopped

- 1 1/2 cups cooked brown rice
- 4 scallions, sliced (green part only)
- 1 large head Bibb lettuce, outer leaves discarded (12 large leaves needed)
- 4 teaspoons sesame seeds
- 1 cup diced red bell pepper

1. In a bowl, whisk together the chile-garlic sauce, sesame oil, soy sauce, hoisin sauce, and vinegar. Set aside.

2. Heat the avocado oil in a large skillet over medium heat. Add the garlic, ginger, and onion and cook for 2–3 minutes, or until mixture is fragrant and onion begins to soften.

3. Add the ground beef and mushrooms and sauté until beef is just cooked through, about 4–5 minutes. Add the chile-garlic sauce mixture and cooked rice. Reduce heat to a simmer and cook, stirring, for 3–4 minutes. Remove from heat and stir in the scallions.

4. Fill each lettuce leaf with 1/4 cup filling. Garnish each serving (3 lettuce cups) with 1 teaspoon sesame seeds and 1/4 cup red pepper divided among the 3 cups.

EXCHANGES/CHOICES 1 Starch
3 Nonstarchy Vegetable
1 Lean Protein
2 Fat

CALORIES	310
CALORIES FROM FAT	110
TOTAL FAT	12.0 g
SATURATED FAT	2.8 g
TRANS FAT	0.3 g
CHOLESTEROL	35 mg
SODIUM	340 mg
POTASSIUM	900 mg
TOTAL CARBOHYDRATE	33 g
DIETARY FIBER	5 g
SUGARS	8 g
PROTEIN	18 g
PHOSPHORUS	325 mg

Peanut Butter–Chocolate Chip Bars p. 230

sweets

Having diabetes does not mean that you can never eat sweets again. But, contrary to popular belief, it also does not mean that you should dive head first into the use of artificial sweeteners. Artificial calorie-free sweeteners, though lacking in calories, pack a super-sweet punch. Several times sweeter than natural sweeteners, no-calorie sweeteners can actually enable your sugar cravings by training your taste buds to need more sweetness…a lot more. Thankfully, you can train your taste buds to enjoy sweets in a healthier way. By limiting the added sugars in your diet and focusing on natural sources of sweetness—such as fruits of all kinds, beets, carrots, squash, and sweet potatoes—as well as natural sweeteners, you can have your cake and eat it too. In this chapter, you'll find decadent recipes that will satisfy your sweet cravings in healthy way. From cobblers and muffins to cookies, cakes, drinks, and even chocolate ice cream, these are treats you can truly feel good about eating.

Cool Weather Cobbler

SERVES: 18 | SERVING SIZE: 3/4 CUP | PREP TIME: 20 MINUTES | COOKING TIME: 40 MINUTES

This is my take on a classic apple crumble, but I wanted to pay homage to the natural sweetness of the fruit instead of lobbing on the sugar. Arrowroot powder thickens this whole-fruit filling and fresh ginger, cinnamon, and orange zest lend robust flavors to this treat. And the topping adds more than just crunch; with oats, whole-wheat flour, pumpkin seeds, almonds, and maple syrup, it's a tasty way to get your nutrients.

FILLING

6 medium pears or apples, peeled, cored, and sliced

1 cup fresh or frozen cranberries and/or pitted cherries

1 tablespoon arrowroot powder

1 teaspoon ground cinnamon

1 teaspoon grated fresh ginger

1 teaspoon freshly grated orange zest

TOPPING

1 cup DIY Nut Flour (page 72, using almonds)

2 cups gluten-free rolled oats

1/2 cup whole-wheat flour

1/4 cup unsalted, toasted pumpkin seeds

1/4 cup raw, unsalted sliced almonds

1 teaspoon ground cinnamon

1/4 teaspoon fine sea salt

2 tablespoons melted coconut oil or canola oil

1 tablespoon extra-virgin olive oil

1/3 cup pure maple syrup (preferably grade B)

1. Preheat the oven to 350°F.

2. To make the filling, toss together all the fruit, the arrowroot powder, cinnamon, ginger, and orange zest in a medium bowl. Spread the filling in the bottom of an 8 x 12-inch baking dish.

3. To make the topping, stir together the almond flour, oats, flour, pumpkin seeds, almonds, cinnamon, and salt in another medium bowl. Drizzle in the coconut oil, olive oil, and maple syrup and mix until evenly combined.

4. Crumble the topping over the filling and bake for 40 minutes, or until the topping is brown and the fruit is bubbling. Remove cobbler from the oven and set aside to cool for 10 minutes before serving.

EXCHANGES/CHOICES	2 Carbohydrate
	1 1/2 Fat
CALORIES	190
CALORIES FROM FAT	80
TOTAL FAT	9.0 g
SATURATED FAT	2.1 g
TRANS FAT	0.0 g
CHOLESTEROL	0 mg
SODIUM	35 mg
POTASSIUM	220 mg
TOTAL CARBOHYDRATE	26 g
DIETARY FIBER	5 g
SUGARS	10 g
PROTEIN	5 g
PHOSPHORUS	135 mg

Almond, Millet, and Pear Cake

SERVES: 18 | SERVING SIZE: 1 RECTANGULAR PIECE | PREP TIME: 10 MINUTES | COOKING TIME: 30 MINUTES

This naturally gluten-free, nutty, orange-scented cake is just as delicious for breakfast as it is for dessert. The cooked millet adds extra fiber and protein. You can swap out the fruit depending on the season, which makes this recipe a winner all year round.

- 2 cups DIY Nut Flour (page 72, using almonds)
- 1 tablespoon aluminum-free baking powder
- 1/2 teaspoon ground cinnamon
- 1/4 teaspoon fine sea salt
- 2 teaspoons freshly grated orange zest
- 1/4 cup freshly squeezed orange juice
- 1/4 cup pure maple syrup (preferably grade B)
- 1/4 cup avocado oil or extra-virgin olive oil
- 2 large eggs
- 1 teaspoon pure vanilla extract
- 1 cup cooked millet (from 1/3 cup dry, see page 157 for instructions)
- 1 pear, cored and diced (skin on)

1. Preheat the oven to 350°F. Line an 8 x 11-inch baking pan with parchment paper.

2. In a large bowl, whisk together the almond flour, baking powder, cinnamon, and salt. Set dry ingredients aside.

3. In a medium bowl, whisk together the orange zest, orange juice, maple syrup, oil, eggs, and vanilla.

4. Add the wet ingredients to the dry ingredients and stir with a wooden spoon or spatula until well combined. Fold in the cooked millet and diced pear. Add mixture to the prepared pan.

5. Bake for 25–30 minutes, or until cake is golden brown and firm to the touch.

6. Remove pan from the oven and let the cake cool slightly, then cut into 18 pieces and serve immediately.

EXCHANGES/CHOICES	1 Carbohydrate
	2 Fat
CALORIES	160
CALORIES FROM FAT	110
TOTAL FAT	12.0 g
SATURATED FAT	1.1 g
TRANS FAT	0.0 g
CHOLESTEROL	20 mg
SODIUM	100 mg
POTASSIUM	155 mg
TOTAL CARBOHYDRATE	11 g
DIETARY FIBER	2 g
SUGARS	5 g
PROTEIN	5 g
PHOSPHORUS	175 mg

Cherry-Cashew Skillet Cake

SERVES: 12 | SERVING SIZE: 1 SLICE | PREP TIME: 5 MINUTES | COOKING TIME: 25 MINUTES

I love this grain-free "cake" and often wow my family and guests with the simple decadence it offers. You can swap out the cashew flour for other nut flours like almond or hazelnut, and you can even mix up the fruit based on what's in season. This ultra-moist, protein-packed dessert is both simple to make and unbelievably yummy.

1 1/2 cups DIY Nut Flour (page 72, using cashews)

1 teaspoon aluminum-free baking powder

1/4 teaspoon fine sea salt

1 teaspoon ground cinnamon

2 large eggs

2 teaspoons freshly grated lemon zest

1/4 cup DIY Nut Milk (page 69, using almonds), or organic, unsweetened almond milk

3 tablespoons pure maple syrup (preferably grade B)

1/4 cup mashed bananas

1 tablespoon extra-virgin olive oil

1/2 cup pitted and sliced fresh cherries

1. Preheat the oven to 375°F.

2. In a large bowl, whisk together the cashew flour, baking powder, salt, and cinnamon. Set dry ingredients aside.

3. Purée the eggs, lemon zest, almond milk, maple syrup, and mashed banana in a blender.

4. Add the wet ingredients to the dry ingredients and stir with a wooden spoon or spatula until the mixture forms a pancake-like batter.

5. In a 9-inch cast iron pan or ovenproof skillet, heat the olive oil over medium heat. Pour the batter into the hot pan, allowing it to cover the entire bottom. Top the batter with the cherries and cook for 3 minutes to set.

6. Transfer pan to the oven and bake for 20–25 minutes, or until cake is golden and a toothpick poked in the center comes out clean.

7. Remove pan from the oven and let cake cool slightly. Then cut into 12 slices and serve immediately.

EXCHANGES/CHOICES	1/2 Carbohydrate 2 Fat
CALORIES	150
CALORIES FROM FAT	100
TOTAL FAT	11.0 g
SATURATED FAT	1.1 g
TRANS FAT	0.0 g
CHOLESTEROL	30 mg
SODIUM	90 mg
POTASSIUM	180 mg
TOTAL CARBOHYDRATE	10 g
DIETARY FIBER	3 g
SUGARS	5 g
PROTEIN	5 g
PHOSPHORUS	145 mg

Ginger-Cardamom Pear Sauce with Pistachios

SERVES: 6 | SERVING SIZE: 1/3 CUP | PREP TIME: 15 MINUTES | COOKING TIME: 40 MINUTES

Move over, applesauce! Since pears are naturally sweeter than apples, there's no need to add sugar, honey, or maple syrup to this healthy dessert. Aromatic spices take this dish to another dimension, and a heart-healthy sprinkling of pistachios is all you need to keep your taste buds excited

2 pounds ripe pears (Bosc, Asian, Anjou, or Bartlett), peeled, cored, and chopped

1 cup water

2 tablespoons freshly squeezed lemon juice

1 1/4 teaspoons ground cardamom

1 teaspoon grated fresh ginger

6 tablespoons roughly chopped raw, unsalted pistachios

1. Combine all the ingredients *except* for the pistachios in a medium, heavy-bottomed saucepan over medium-high heat. Cover the pan and bring the mixture to a boil; then reduce heat to medium-low and simmer for 30 minutes, or until pears are very tender.

2. Remove pan from the heat and let the sauce cool slightly. Transfer the cooled sauce to a blender or food processor and purée until smooth.

3. Top each serving with 1 tablespoon of chopped pistachios.

EXCHANGES/CHOICES	1 1/2 Fruit
	1/2 Fat
CALORIES	130
CALORIES FROM FAT	30
TOTAL FAT	3.5 g
SATURATED FAT	0.5 g
TRANS FAT	0.0 g
CHOLESTEROL	0 mg
SODIUM	0 mg
POTASSIUM	250 mg
TOTAL CARBOHYDRATE	24 g
DIETARY FIBER	5 g
SUGARS	14 g
PROTEIN	2 g
PHOSPHORUS	55 mg

Carrot, Ginger, and Peach Popsicles

SERVES: 6 | SERVING SIZE: 1 POPSICLE | PREP TIME: 5 MINUTES | FREEZING TIME: AT LEAST 4 HOURS

Take your everyday popsicles to a new level with this recipe! Ginger and peach are playfully paired with sweet carrots in this recipe to create a tantalizing flavor profile that packs a nutritional punch!

1 cup unsweetened 100% carrot juice

1 1/2 cups fresh or frozen peaches

1/2 cup fresh or frozen mango cubes

2 teaspoons grated fresh ginger

1 cup DIY Nut Milk (see page 69, using almonds), or organic, unsweetened almond milk

1. Purée all ingredients in a blender until smooth. Pour the mixture into 6 (4-ounce) popsicle molds. Freeze for at least 4 hours.

EXCHANGES/CHOICES	1/2 Carbohydrate
CALORIES	45
CALORIES FROM FAT	5
TOTAL FAT	0.5 g
SATURATED FAT	0.1 g
TRANS FAT	0.0 g
CHOLESTEROL	0 mg
SODIUM	15 mg
POTASSIUM	235 mg
TOTAL CARBOHYDRATE	10 g
DIETARY FIBER	1 g
SUGARS	8 g
PROTEIN	1 g
PHOSPHORUS	30 mg

Green Orange Cream Pops

SERVES: 6 | SERVING SIZE: 1 POPSICLE | PREP TIME: 5 MINUTES | FREEZING TIME: AT LEAST 4 HOURS

Harness your childhood in this tasty pop that is green with goodness!

1 1/2 cups fat-free, vanilla strained
   yogurt (such as Siggi's)

1 cup fresh squeezed orange juice

1 cup baby kale

1. Purée all ingredients in a blender until smooth. Pour the mixture into 6 (4-ounce) popsicle molds. Freeze for at least 4 hours.

EXCHANGES/CHOICES	1/2 Carbohydrate
	1 Lean Protein
CALORIES	60
CALORIES FROM FAT	0
TOTAL FAT	0.0 g
SATURATED FAT	0.1 g
TRANS FAT	0.0 g
CHOLESTEROL	5 mg
SODIUM	25 mg
POTASSIUM	180 mg
TOTAL CARBOHYDRATE	9 g
DIETARY FIBER	0 g
SUGARS	7 g
PROTEIN	6 g
PHOSPHORUS	85 mg

Peanut Butter–Chocolate Chip Bars

SERVES: 16 | SERVING SIZE: 1 BAR | PREP TIME: 5 MINUTES | COOKING TIME: 30 MINUTES

I amped up this version of a "blondie" with the bonus of peanut-buttery goodness. These bars are a great example of a dessert that is just sweet enough, yet ridiculously satisfying!

Nonstick cooking spray

1 large egg

1 egg white

1/3 cup melted coconut oil or avocado oil

1/3 cup pure maple syrup (preferably grade B)

1/4 cup mashed banana

1/4 cup DIY Nut Milk (page 69, using almonds), or organic, unsweetened almond milk

1 teaspoon pure vanilla extract

1/2 cup DIY Nut Butter (page 71, using peanuts), or organic, no-sugar-added peanut butter

3/4 cup DIY Nut Flour (page 72, using almonds)

3/4 cup chickpea flour (or spelt flour)

2 tablespoons ground flaxseed

1 teaspoon aluminum-free baking powder

1/2 teaspoon baking soda

1/3 cup no-sugar-added dark chocolate chips

1. Preheat the oven to 350°F. Coat a 9 x 9-inch baking dish with nonstick cooking spray.

2. In the bowl of an electric mixer, or with a hand mixer, beat together the egg, egg white, oil, maple syrup, banana, almond milk, vanilla, and peanut butter until smooth. Set wet ingredients aside.

3. In a separate large bowl, whisk together the almond flour, chickpea flour, flaxseed, baking powder, and baking soda.

4. Add the dry ingredients to the wet ingredients and stir with a wooden spoon or spatula until well combined. Fold in the chocolate chips. Scrape batter into the prepared baking dish and spread it out evenly.

5. Transfer pan to the oven and bake for 30 minutes, or until a toothpick poked into the center comes out clean.

6. Remove pan from the oven, let it cool slightly, then cut into 16 bars.

EXCHANGES/CHOICES	1 Carbohydrate
	2 1/2 Fat
CALORIES	180
CALORIES FROM FAT	120
TOTAL FAT	13.0 g
SATURATED FAT	2.0 g
TRANS FAT	0.0 g
CHOLESTEROL	10 mg
SODIUM	120 mg
POTASSIUM	185 mg
TOTAL CARBOHYDRATE	13 g
DIETARY FIBER	3 g
SUGARS	5 g
PROTEIN	5 g
PHOSPHORUS	120 mg

Orange, Ginger, Almond Quinoa Cookies

SERVES: 12 | SERVING SIZE: 1 COOKIE | PREP TIME: 10 MINUTES | COOKING TIME: 30 MINUTES

As they bake, these cookies fill the house with the most comforting aroma of citrus, almonds, and spice. Plus, they provide you with a healthy serving of protein and fiber from the quinoa, and the addition of fresh ginger may help give your immune system an extra boost.

1 1/4 cups DIY Nut Flour (page 72, using almonds) or store-bought almond flour

1/2 teaspoon aluminum-free baking powder

1/2 teaspoon fine sea salt

1 teaspoon freshly grated orange zest

1 teaspoon grated fresh ginger

2 tablespoons avocado oil

1/2 cup Siggi's nonfat Orange & Ginger yogurt

2 tablespoons honey

2 tablespoons freshly squeezed orange juice

1 large egg

1/4 teaspoon almond extract

1/2 teaspoon vanilla extract

1 cup cooked quinoa, chilled

1. Preheat the oven to 375°F. Line a baking sheet with parchment paper.

2. In a medium bowl, whisk together the almond flour, baking powder, and salt. Set flour mixture aside.

3. In a separate bowl, whisk together the orange zest, ginger, avocado oil, yogurt, honey, orange juice, egg, almond extract, and vanilla extract.

4. Stir the flour mixture into the wet mixture with a wooden spoon, then fold in the quinoa just until fully incorporated.

5. Using a spoon or a tablespoon measure, scoop the cookie dough onto the prepared baking sheet in 2-tablespoon portions, spacing them about 2 inches apart. Bake for 15–20 minutes, or until golden brown.

6. Remove cookies from the oven and transfer them to a wire rack to cool. Serve.

EXCHANGES/CHOICES	1/2 Carbohydrate 2 Fat
CALORIES	130
CALORIES FROM FAT	80
TOTAL FAT	9.0 g
SATURATED FAT	0.9 g
TRANS FAT	0.0 g
CHOLESTEROL	15 mg
SODIUM	120 mg
POTASSIUM	140 mg
TOTAL CARBOHYDRATE	10 g
DIETARY FIBER	2 g
SUGARS	5 g
PROTEIN	5 g
PHOSPHORUS	120 mg

Sweet Potato Skillet Corn Bread

SERVES: 12 | SERVING SIZE: 1 WEDGE | PREP TIME: 50 MINUTES | COOKING TIME: 45 MINUTES

Who needs sugar when you've got vegetables like sweet corn and sweet potatoes? In this corn bread recipe, whole foods take center stage, infusing each bite with robust flavor. More savory than sweet, this corn bread can hold its own as a side dish to chili or as a satisfying snack.

- 2 tablespoons avocado oil, divided
- 1 pound red-skinned sweet potatoes
- 2 cups yellow cornmeal
- 1 cup frozen (or cooked fresh) sweet corn kernels
- 1/4 cup pure maple syrup (preferably grade B)
- 1 tablespoon aluminum-free baking powder
- 1/2 teaspoon fine sea salt
- 1/2 teaspoon baking soda
- 1 teaspoon grated fresh ginger
- 2 large eggs
- 1 cup fat-free, plain strained yogurt (Greek or skyr)
- 1/2 cup fat-free milk

1. Preheat the oven to 375°F. Coat a 12-inch cast iron skillet with 1 tablespoon avocado oil.

2. Pierce the sweet potatoes all over with a fork or knife. Place them right on the oven rack (you can wrap them in foil if you'd like) and roast for 45 minutes, or until they are very tender. Carefully remove sweet potatoes from the oven, transfer to a cutting board, slice them open, and remove the skin. When they are cool enough to handle, mash them in a large bowl using a potato masher.

3. In the bowl of a food processor: Combine the cornmeal, corn kernels, maple syrup, baking powder, salt, baking soda, and ginger; process until smooth. Empty the contents of the food processor into another large bowl.

4. Using the same food processor; combine 1 cup mashed sweet potatoes with the eggs, yogurt, milk, and remaining 1 tablespoon oil. Refrigerate remaining mashed sweet potatoes for another recipe. Purée the potato mixture; then add to the cornmeal mixture. Stir gently to just combine.

5. Pour the batter into the prepared skillet. Transfer skillet to the oven and bake until the cornbread is golden brown on top and a toothpick inserted into the center comes out clean, about 45 minutes.

6. Remove skillet from the oven, let it cool slightly, and then cut the cornbread into 12 equal wedges.

EXCHANGES/CHOICES	1 1/2 Starch
	1/2 Carbohydrate
	1/2 Fat
CALORIES	180
CALORIES FROM FAT	30
TOTAL FAT	3.5 g
SATURATED FAT	0.6 g
TRANS FAT	0.0 g
CHOLESTEROL	30 mg
SODIUM	270 mg
POTASSIUM	220 mg
TOTAL CARBOHYDRATE	31 g
DIETARY FIBER	2 g
SUGARS	7 g
PROTEIN	6 g
PHOSPHORUS	210 mg

Blueberry Yogurt Lemon Bars

SERVES: 16 | SERVING SIZE: 1 SQUARE | PREP TIME: 10 MINUTES | COOKING TIME: 35–45 MINUTES

A crunchy, graham cracker crust is the perfect foundation for this creamy, citrus-scented bar. A cross between cheesecake and a lemon bar, this sweet treat is sure to evoke some childhood memories!

Nonstick cooking spray

1 1/2 cups unsweetened graham cracker flour (see tip)

3 tablespoons avocado oil

1 tablespoon plus 2 teaspoons freshly grated lemon zest, divided

1/4 teaspoon fine sea salt

1 whole egg

3 egg whites

2 cups Siggi's nonfat blueberry yogurt OR 2 cups fat-free vanilla Greek yogurt (and no added maple syrup)

1 teaspoon maple syrup

1/4 cup freshly squeezed lemon juice

1 tablespoon freshly grated lemon zest

3/4 cup fresh blueberries

1. Preheat the oven to 350°F.

2. Line an 8-inch baking dish with parchment paper, then coat it with nonstick cooking spray.

3. To make the crust, add graham cracker flour, avocado oil, 2 teaspoons lemon zest, and salt to the bowl of a food processor; pulse to combine. Press mixture into the bottom of the prepared pan. Bake for 10–15 minutes, or until crust is golden brown. Then remove pan from the oven and set aside to cool.

4. To make the filling, process the egg, egg whites, yogurt, maple syrup, lemon juice, and remaining 1 tablespoon lemon zest in a blender until smooth. Stir in the fresh blueberries. Pour the filling onto the prebaked crust.

5. Transfer pan to the oven and bake for 25–30 minutes, or until the center is set. Remove pan from the oven and place on a wire rack to cool completely. Cut into 16 equal-sized squares and serve chilled or at room temperature.

tip: To make graham cracker flour, add 15 graham crackers to a food processor and process until they reach a flour-like consistency. Yields 1 1/2 cups.

EXCHANGES/CHOICES	1/2 Carbohydrate 1 Fat
CALORIES	90
CALORIES FROM FAT	35
TOTAL FAT	4.0 g
SATURATED FAT	0.5 g
TRANS FAT	0.0 g
CHOLESTEROL	15 mg
SODIUM	105 mg
POTASSIUM	75 mg
TOTAL CARBOHYDRATE	10 g
DIETARY FIBER	0 g
SUGARS	6 g
PROTEIN	4 g
PHOSPHORUS	55 mg

Zucchini and Carrot Mini Muffins

SERVES: 12 | SERVING SIZE: 2 MINI MUFFINS | PREP TIME: 10 MINUTES | COOKING TIME: 25 MINUTES

I am a huge fan of adding vegetables to anything and everything—including dessert! The shredded carrots and zucchini in this recipe add moisture and flavor—as well as a bundle of nutrients. Make a batch of these muffins and freeze half; this is a great way to avoid overindulging, plus then you know you have some backup healthy snacks on hand in a pinch.

Nonstick cooking spray

1 cup unbleached spelt flour or gluten-free flour mix

1/2 teaspoon ground cinnamon

1/4 teaspoon fine sea salt

1 teaspoon baking soda

2 tablespoons avocado oil

1/2 cup unsweetened applesauce

2 tablespoons pure maple syrup (preferably grade B)

1 large egg, beaten

1 teaspoon vanilla extract

1 cup finely grated zucchini

1/2 cup finely grated carrot

1. Preheat the oven to 350°F. Place a rack in the middle of the oven. Coat a mini muffin pan with nonstick cooking spray.

2. In a medium bowl, whisk together the flour, cinnamon, salt, and baking soda. Set flour mixture aside.

3. In a large bowl, using a wooden spoon, mix together the oil, applesauce, maple syrup, egg, and vanilla extract. Add the flour mixture to the wet ingredients and stir until just barely combined, then fold in the zucchini and carrot until just distributed.

4. Fill each cup in the mini muffin pan approximately 3/4 of the way full (I use a small cookie scoop).

5. Bake for 20–25 minutes, or until a toothpick inserted in the center of a muffin comes out clean. Serve warm.

EXCHANGES/CHOICES	1 Carbohydrate
	1/2 Fat
CALORIES	90
CALORIES FROM FAT	25
TOTAL FAT	3.0 g
SATURATED FAT	0.5 g
TRANS FAT	0.0 g
CHOLESTEROL	15 mg
SODIUM	160 mg
POTASSIUM	100 mg
TOTAL CARBOHYDRATE	12 g
DIETARY FIBER	2 g
SUGARS	3 g
PROTEIN	2 g
PHOSPHORUS	25 mg

Summer Melon Aqua Fresca

SERVES: 4 | SERVING SIZE: 1 CUP | PREP TIME: 5 MINUTES | COOKING TIME: NONE

Banish summer exhaustion with this refreshing and juicy drink. You are just a blender whirl away from some thirst-quenching goodness.

2 cups cubed, seeded watermelon

2 cups cubed cantaloupe

1/2 cup cold water

2 tablespoons freshly squeezed lime juice

2 tablespoons chopped fresh mint

2 cups seltzer water

4 lime slices (for garnish)

1. In a blender or food processor, combine the watermelon, cantaloupe, water, lime juice, and mint. Purée until smooth and uniform in color, then stir in the seltzer water. Serve over ice with lime slices for garnish.

EXCHANGES/CHOICES	1 Fruit
CALORIES	50
CALORIES FROM FAT	0
TOTAL FAT	0.0 g
SATURATED FAT	0.1 g
TRANS FAT	0.0 g
CHOLESTEROL	0 mg
SODIUM	40 mg
POTASSIUM	310 mg
TOTAL CARBOHYDRATE	13 g
DIETARY FIBER	1 g
SUGARS	11 g
PROTEIN	1 g
PHOSPHORUS	20 mg

Hibiscus, Citrus, and Berry Cooler

SERVES: 8 | SERVING SIZE: 1 CUP | PREP TIME: 5 MINUTES | REFRIGERATION TIME: AT LEAST 1 HOUR

In this cooler, which can be made year-round using frozen fruit, I pair naturally sweet hibiscus tea with raspberries and citrus juices for a burst of tangy-sweet flavor without any added sweeteners.

4 herbal hibiscus tea bags

4 cups boiling water

1 cup raspberries (fresh or frozen)

1/2 cup freshly squeezed orange juice

1 tablespoon freshly squeezed lime juice

3 cups cold water

8 orange slices (for garnish)

1. In a teapot or saucepan, steep the tea bags in the simmering water for 5 minutes.

2. While tea is steeping, combine the berries, orange juice, lime juice, and cold water in a blender. Process on high speed until mixture is as smooth as possible. Pour mixture through a fine-mesh strainer into a 2-quart serving pitcher. Add the tea to the pitcher and refrigerate for at least 1 hour or until chilled.

3. Serve over ice with orange slices as garnish.

EXCHANGES/CHOICES	Free food
CALORIES	15
CALORIES FROM FAT	0
TOTAL FAT	0.0 g
SATURATED FAT	0.0 g
TRANS FAT	0.0 g
CHOLESTEROL	0 mg
SODIUM	0 mg
POTASSIUM	65 mg
TOTAL CARBOHYDRATE	4 g
DIETARY FIBER	1 g
SUGARS	2 g
PROTEIN	1 g
PHOSPHORUS	5 mg

Grilled Peaches with White Balsamic and Mascarpone Cream

SERVES: 8 | SERVING SIZE: 1 PEACH HALF, 2 TABLESPOONS MASCARPONE CREAM, AND 1 TABLESPOON NUT CRUMBLE
PREP TIME: 10 MINUTES | COOKING TIME: ABOUT 15 MINUTES

When they're tossed on the grill, peaches develop a rich, jam-like flavor, which is divine when paired with mascarpone cheese and a drizzle of balsamic and honey.

4 peaches, halved, pits removed

1 tablespoon vegetable oil

1/2 cup white balsamic vinegar

1 cup fat-free, plain strained yogurt (Greek or skyr)

2 tablespoons mascarpone cheese

1 tablespoon honey

1/4 teaspoon vanilla extract

1/4 cup chopped walnuts

2 teaspoons ground cinnamon

1. Preheat an outdoor grill or grill pan to medium-high. Preheat the oven to 400°F.

2. In a large bowl, toss the peaches with the oil until well coated. Grill peaches cut-side down until charred, 2–3 minutes, then transfer them to a baking dish, cut-side up, and drizzle with the white balsamic vinegar.

3. Roast the peaches, uncovered, for 10–15 minutes, or until tender.

4. Meanwhile, in the bowl of a food processor, combine the yogurt, mascarpone, honey, and vanilla. Purée until smooth.

5. In a blender, pulse together the walnuts and cinnamon to form a crumble.

6. Remove peaches from the oven and serve each peach half with 2 tablespoons mascarpone cream and 1 tablespoon nut crumble.

EXCHANGES/CHOICES	1 Carbohydrate
	1 Fat
CALORIES	130
CALORIES FROM FAT	50
TOTAL FAT	6.0 g
SATURATED FAT	1.4 g
TRANS FAT	0.1 g
CHOLESTEROL	5 mg
SODIUM	15 mg
POTASSIUM	220 mg
TOTAL CARBOHYDRATE	15 g
DIETARY FIBER	2 g
SUGARS	13 g
PROTEIN	4 g
PHOSPHORUS	75 mg

Chocolate, Cinnamon, and Almond "Ice Cream"

SERVES: 6 | SERVING SIZE: 1/2 CUP | PREP TIME: 5 MINUTES | COOKING TIME: 10 MINUTES

I love this play on ice cream! Frozen, creamy bananas are blended with the sophisticated flavors of chocolate and cinnamon. Earthy, sweet, and savory, this "ice cream" is really delicious. Craving some crunch? Top it off with a sprinkle of the Everyday Cinnamon Walnut Crumble on page 68.

4 small frozen bananas, peeled and cut into quarters

1/4 cup unsweetened vanilla almond milk

1 tablespoon almond butter

2 tablespoons dark cacao powder (or cocoa powder)

1/4 teaspoon cinnamon

1. Place bananas, almond milk, almond butter, cocoa powder, and cinnamon into a food processor. Let sit for 5 minutes so bananas start to soften. Pulse/process until smooth and creamy. You may need to push down the sides of the processor a few times.

2. Serve as is or place in a freeze-safe container and freeze for 1 hour for a more "scoop-able" texture.

EXCHANGES/CHOICES	1 Fruit
	1/2 Fat
CALORIES	80
CALORIES FROM FAT	20
TOTAL FAT	2.0 g
SATURATED FAT	0.3 g
TRANS FAT	0.0 g
CHOLESTEROL	0 mg
SODIUM	10 mg
POTASSIUM	300 mg
TOTAL CARBOHYDRATE	17 g
DIETARY FIBER	3 g
SUGARS	8 g
PROTEIN	2 g
PHOSPHORUS	40 mg

Peppered Strawberries with Balsamic Glaze

SERVES: 4 | SERVING SIZE: 3/4 CUP STRAWBERRIES AND 1 TEASPOON GLAZE | PREP TIME: 5 MINUTES | COOKING TIME: NONE

Strawberries are a naturally sweet treat that can be enjoyed on their own or dressed up with a few simple ingredients. I love the way the freshly ground black pepper plays with the sweetness of the berries and balsamic in this recipe to create a festive, almost savory treat.

3 cups strawberries, hulled and halved

1 teaspoon freshly grated orange zest

1 tablespoon freshly squeezed orange juice

1/4 teaspoon freshly ground black pepper

4 teaspoons balsamic glaze

1. In a small bowl, combine the strawberries, orange zest, orange juice, and pepper. Divide the berries into 4 (3/4-cup) servings and drizzle each with a teaspoon of balsamic glaze.

EXCHANGES/CHOICES	1 Fruit
CALORIES	50
CALORIES FROM FAT	5
TOTAL FAT	0.5 g
SATURATED FAT	0.0 g
TRANS FAT	0.0 g
CHOLESTEROL	0 mg
SODIUM	0 mg
POTASSIUM	200 mg
TOTAL CARBOHYDRATE	11 g
DIETARY FIBER	2 g
SUGARS	7 g
PROTEIN	1 g
PHOSPHORUS	30 mg

Oven-Roasted Figs with Cinnamon Walnut Crumble

SERVES: 8 | SERVING SIZE: 2 FIGS | PREP TIME: 5 MINUTES | COOKING TIME: 15 MINUTES

I love roasted fruit. While simple, this cooking technique truly bolsters fruit's natural yum factor. I am also a fan of recipes with minimal ingredients, and this recipe surely fits the bill. Quick enough for a weekday treat and elegant enough for entertaining, this fig dish is a keeper.

16 medium figs

2 tablespoons white balsamic vinegar

2 teaspoons melted butter

1/2 cup Everyday Cinnamon Walnut
   Crumble (page 68)

1. Preheat the oven to 425°F.

2. Rinse the figs and pat them dry. Cut off the stems and, without cutting through the base, halve them from top to bottom and place them in a medium bowl.

3. Toss the figs gently with the vinegar and butter. Set the figs upright and snug in a rimmed baking dish. Roast for 10 minutes.

4. Remove figs from the oven and sprinkle 1/2 tablespoon cinnamon crumble into each. Bake an additional 3–5 minutes. Serve warm.

EXCHANGES/CHOICES	1 1/2 Fruit
	1 1/2 Fat
CALORIES	150
CALORIES FROM FAT	70
TOTAL FAT	8.0 g
SATURATED FAT	1.3 g
TRANS FAT	0.0 g
CHOLESTEROL	5 mg
SODIUM	10 mg
POTASSIUM	280 mg
TOTAL CARBOHYDRATE	22 g
DIETARY FIBER	4 g
SUGARS	17 g
PROTEIN	2 g
PHOSPHORUS	50 mg

index